INSTITUTIONAL FOUNDATIONS OF PUBLIC FINANCE

David F. Bradford (1939–2005)

Alan J. Auerbach and Daniel N. Shaviro, Editors

Institutional Foundations of Public Finance

Economic and Legal Perspectives

HARVARD UNIVERSITY PRESS

Cambridge, Massachusetts, and London, England 2008

Frontispiece: Copyright Jon Roemer for Woodrow Wilson School, Princeton University, 2004.

Library of Congress Cataloging-in-Publication Data

Institutional foundations of public finance : economic and legal perspectives / edited by Alan J. Auerbach and Daniel N. Shaviro.

p. cm.

"The contents of this volume were originally presented at a conference entitled 'Key Issues in Public Finance: A Conference in Honor of David Bradford,' that was held at NYU Law School on May 5, 2006"—Intro.

Includes index.

ISBN 978-0-674-03097-8 (alk. paper)

1. Finance, Public. 2. Fiscal policy. I. Auerbach, Alan J. II. Shaviro, Daniel N.

HJ141.I56 2008

339.5'2—dc22 2008021505

Contents

Acknowledgments

The chapters in this volume were initially presented at a conference entitled "Key Issues in Public Finance: A Conference in Honor of David Bradford," which was held at NYU Law School on May 5, 2006. We are grateful to David Wise, the Special Events Coordinator at NYU Law School, for his outstanding work in arranging the conference, and to the following sponsors who provided financial support for the conference: the Burch Center for Tax Policy and Public Finance, UC Berkeley; the Fund for Tax and Fiscal Research, Harvard Law School; the American Enterprise Institute; and NYU Law School.

INSTITUTIONAL FOUNDATIONS OF PUBLIC FINANCE

CHAPTER 1

Introduction

ALAN J. AUERBACH

DANIEL N. SHAVIRO

The late David Bradford was involved in many areas of public finance and public policy, to which he consistently brought an understanding of the importance of institutions. It is natural, therefore, in his memory, to review and reflect on the major developments in recent years on the core topics he studied, and to do so in an institutionally grounded fashion that integrates economic and legal perspectives. This volume offers assessments and fresh contributions on a number of important tax and fiscal policy issues, with chapters and commentaries by leading economists and law professors, all of whom knew and admired David Bradford and were inspired by him in developing their own often divergent ideas. The contents of this volume were originally presented at a conference entitled "Key Issues in Public Finance: A Conference in Honor of David Bradford," which was held at NYU Law School on May 5, 2006.

Bradford is best known today for his extensive, pathbreaking, and influential work on the choice between income and consumption taxation. We devote Part I of the volume to this topic, trying as best we can in limited space to touch on a variety of the different aspects that his work illuminated. Part I includes explorations not only of the steady state abstract differences between the systems, but of questions of transition and implementation.

In Part II we turn to several other areas to which Bradford made important contributions. These topics include fiscal federalism, which his early work emphasized and helped to advance; corporate finance, in which he helped develop the so-called "new view" of dividend taxation; and fiscal language, a topic of lasting interest to him in which the conceptual breakthroughs that he proposed or helped develop arguably remain underappreciated.

1. Choice of Tax Base

The choice between income and consumption taxation has been at the forefront of tax reform debate for many decades. Over time, the voluminous literature on this subject has continued to generate new insights concerning such critical aspects of the choice as the theoretical differences between the two systems, the question of how a consumption tax could be implemented, and issues of transition from an income to a consumption tax. Bradford (1996, 1998, 2004) made important contributions in all three areas. The next three chapters of this book address, in turn, the grounds for choosing between the systems, implementation methods, and transition issues.

In Chapter 2, "The Choice between Income and Consumption Taxes: A Primer," Alan Auerbach surveys the literature with an eye both to identifying the key economic issues raised by the differences between the systems, and to reviewing what we know about these issues. The analysis is complicated, he notes, by the fact that not all prototypes commonly regarded as consumption taxes are identical economically in how they bear on risk-taking, economic rents, and the normal return to capital. In addition, fundamental economic questions, such as the optimal tax rate on capital income, remain unresolved. Thus, while prominent models (e.g., Atkinson and Stiglitz, 1976; Judd, 1985; Chamley, 1986) support a zero tax rate on capital, this conclusion can be challenged in a dynamic setting where such a tax raises the cost to high-ability individuals of opting out of the labor market once they have set aside resources (Golosov et al., 2003). More generally, Auerbach finds that any efficiency gains from shifting to a consumption tax are highly sensitive to the implementation method and to the treatment of assets in the transition.

Glenn Hubbard and Alvin Warren, in commenting on Auerbach's chapter, take very different approaches despite agreeing that it provides an excellent primer on the issues raised by choosing between income and consumption taxation. Hubbard emphasizes the essay's demonstration that "the devil is in the details" of a given tax reform proposal, and that further theoretical and empirical research is needed. Warren argues that the academic literature surveyed will not influence public policy debate to the extent that participants in it might desire unless more care is taken to explain and justify key analytic moves, such as disaggregating financial flows into their conceptual components and assuming full marketplace responses to government policy changes.

Whether under an income or a consumption tax, a number of design choices, such as individual- versus business-level collection and the treatment of cross-border transactions, can have first-order significance. In Chapter 3, "Implementing Income and Consumption Taxes," David Weisbach examines some of the main design choices under either system. To orient his analysis, Weisbach sets forth the "parallel implementation hypothesis," under which any method of implementing either an income or a consumption tax would have a corresponding method for implementing the other base, modified only with respect to the measurement of time value returns. Practical administrative considerations prevent this hypothesis from holding entirely in practice, but it sheds light not only on the choice between systems and on how a consumption tax might best be implemented, but also on the sources of complexity under existing law. In the international realm, for example, income taxation invites (even if it does not require) overlapping individual- and business-level taxes, along with efforts to implement some degree of business-level capital export neutrality, that interact to make extreme complexity close to unavoidable.

Edward McCaffery and Joel Slemrod, in commenting on the Weisbach paper, both use the parallel implementation hypothesis as a starting point for exploring why, in practice, the choice of implementation method actually does matter. McCaffery argues that demonstrating theoretical equivalence between two implementation methods does not establish that they are normatively equivalent, given perceptual and transaction cost differences. In his view, taxing people when they consume is normatively preferable to taxing them when they earn even if it penalizes "lumpy" consumption. Slemrod discusses the administrative principles that should guide implementation, such as relying on transactions in which the filings by parties with adverse interests can be cross-checked. He also notes that withholding by firms, including differential withholding that depends on the attributes of the counterparty, can be used to bridge many of the differences between implementation methods.

Even if one would prefer a consumption tax starting from a blank slate, transition issues are critical to tax reform decisions in any jurisdiction that starts out with an income tax in place. Some regard the dislocations that might accompany shifting from an income tax to a consumption tax as decisive against imposing the shift. Others view the transition, which can include a capital levy on existing wealth when the consumption tax is enacted, as a crucial or even indispensable advantage, by reason of its permitting the imposition of a one-time lump sum wealth tax.

In Chapter 4, "Capital Levies and Transition to a Consumption Tax," Louis Kaplow discusses the merits of imposing the capital levy, which he finds depend on the likelihood of repetition, the extent of anticipation, and the levy's effects on distribution. Kaplow concludes that, while political economy concerns are crucial, there is reason to be skeptical about the advantages attributed to the capital levy. The anticipation problem may be acute, repetition is potentially a serious concern, and alternative policies might be distributively superior as a result of not depending in their application on whether one saved just before or just after the switch between tax bases. Kaplow also explores subsidiary transition issues raised by the capital levy, such as the significance of subsequent consumption tax rate changes and the argument (which he challenges) that taxpayers subject to the levy would relevantly be compensated by increased after-tax returns under the new system.

In their commentaries, James Hines and Kyle Logue emphasize the importance of the little-understood empirical question of how expectations would actually be affected by a given income to consumption tax transition. Many different possibilities are plausible, given the difficulty of predicting future government behavior or even interpreting particular inputs to any prediction. Hines notes as well the importance of developing a better understanding of the transition levy on existing human capital that may result from a tax law change. Logue suggests further inquiry into the feasibility and merits of government precommitment to restrict capital levies to predetermined and objectively verifiable circumstances, such as war or natural disaster, where the need for revenue is especially great.

2. Fiscal Federalism, Corporate Finance, and Fiscal Language

Fiscal federalism—the study of the interrelationships of fiscal policies at different levels of government—is a prominent topic in the field of public finance, dating at least from the classic paper by Tiebout (1956). Tiebout showed how competing local jurisdictions might elicit consumer preferences for local public spending in a manner that could not be done at the central government level. With Europe evolving toward a federal system more like that of the United States, and many large countries such as China confronting the problems of regional heterogeneity, fiscal federalism has taken on even more policy relevance in recent years.

Taking up the state of fiscal federalism research in Chapter 5, "On the Theory and Practice of Fiscal Decentralization," Wallace Oates begins with his oft-cited Decentralization Theorem (Oates, 1972), which demonstrates that, under certain conditions, it is more efficient for lower levels of government to provide local public goods than for central governments to do so. The key intuition for favoring decentralization is that local governments can adjust spending levels to reflect variations in preferences and costs in a manner that is difficult to do at the federal level. As illustrated by Bradford and Oates (1974), the efficiency gains from local provision are potentially quite significant. After reviewing what the traditional literature had to say about the validity of the Decentralization Theorem using standard public finance analysis, Oates considers the recent literature, which has focused more on the political economy of government decisions and intergovernmental relations. A key issue identified in this literature is the extent to which central governments can impose "hard" budget constraints on local governments when such governments are ceded the responsibility for making public spending decisions. If such constraints cannot be made credible, then letting local governments determine spending may lead to very unfortunate fiscal outcomes, with "soft" budget constraints leading to an irresponsible raiding of the national "commons." Ironically, then, it is easier for strong central governments, which can make credible commitments to enforce budget constraints, to grant more decision-making authority to local governments; private markets can also contribute to making decentralization work by punishing bad choices by local governments in debt and property markets.

Charles McLure and Harvey Rosen offer their own perspectives on the issues that Oates raises. Rosen argues that, in reviewing various criticisms of the Decentralization Theorem, Oates may cede too much ground. In Rosen's view, there are many arguments in favor of decentralized local public goods provision, including the informational requirements of centralized provision and the ability of local variations in public goods choices to serve as a laboratory for national decisions. Rosen also discounts one of the standard criticisms of local provision—its inability to deal with interjurisdictional spillover effects—on two grounds: first, local provision has not led to the predicted "race to the bottom" that certain tax spillovers would predict; second, when federal government intervention in local decisions does occur, it shows little evidence of being related to addressing spillovers. McLure focuses on three aspects of decentralization: tax exporting, tax assignment, and the impact of public employee unions. He reminds us that tax exporting is endogenous with respect to federal government policy, notably the deductibility of state and local taxes from the federal income tax, so that interjurisdictional spillovers and hence the performance of state and local governments can be significantly affected by federal tax policy. McLure sees current federal tax policy as encouraging growth of the state and local government sectors, and suggests that the strength of public sector unions also may be contributing to this growth, in part by contributing to the softening of state and local budget constraints.

How do taxes on dividends affect the financial policy, investment decisions, and market valuation of corporations? Traditionally, dividend taxes were thought to discourage dividends and weaken investment while exerting downward pressure on share values during a period of adjustment to the new tax system. A challenge to this perspective arose from the "new view" of dividend taxation developed in the work of King (1977), Auerbach (1979), and Bradford (1981), which argued that dividend taxes should be largely nondistortionary with respect to the decisions of mature firms with pools of retained earnings sufficient to supply the equity funds needed for new investment. For such firms, according to this view, the dividend tax should be capitalized into share values but have little impact on investment or dividend policy.

In Chapter 6, "Dividends and Taxes," Roger Gordon and Martin Dietz assess the empirical support for the new view of dividend taxation, along with that for an alternative, the dividend-signaling model. They find that each model is consistent with some empirical observations, but not others. For example, the signaling model can explain the coexistence of share repurchases and dividends, while this is more of a problem for the new view. On the other hand, the observed negative impact of dividend taxes on firm values, while consistent with the new view, is not forecast by the signaling model. Both models can explain why firms might increase dividends in response to a reduction of the dividend tax rate (under the signaling model in response to a reduced cost of signaling and under the new view to the extent that the tax rate reduction is not seen as completely permanent), but neither model can explain why firms would issue shares and pay dividends simultaneously, as some firms are observed to do. Thus each model has only partial support from the data, suggesting that some other model, perhaps incorporating certain elements of the new view and the signaling model, is needed to capture fully the impact of dividend taxation on corporate behavior and valuation.

William Andrews and George Zodrow, in reviewing the Gordon-Dietz contribution, suggest that the authors overstate the strength of the evidence against the new view. Andrews argues that the Gordon-Dietz characterization of the new view is overly restrictive. He notes that the stability of dividends is perfectly consistent with the new view, once one incorporates borrowing in the model, since fluctuations in debt (or liquid assets) can be used to cushion fluctuations in real investment. He also argues that the continued use of dividends in lieu of more favorably taxed repurchases is something of a puzzle for other models as well, and that the new view applies to the extent that dividends are paid. Zodrow argues that the empirical regularities typically cited as evidence against the new view, such as the stability of dividends, the presence of share repurchases, and the responsiveness of dividends to tax rate changes, are not compelling, and cites various recent contributions that have provided empirical evidence in favor of the new view and against the signaling view.

Fiscal policy evaluation depends on fiscal language, but, as emphasized by Bradford (2003), the language of fiscal policy is often ambiguous and confusing. Recent policy debates contain many familiar examples of this ambiguity. When taxes on social security benefits were increased during the 1990s, did this constitute a reduction in benefits and hence in government spending, or an increase in taxes? While each characterization seems equally valid and the choice is irrelevant in terms of the underlying policy, inferences based on the resulting "size of government" would differ. When the Medicare program was expanded in 2003 to include a future prescription drug benefit with little dedicated funding, did this represent a new obligation of the U.S. government? It would have had the government immediately issued vouchers to beneficiaries to purchase the drugs, but as the program was structured the budgetary cost would be recognized only when the drug purchases occurred, rather than when the commitment was made. Again, the difference in the two methods of implementation is irrelevant, but conclusions based on the immediate impact on the budget deficit would have been quite different in the two cases.

While the existence of such ambiguities is recognized by economists and policy makers, their pervasiveness may not be. In Chapter 7, "On the General Relativity of Fiscal Language," Jerry Green and Laurence Kotlikoff argue that the range of standard fiscal measures, including the deficit, taxes, and transfer payments, are economically ill defined; that is, for a given underlying government policy, each of these measures can take on arbitrary values. As a corollary, derivative measures such as disposable income, private assets, and personal saving can change arbitrarily as a result of labeling conventions, without any change in underlying policy. Although these points are not new to the literature (e.g., Kotlikoff, 1986; Auerbach and Kotlikoff, 1987; Kotlikoff, 2002), Green and Kotlikoff offer a more general model showing how equivalent policies can be stated in alternative fashions depending on arbitrary choices of baseline.

In their commentaries, Daniel Shaviro and Kent Smetters each accept the logic of the Green-Kotlikoff analysis while questioning its generality and empirical significance. Shaviro notes that even the concept of net taxes used in generational accounting is formally ambiguous if the initial entitlement to market incomes can be arbitrarily assigned to government or individuals. But, he argues, there is a much more natural baseline assumption in this case (that the government starts with no claim on individual incomes) than in other instances where fiscal language can be faulted, as in the distinction between tax cuts and spending increases. Smetters takes issue with the assumptions implicit in the Green-Kotlikoff proposition, arguing that the purported economic invariance to changes in fiscal language requires that market opportunities and constraints not be affected by the changes in language. Where changes in legal rights are involved, for example, real differences in outcomes may arise.

David Bradford will be missed, both personally and intellectually, by people working in all the areas that this volume discusses. In addition to being grateful for his contributions, however, we are confident that intellectual progress will continue on all fronts, perhaps even leading to improvements in public understanding and public policy. We hope that the readers of this volume will find its contributions to be provocative and stimulating instances of the spirit of open inquiry that David always exemplified.

REFERENCES

Atkinson, Anthony B., and Joseph E. Stiglitz. 1976. "The Design of Tax Structure: Direct versus Indirect Taxation." *Journal of Public Economics* 6(1–2): 55–75.

Auerbach, Alan J. 1979. "Wealth Maximization and the Cost of Capital." *Quarterly Journal of Economics* 93: 433–446.

Auerbach, Alan J., and Laurence J. Kotlikoff. 1987. *Dynamic Fiscal Policy*. Cambridge: Cambridge University Press.

Bradford, David F. 1981. "The Incidence and Allocation Effects of a Tax on Corporate Distributions." *Journal of Public Economics* 15: 1–22.

Bradford, David F. 1996. "Consumption Taxes: Some Fundamental Transition Issues." In Michael J. Boskin (ed.), *Frontiers of Tax Reform* (pp. 123–150). Stanford, CA: Hoover Institution Press.

Bradford, David F. 1998. "Transition to and Tax Rate Flexibility in a Cash-Flow Type Tax." In James Poterba (ed.), *Tax Policy and the Economy* (vol. 12, pp. 151–172). Cambridge, MA: MIT Press.

Bradford, David F. 2003. "Reforming Budgetary Language." In Sigbren Cnossen and Hans-Werner Sinn (eds.), *Public Finance and Public Policy in the New Century.* Cambridge, MA: MIT Press.

Bradford, David F. 2004. *The X-Tax in the World Economy: Going Global with a Simple, Progressive Tax.* Washington, DC: AEI Press.

Bradford, David F., and Wallace E. Oates. 1974. "Suburban Exploitation of Central Cities and Governmental Structure." In H. Hochman and G. Peterson (eds.), *Redistribution through Public Choice* (pp. 43–90). New York: Columbia University Press.

Chamley, Christophe. 1986. "Optimal Taxation of Capital Income in General Equilibrium with Infinite Lives." *Econometrica* 54(3): 607–622.

Golosov, Mikhail, Narayana Kocherlakota, and Aleh Tsyvinski. 2003. "Optimal Indirect and Capital Taxation." *Review of Economic Studies* 70(3): 569–587.

Judd, Kenneth L. 1985. "Redistributive Taxation in a Simple Perfect Foresight Model." *Journal of Public Economics* 28(1): 59–83.

King, Mervyn. 1977. *Public Policy and the Corporation.* London: Chapman and Hall.

Kotlikoff, Laurence J. 1986. "Deficit Delusion." *The Public Interest* (Summer): 53–65.

Kotlikoff, Laurence J. 2002. *Generational Policy.* Cambridge, MA: MIT Press.

Oates, Wallace E. 1972. *Fiscal Federalism.* New York: Harcourt Brace Jovanovich.

Tiebout, Charles M. 1956. "A Pure Theory of Local Expenditures." *Journal of Political Economy* 64 (October): 416–424.

PART I

Choice of Tax Base

CHAPTER 2

The Choice between Income and Consumption Taxes: A Primer

ALAN J. AUERBACH

1. Introduction

It has now been nearly three decades since the publication of two important volumes that laid out many of the details of how one might implement a progressive consumption tax. *The Structure and Reform of Direct Taxation* (Institute for Fiscal Studies, 1978; hereafter referred to as the Meade Committee Report) was produced in the United Kingdom by a group of economists and other academics. *Blueprints for Basic Tax Reform* (U.S. Treasury, 1977, reprinted as Bradford et al., 1984; hereafter *Blueprints*) came from the staff of the U.S. Treasury, working under David Bradford, who was Deputy Assistant Secretary for Tax Analysis while the report was being prepared. Both reports focused on the direct individual consumption tax envisaged by such earlier authors as Fisher (1939), Kaldor (1955), and Andrews (1974), rather than on the indirect consumption taxes already in place, notably value-added taxes (VAT). Since the publication of these two volumes, though, there have been new ideas about how to combine the simplicity of indirect taxation and the progressivity and flexibility of direct taxation, notably the flat tax (Hall and Rabushka, 1985) and the X-tax (Bradford, 1986).

Over the years, there have been many, many contributions analyzing the mechanics of the different variants of consumption taxation, the potential efficiency and distributional effects of their adoption, the issues of administration and transition from the current tax system, and the problems relating to certain types of transactions. We now have a better idea of how to implement a consumption tax, and of what adopting a consumption tax would mean for the economy. But much of what we "know," from the recent literature and indeed from the Meade Committee and *Blueprints*, is not part of the general policy discussion, and there are important issues that the literature has recognized but still not resolved. My aim in this chapter is not to survey the vast literature on consumption taxes, but to lay out some of the key economic issues involved in deciding whether and how to adopt a consumption tax, and to discuss what theory and evidence have told us and could tell us about these issues.

2. What Is a Consumption Tax?

It may seem tautological that a consumption tax is a tax on consumption, but no tax currently in effect or realistically proposed is a consumption tax by that simple definition. To show this, we start with the product and income sides of the national income identity for Gross National Product (GNP),[1]

$$\text{GNP} = C + I + G + X - M + R^f = W + R + R^f \tag{2.1}$$

where C is consumption, I is gross domestic investment, G is government spending, X is exports, M is imports, W is wage income, R is domestic gross capital income, and R^f is net foreign income (i.e., foreign income of domestic residents less domestic income of foreign residents).[2] The standard method for imposing consumption taxes, as under the VAT, is to start on the income side, taxing all factor returns but then forgiving taxes on sales that do not represent consumption, in particular:

$$C = W + R - I - G - X + M \tag{2.2}$$

so that sales for investment and export are free of tax while tax is imposed on imports.

In principle, government purchases should also be excluded from the tax base, although this will not matter if the government budget adjusts to the treatment of government purchases. That is, if government purchases are added to the tax base, and the government budget is then expanded to cover the additional cost of government purchases, there will be no real impact—there need be no change in the quantities of goods and services the government purchases. Of course, if the government budget does not adjust, or if the federal government taxes the purchases of state and local governments and makes no compensating transfers to these lower-level governments, then taxing government purchases will reduce real government budgets. While this issue may be quite important in evaluating specific tax proposals, it is straightforward conceptually. For the remainder of the discussion, then,

I will ignore this issue, assume that the consumption tax has no impact on government purchases, and simply leave government spending out when using the national income identity, starting instead from expression (2.2′):

$$C = W + R - I - X + M \tag{2.2'}$$

It is useful to introduce another identity, the international accounts identity, which requires that the current and capital accounts must balance:[3]

$$(X - M + R^f) + (-I^f) = 0 \tag{2.3}$$

where I^f is net foreign investment. Combining (2.3′) and (2.3) yields:

$$C = W + (R - I) + (R^f - I^f) \tag{2.4}$$

which emphasizes that a consumption tax can also be conceived as a tax on wages plus taxes on the net cash flows (gross income less gross investment) from domestic and foreign activities.

The simplest manner in which "consumption" taxes do not tax consumption is by omitting certain elements of consumption from the tax base. It is common for VATs to "zero rate" certain commodities, for example, with the objective of achieving more progressive taxation, notwithstanding the weak theoretical arguments for relying on variations in indirect tax rates for this purpose in the context of a broader system that includes progressive direct taxes. But the more complex deviations from consumption taxation occur through the exclusion of certain elements of the cash flows, i.e., $(R - I) + (R^f - I^f)$.

2.1. Consumption Taxes and Wage Taxes

For a zero-present-value investment made today, the future additions to R or R^f are equal in present value to the cost of today's investment added to I or I^f. Thus, with tax rates constant over time, the decision of whether to include or exclude these cash flows would have no impact on the present value of government revenues, nor would it have any impact on the incentive to undertake these marginal investments—the effective tax rate on such investments would be zero under both approaches.

Both *Blueprints* and the Meade Committee recognized this equivalence and envisioned giving taxpayers a choice under a personal expenditure tax of whether assets held at arm's length would be subject to cash flow taxation or simply tax exempt, with both investments and returns ignored by the tax system.[4] Indeed, both volumes saw an advantage in giving taxpayers a choice when tax rates *do* vary over time and hence the present value of cash flow taxation is not zero for marginal investments. Under a progressive expenditure tax for which marginal tax rates could vary over time, the ability of taxpayers to choose between the two forms of tax treatment would provide an averaging device, allowing taxpayers to shift their tax bases from high-rate to low-rate years while holding the present value of the tax base constant.

As the subsequent literature has clarified and elucidated (e.g., Gordon, 1985; Kaplow, 1994; Warren, 1996; Weisbach, 2004), the same equivalence holds for risky assets, assuming that taxation of gains and losses is symmetric and that investors can scale up holdings to offset the government's implicit equity position. The investor would simply increase holdings of risky assets in order to undo the reduction in risk and out-of-pocket cost that the cash flow tax would produce, with the result that after-tax cash flows would be identical under the two alternative approaches to taxation. This equivalence at the investor level, however, leaves open what happens to risk-taking in the economy as a whole. The answer depends on whether capital markets efficiently pool risks, a question to which I return below. If asset markets are efficient, the increased riskiness of the government's share of risky assets under the cash flow tax could not be reduced by pooling; once the government transmitted this risk back to the economy, the added "background" risk would offset the propensity for increased individual purchases of risky assets, leaving the equilibrium unaffected by the decision of whether to include the cash flows from risky assets in the tax base.

Another conclusion of this literature, to which I also return below, is that the income tax differs from the consumption tax only in its taxation of the safe rate of return on assets. To the extent that an asset's return is simply an excess return that compensates for risk-taking, the investor can undo the income tax by scaling up the position in the risky asset. Only the tax on the safe rate of return cannot be undone by this portfolio shift, and thus only the tax on the safe rate of return is relevant in assessing the distortion of an individual's intertemporal decisions.

Thus, whether investments are safe or risky, excluding from a consumption tax the cash flows on new, marginal investments would, to a first approximation, have no impact on the economy. But there are remaining components of the cash flows, $(R - I) + (R^f - I^f)$, which may be grouped into two categories: normal returns (including recovery of principal) from earlier investments and supernormal economic rents. It is useful to distinguish these two sources because opinions vary as to how these elements of the cash flow tax base should be treated in a transition from the income tax to the consumption tax. In particular, some view the tax on returns to existing capital as an unfair by-product of the transition from one tax base to another, as only the net returns, rather than the recovery of capital, would be taxed under the income tax. Imposing a consumption tax therefore introduces a levy on the value of existing assets. The taxation of economic rent, however is typically not viewed with such concern, because rent would be taxed equally under an income tax or a consumption tax. There may also be different incentive effects if these taxes are anticipated prior to their enactment, because an anticipated levy on the recovery of capital is effectively a capital income tax.

For some assets, notably owner-occupied housing and other consumer durables, it would be difficult to impose a cash flow tax because this would require the taxation of imputed rental income. That is, we observe the investment flows as components of I but we do not observe all the components of R, just the subsequent asset sales, not the flow of imputed rental income during the period of ownership. Thus, both *Blueprints* and the Meade Committee viewed the unregistered/nonqualified treatment as necessary for these assets. For other assets, such as closely held businesses, the ease of shifting factor payments between wages and returns to capital suggested that such assets be subject to cash flow taxation, with no option for owners to leave such assets outside the system.

2.2. Origin versus Destination Basis

One particular element of cash flows about which there has been considerable debate is those from net foreign assets, $(R^f - I^f)$. Under a standard destination-based VAT, these would be included indirectly through the border tax adjustments on imports and exports, since the current and capital accounts balance. But some taxes, notably the Hall-Rabushka flat tax, would be imposed on an origin basis and hence would provide no special treatment for the cash flows associated with cross-border investments. From the analogy with other types of asset cash flows, it should be evident that the distinction between these two tax bases lies in the treatment of rents and the normal returns to existing assets. There should be no impact on the incentives for inbound or outbound investment, just on asset values and the present value of government revenues.[5] Because there should be no impact on cross-border investments, there is no reason why trade flows should be affected either; with an immediate adjustment of exchange rates, this irrelevance should be what we observe. That is, assuming no differences between the two tax systems in terms of domestic or foreign price levels, a switch from an origin-based VAT to a destination-based VAT should lead to a currency appreciation for the adopting country that should just offset the incipient advantage of exporters and disadvantage of importers under the destination-based system.[6]

To understand why the exchange rate would change in this manner, consider the hypothetical experiment in which the exchange rate rose by less than the predicted amount, or not at all. The reduced relative price of domestic goods and services would lead to an improvement of the trade balance that, by expression (2.3), would have to be offset by a reduction in the capital account balance. But, assuming no change in the future expected path of currency appreciation or depreciation, there would be no wish on the part of international investors to shift from their previous investment choices. Thus, there would be an imbalance in the international accounts leading to a further adjustment in the exchange rate until the potential change in trade flows disappeared.

The simplicity of this analysis has done little to offset the skepticism of policy makers and trade "experts." Many skeptics simply refuse to acknowledge the predictions of economic theory or the validity of the national income identity. Others confuse the effects of adopting a consumption tax with the effects of border adjustments per se. From (2.2′), it is clear that any tax policy that reduces consumption, as a shift to consumption taxation might, will increase the trade balance, holding constant income and domestic investment. Some confuse the impact of uniform border adjustments with the impact of industry-specific border adjustments. If border adjustments only apply in a particular industry, for example, the exchange rate cannot fully adjust in response, because this would reduce net export demand in other industries and hence overall. Thus, there would be only a partial exchange rate adjustment and a shift in net exports to the industries covered by the border adjustments. And there are those who might think that border adjustments would have the same impact as tariffs, which incorporate one part of the border adjustment (the import tax) but not the other (the export subsidy).

Some skeptics also rely on more sophisticated (but not more compelling) arguments to promote the importance of border adjustments. One argument, for example, is that the analysis given above does not apply in a world where countries peg their exchange rates to the dollar. In that case, dollar appreciation under a destination-based VAT would be held in check by the reserve transactions of foreign governments and central banks. While such transactions would, indeed, lead to a violation of the assumptions needed for the equivalence of the two tax systems to hold, proponents of this argument do not explain why a foreign government would choose to ignore changes in the real exchange rate when setting its currency peg. For example, suppose a foreign government seeks to enforce an exchange rate of e units of its currency per dollar under an origin-based tax at rate t. Then, the United States shifts to a destination-basis for its tax, and the border adjustments increase the relative price of foreign goods by a factor of $(1 + t)$ if the exchange rate is unchanged. If the foreign government wishes to maintain its competitive position, it will seek to devalue its currency by a factor of $(1 + t)$ to $e(1 + t)$, which should be easy to accomplish because this should be the result if the previous level of reserve operations is maintained. Put another way, if the government's opportunity set has not changed, then why should its choice from this set?

The equivalence of destination-based and origin-based taxes is not exact because of the different treatment of net cash flows under the two systems. As discussed, a destination-based tax would expand the tax base by the present value of rents and normal returns to existing capital associated with a country's net foreign asset position. For the United States today, the net foreign asset position is negative, so the destination-based tax would tend to reduce revenues in present value, to the extent that rates of return on U.S. and foreign assets are equal.[7,8] To the extent that a country's net asset position is close to zero, this would make little difference in terms of tax revenues. But there could still be a big difference in terms of the impact on asset values, even with a zero net international investment position, because the valuation effects would apply to gross asset positions. The cash flows of all U.S.-owned assets held abroad would be hit by the cash flow tax included in the destination-based VAT, and those of foreign-owned assets held in the U.S. would be subsidized. The fact that the taxes would be collected on traded commodities rather than on the capital flows themselves is irrelevant, because the exchange rate adjustment would shift the incidence of the taxes onto the asset holders.[9]

As an example of the size of the potential asset revaluations associated with border adjustments, consider the case of the United States at the end of 2004, when, according to the Bureau of Economic Analysis, foreign-owned assets in the United States totaled \$11.5 trillion and U.S.-owned assets abroad were \$9.1 trillion.[10] The border adjustment of a domestic VAT at a rate, say, of 30 percent, would require a 30 percent depreciation of foreign currencies relative to the dollar—a \$2.7 trillion loss for U.S. holders of foreign assets, and a gain of \$4.9 (\$11.5/0.7 – \$11.5) trillion for foreign-asset holders, relative to a 30 percent VAT with no border adjustment.

2.3. The Treatment of Financial Assets and Liabilities

Following expression (2.4), a tax on consumption requires that gross private income be taxed and that gross investment purchases be deductible or in some other manner effectively excluded from the tax base. Except to the extent that they represent holding of foreign assets, financial positions do not show up in expression (2.4) because they net out. That is, we could also write expression (2.4) as:

$$C = W + (R - I) + (R^f - I^f) + (F - J) \tag{2.4'}$$

where F is net flows from financial assets and J is net purchases of financial assets, and these would both equal zero if we were considering the economy as a whole.

Note that, as in the case of net foreign assets, the fact that F and J are each zero in the aggregate does not imply the absence of wealth effects from a decision to tax the component flows, simply that these wealth effects cancel. Imposing a cash flow tax on all financial assets and liabilities places a tax on the returns to all existing financial assets and presents a subsidy of equal magnitude to those with financial liabilities. Indeed, this effect would occur even if F and J were not included explicitly in the tax base, if the price level rose and the financial assets and liabilities were not indexed to the price level. Some have argued that the adoption of a VAT would raise the price level by the extent of the tax; such a price increase would simulate the imposition of a cash flow tax on net financial assets (and indeed on all positions not indexed to the price level). It follows, of course, that including financial flows in the tax base *and* having the price level rise by the extent of the tax would effectively impose the cash flow tax on net asset positions twice.

Leaving aside these distributional effects of including financial flows in the cash flow tax base, these flows would not equal zero if we considered only the flows of the private sector, for then the net cash flows between the private sector and the government would be included in the tax base. This would have the effect of adding the present value of cash flows from existing government debt to the tax base; once again, nominal assets would be hit twice if the price level rose, in this case raising the present value of tax collections twice because the tax applies to a positive net asset position.

Another variation in the taxation of financial flows would be to apply a cash flow tax in full to the business sector. Cash flows within the business sector would, again, cancel out in terms of revenue, assuming all businesses are subject to the same tax rate, but flows between the business sector and the household sector would not cancel out. As the business sector is a net debtor to the household sector, this would have the effect of reducing the cash flow tax base by the present value of interest on net existing liabilities, assuming no special transition provisions. Such a variant of the cash flow tax was described by the Meade Committee as an "$R + F$" base cash flow tax.

An administrative advantage of the $R + F$ base is that it makes it easier to tax the income generated by the financial services sector. Recall that the objective of the consumption tax is to include all capital income components of GNP, R, in the tax base. But some components of capital income may be disguised as interest payments. Including all elements of $R + F$ in the tax base obviates the need to identify components of F that should really be included in R. Thus, an $R + F$ base VAT applied to a financial services company would automatically tax interest-rate spreads that compensate the company for the services it renders, and would eliminate the incentives of an integrated company offering both real and financial services to shift profits from real to financial activities.

Unfortunately, as it eliminates one complicating distinction, the $R + F$ base introduces another. As the Meade Committee Report (Chapter 12) observed, the transactions of the business sector are related by an identity which, using our notation, may be written

$$(R - I) + (F - J) + S = 0 \tag{2.5}$$

where S equals net transactions in corporate shares and dividend payments (i.e., the net flows between firms and their shareholders). Under an R base tax that ignores financial transactions between the business and household sectors, both $(F - J)$ and S are omitted from the tax base. Thus, transactions between a firm's creditors and shareholders are treated identically. Just as new share issues and dividends are excluded from the tax base, so are borrowing and interest payments. But, once $(F - J)$ is included in the tax base, transactions with creditors are subject to a cash flow tax—with taxes on borrowing and deductions for interest expenses and repayment of principal—while transactions with shareholders are still ignored.

How serious a problem this distinction in how the sources of funds are treated under the $R + F$ base depends on the extent to which firms can manipulate payments between debt and equity; for example, by issuing debt and equity to the same party and overstating deductible interest payments while understating nondeductible dividends. The problem is similar to that under the R base of shifts on the output side between the firm's real and financial activities, so the decision of whether to group financial flows with the firm's transactions with its customers or with the firm's transactions with its shareholders depends in part on where the problem of manipulation is greater.

There is also an analogy here to the problems attendant upon a decision to allow a choice under an individual expenditure tax between registered/qualified assets and unregistered/unqualified assets, to the extent that cash flows associated with individual assets can be manipulated.[11]

2.4. The Timing of Tax Payments

Aside from the differences in their treatment of rents and normal returns to existing assets, the cash flow and tax-exempt approaches also differ with respect to the timing of tax collections. While tax-exempt treatment simply imposes no taxes, cash flow treatment arrives at the same zero present value through deductions and taxes that offset. This distinction has two potentially important effects.

First, with truncated windows for revenue calculations, the tax-exempt approach appears less costly. The result can be distorted policy decisions, an example of which is the trend away from traditional IRAs (which provide cash flow treatment to contributed funds) to Roth IRAs (which provide tax-exempt treatment) in recent years in the United States, including the use as a revenue "source" of provisions encouraging investors to switch from the former to the latter. Another example, already cited above, is viewing border adjustments as a source of revenue when, in present value, they likely would involve a net revenue loss.

Second, with tax rates that vary over time, the cash flow tax no longer imposes a zero effective tax rate on capital accumulation. Indeed, the effective tax rates could be very positive or negative if large tax rate changes occur over short periods, given that gross investment is fully deductible in one year and gross returns are fully subject to taxation in others. This led Bradford (1998), among others, to suggest replacing the immediate deduction of investment with a procedure for carrying the basis of investment forward with interest and taking depreciation deductions in accordance with the timing of economic depreciation. While the deductions would have the same present value as expensing with tax rates constant, their timing would eliminate the distortion of investment decisions: marginal investments would face a zero effective tax rate, as only supernormal rents would be subject to taxation in any period.

This "basis with interest" approach thus combines the insulation from tax rate changes and the timing of revenues of the tax exemption approach with the taxation of rents present under the cash flow tax. However, this compromise has a major drawback relative to the simple cash flow tax (and, obviously, relative to tax exemption) of requiring that investors keep track of asset bases and calculate depreciation allowances over time.

Not having to measure capital income has generally been viewed as one of the major simplifications of cash flow taxation. Indeed, rather than attempting to make a cash flow tax look more like an income tax, Auerbach and Bradford (2004) adopted the opposite approach of considering how to make an income tax look more like a cash flow tax. They developed a method of using the cash flow tax with rising tax rates over time to simulate an income tax, suggesting that the advantages of eliminating basis could outweigh the disadvantage of susceptibility to time-varying tax rates, particularly with financial innovation making the identification of specific assets more difficult.

2.5. Individual versus Business Taxation

Consumption taxes can be imposed either at the business level or at the individual level. The working of the business-level VAT has already been discussed. A cash flow personal expenditure tax, sometimes called a consumed income tax, would start with the individual income base and subtract net saving. Assuming that saving is measured consistently with income, all income that is not saved is consumed, so the result would be a consumption tax. Similarly, one can adopt a mixed approach, as under the flat tax or the X-tax, that starts with a VAT and shifts the taxation of wages from the business to the individual level. While these approaches are all equivalent at the abstract level, they would likely differ in practice.

First, the business–household borderline is not clear, and some income-producing activities might be included in the household sector under a business level consumption tax. For example, how would a household's speculative holding of land be treated?

Second, progressive taxation based on an individual's circumstances can, realistically, only be applied to taxes at the individual level. Hence, the flat tax and the X-tax transfer the wage component of the tax base to households in order to apply progressive rate schedules to that base.

Third, the difference in statutory incidence would also affect the measured price level. A value-added tax, or a retail sales tax, added to factor incomes, would have a higher measured price level than if the same tax were collected from individual consumers through a consumed income tax. Although this difference simply reflects a convention in how the price level is measured—including indirect taxes but excluding direct taxes—it would have real effects to the extent that the price level matters as, for example, in the indexation of transfer payments. It would also matter to the extent that wages were sticky, either through explicit rigidities due to contract and minimum wage provisions, or due to other sources of sluggish adjustment.

Fourth, market prices of assets will differ according to the level at which taxes are collected. In comparing the impact on market values of a VAT and a consumed income tax, it is helpful to consider the treatment of traditional IRAs under current law. The securities inside an IRA have one market value, but this is not the after-tax value of the IRA to its owner (i.e., what the holder of the IRA could sell the account for if the future tax liability due on withdrawals was transferred along with the asset). If all investments were through IRAs, as effectively would be the case under an individual level consumption tax, the after-tax value of the existing IRA to the investor would fully capitalize these deferred taxes, because a new IRA composed of the same portfolio of securities would face no taxes in present value under a system with constant tax rates over time.[12] If the taxes were payable not by individuals holding the IRAs, but instead by the firms issuing the securities held in the IRAs, then the market values of the securities would already reflect the deferred taxes. There would be no difference in the after-tax value of the securities to investors, but the market values would adjust to offset the shift in statutory incidence of the tax from investors to firms.[13]

Because market values under economically equivalent consumption taxes can vary significantly, the impact on market values of adopting a consumption tax depends very much on how the tax is imposed, even if the ultimate economic impact of the tax does not. Consider a shift from the current U.S. tax system to a consumption tax. As discussed above, a consumption tax without transition relief incorporates a form of capital levy in its tax on rents and the normal returns to existing assets. This capital levy, in itself, would cause the after-tax values of assets to fall. An offsetting effect on asset values comes from an increase in asset demand due to a shift to the more favorable treatment of new investment. Still, it is likely that the after-tax values of existing assets to investors would fall.[14] However, the *market* values of the assets could rise if some taxes were shifted from the business level to the individual level. Given that the depreciation provisions of the current U.S. corporate income tax favor new assets over existing assets, the values of corporate shares should capitalize this difference, simulating the impact of partial cash flow taxation.[15] Going to full cash flow taxation but shifting the entire tax to the individual level, by replacing the current corporate and personal income taxes with a consumed income tax for example, would lower the after-tax values of these assets to investors, but *raise* their market values, because the taxes on asset sales would be due *after* the assets were sold.

Finally, some have argued that indirect consumption taxes are a more effective method of collecting taxes from individuals who do not report income or pay tax under the income tax. The logic is that these individuals currently pay no tax, but would be hit by sales tax or VAT on their purchases. Presumably, this supposed benefit of indirect consumption taxes would not apply to a household-level consumed income tax, for the tax evader would be no more likely to file a tax return than before. But the underlying logic itself is flawed, as the following discussion illustrates.

2.6. Activities Outside the Tax System

In a simple world without intermediate inputs or investment, where income equals consumption, it is easy to see the flaw in the previous logic. Imagine that there are two sectors, sector 1 is covered by the tax system and sector 2 is not covered. Under the income tax, sector 1 pays taxes while sector 2 does not. Under an indirect consumption tax, sector 1 again pays taxes, while sector 2 does not. Thus, there has been no change in the tax base, and hence no possible reason for any change in tax incidence.

A somewhat more sophisticated analysis that takes intermediate inputs into account does not change the basic story. Suppose now that the first sector produces both investment goods and consumption goods; that the investment goods serve as capital in both sectors; and that both sectors are competitive, so that price equals marginal cost. Then, under an income tax, the costs of production and hence prices in the covered and uncovered sectors will be, respectively:

$$p_1 = \frac{w}{1-t} l_1 + p_1 \frac{r}{1-t} k_1 \tag{2.6.1}$$

$$P_2 = wl_2 + p_1 rk_2 \tag{2.6.2}$$

where w and r are the required after-tax returns to labor and capital, t is the income tax rate, and l_i and k_i are unit labor and capital requirements, respectively, in each sector. Under an indirect consumption tax at rate τ, the effective tax rate on capital income becomes zero in the covered sector, so these expressions become:

$$p_1 = \frac{w}{1-\tau} l_1 + p_1 rk_1 \tag{2.7.1}$$

$$p_2 = wl_2 + p_1 rk_2 \tag{2.7.2}$$

Assuming that the tax change is revenue-neutral in present value, τ must be enough higher than t to make up for the revenue lost by setting the effective tax rate on capital to zero. Since only sector 1 is subject to taxation, this equal-revenue requirement implies that, for given values of w and r, the solution for p_1 in expressions (2.6.1) and (2.7.1) must be the same; hence, so are the solutions for p_2 in (2.6.2) and (2.7.2). Thus, with no change in w and r, there will be no change in the relative production costs or prices of the commodities produced by the covered and uncovered sectors. However, the reduction in the cost of capital relative to labor in sector 1 will encourage a shift from labor to capital in production, and this increased demand for capital relative to labor will raise r relative to w. As discussed further in Hines (2004), this change will raise relative costs in whichever sector is more capital intensive, quite plausibly the covered sector. Thus, the shift to an indirect consumption tax like a VAT may actually encourage the expansion of activity in the uncovered sector.

2.7. *Hybrid Tax Systems*

It is frequently asserted that tax systems that have some of the characteristics of an income tax and some of the characteristics of a consumption tax have effects on behavior that lie between those of an income tax and those of a consumption tax. For example, the 2006 *Economic Report of the President* says: "the personal income tax is actually a hybrid income-consumption tax, so that some of the taxes collected through the U.S. tax system, and those of other countries, might be thought of as taxes on consumption" (p. 115). The provisions to which this passage refers include tax-sheltered saving such as IRAs and relatively low rates of tax on dividends and capital gains. But having favorable treatment for some types of capital income, while it does reduce taxes on capital income, reduces taxes in a different way than, say, shrinking the income tax and replacing the lost revenue with a consumption tax. First, the differential treatment of assets distorts the allocation of capital. Second, the differential treatment of assets and liabilities and, in particular, the full deductibility of interest combined with reduced taxation of capital income, encourages borrowing to invest in tax-favored assets, rather than saving.[16]

3. The Consumption Tax and Economic Efficiency

There are several strands of the literature arguing that a consumption tax would be more efficient than an income tax. I will not attempt a detailed survey of this rich literature here, but will simply try to highlight some key results to provide a flavor of where things stand.[17]

One of the most frequently cited papers in this literature is that of Atkinson and Stiglitz (1976). They showed, under the assumption that preferences are weakly separable into consumption and leisure, that a progressive labor income tax is optimal by itself, i.e., that no variation in commodity taxes can improve social welfare. Although weak separability of preferences is not assured, it is a relatively mild restriction and it is not clear in which direction deviations would point in terms of differential commodity taxes. If one interprets the different consumption goods in the Atkinson-Stiglitz analysis as consumption in different periods, then the result may be interpreted as calling exclusively for a progressive tax on labor income or, in their model equivalently (because there are no initial assets and no transfers to other individuals), a progressive tax on lifetime consumption.

Even if the Atkinson-Stiglitz restriction on preferences is not satisfied, this violation does not necessarily imply that one would want to have higher taxes on future consumption than on current consumption, as would be effectively imposed by a capital income tax. A priori, a capital income subsidy is just as likely to be optimal as a capital income tax. Indeed, as the household's horizon lengthens, in the limit to the infinite horizon, the case against any significant tax on capital income is strengthened by another important result in the literature.

Perhaps the most striking result from infinite horizon models is the finding of Judd (1985) and Chamley (1986) that, for a system with taxes on labor and capital income, the long-run tax on capital income should be zero. Thus, leaving aside the distinction already discussed between consumption and wage taxes relating to the treatment of initial assets and rents, the result calls for consumption tax treatment in the long run. This conclusion is quite general in some respects; it does not depend on individual preferences taking a particular form, for example. The intuition is also very simple. For any given set of individual preferences, we might improve efficiency by taxing consumption in different periods at different rates. Taxing future consumption more heavily than current consumption could be achieved by taxing capital income, but it is implausible that we would want to tax consumption more and more heavily as we move into later and later periods, as would be the case if positive capital income taxes continued to apply. Thus, at some point, regardless of the exact form of preferences, the capital income tax will have to converge to zero.

Although Judd and Chamley derived their results in simple representative agent models without ability differences or progressive taxation, the logic would apply just as well in the Atkinson-Stiglitz framework: even if one did not want uniform consumption taxation, one would not want to have arbitrarily large distortions facing consumption at distant future dates. Further, the intuition associated with the Judd-Chamley result still resonates for finite horizon models, in that a positive capital income tax in every year would still impose a very high effective tax rate on consumption, say, 50 years in the future.

Aside from the usual restrictions that any modeling assumptions impose, however, there are particular problems in applying the Atkinson-Stiglitz result to the design of taxation over time. First, Atkinson and Stiglitz assume that each household has just one form of labor supply. Leaving aside the issue of how different members of a household should be treated at a given point in time, this assumption also ignores the fact that there is labor income in different periods. Even if consumption were separable from all forms of leisure, there is no presumption that leisure at different dates should be subject to the same tax schedule. One might, for example, think that age-specific labor income tax schedules would make sense.[18] But, more important, applying a static analysis like that in the Atkinson-Stiglitz paper to behavior over time ignores the fact that we observe the labor supply and consumption decisions of early periods before those of later ones. Thus, we might wish to implement a tax system in future periods that is conditioned on current decisions.[19] Considering such a dynamic model, Golosov, Kocherlakota, and Tsyvinski (2003) found that the Atkinson-Stiglitz result about uniform commodity taxation still applied across commodities *within* a given period, but that a positive capital income tax was generally optimal. The intuition is that higher capital income makes it more difficult for the government to impose redistributive labor income taxation, because the cost to high-ability individuals of not working hard is reduced by the presence of additional resources. Taxing capital income therefore weakens the self-selection constraints that the government's tax system must satisfy, allowing it more scope for redistribution.

Although capital income taxes distort consumption more and more over the infinite horizon, zero taxes on capital income may not be desirable if we seek to implement a plan for redistributive taxation. On the other hand, the literature lacks results suggesting that labor income and capital income should be treated equally by the tax system, and there is no obvious intuition suggesting that such a result might make sense, leaving aside practical difficulties that arise in distinguishing capital income and labor income. It is no accident that the literature has focused on whether it is efficient for capital income taxes to be zero, rather than on whether there should be equal taxes on capital income and labor income. Even with all the complications in the literature, there is a strong theoretical basis for thinking that consumption taxes will be more efficient than income taxes. But theory typically fails to tell us how great the efficiency difference might be. Given the transition costs of moving from one tax system to another, it could easily be the case that a small efficiency gain in moving to a consumption tax could be outweighed by the transition costs of doing so.

3.1. Previous Results from Simulation Models

Because the magnitude of the potential efficiency gain from adopting a consumption tax is important and yet difficult to discern from theory, there have been substantial efforts to assess the relative efficiency of income and consumption taxes using numerical simulation models with an empirical basis for their parameter assumptions. One model commonly used for this purpose is that of Auerbach and Kotlikoff (1987). In addition to their results, which compared the transition from an income tax to either a wage tax or a consumption tax, subsequent researchers have considered transitions from more realistic versions of the current tax system to a variety of specific tax systems, such as the flat tax or the X-tax, in both the original Auerbach-Kotlikoff model (Auerbach, 1996) or an extended version of the model that has individuals varying with respect to ability and lifetime income (Altig et al., 2001).

The findings in Auerbach and Kotlikoff (1987) are that a shift from an income tax to a consumption tax would increase economic efficiency, while a shift to a wage tax would reduce economic efficiency. The key difference between the two results for apparently similar tax systems is the treatment of assets in transition. Both a consumption tax and a wage tax would remove the distortion facing intertemporal consumption decisions, a change for which the literature would lead us to expect an efficiency gain. But a consumption tax would include in the tax base the returns to existing capital (there are no economic rents in the model), which increases the estimated efficiency gain under the model's assumption that this tax is an unanticipated capital levy that can be used to further reduce distortionary taxes. A wage tax provides no such capital levy. Further, by eliminating capital income taxes that those accumulating wealth had expected to pay, adoption of a wage tax in a sense provides a capital bonus, which has the opposite impact on efficiency compared with a capital levy, and works against the efficiency gains from eliminating the intertemporal consumption distortion. Thus, as the simulations confirm, it is possible for a shift to wage taxation to reduce economic efficiency even as it removes the intertemporal distortion of consumption.

These simulation results do not tell us how large the potential efficiency gains are exclusively from eliminating the intertemporal consumption distortions, because they combine this change with a change in the treatment of existing assets. But the fact that the treatment of existing assets can determine whether the overall efficiency gain is positive or negative suggests that the choice of transition provisions is critical. Auerbach (1996) confirms that providing transition relief within a given system, such as the flat tax, can have a significant impact on long-run output and economic efficiency, in some instances making the efficiency gains disappear entirely. Altig et al. (2001) do not estimate efficiency effects but find generally similar results with respect to the effects of transition relief on long-run output.[20]

None of the simulation results just cited incorporates the potential benefits of consumption taxation that taxes capital income more uniformly (at a rate of zero, in this instance). On the one hand, such benefits might be considerable, given the significant variation in effective tax rates on different investments. On the other hand, such benefits may be largely possible under the income tax. Although one of the argued advantages of the consumption tax is that it is much easier to tax asset income uniformly under that system, many of the very large distortions under the current income tax, such as the distinctions between debt and equity and between owner-occupied housing and other assets, could be substantially reduced without forsaking the income tax.

For example, Hubbard (1997) argues that one should think of the switch from our current tax system to a consumption tax in terms of two steps: the first, to a clean, broad-based income tax that removes the inter-asset distortions of the current tax system, and the second from this reformed income tax to a consumption tax. This decomposition gives credit for removing inter-asset distortions to the initial tax reform step rather than to adopting a consumption tax.

Hubbard argues further that since both the income tax and the consumption tax hit economic rents, and since both tax the returns to risk-taking in the same manner, the only distinction between their treatments of capital income is the income tax on the safe rate of return. As this safe rate of return is not large, the distinction between the income tax and consumption tax does not appear to be large either.

3.2. New Simulation Results

If the safe rate of return is close to zero, how large can the gains from reducing the tax rate on this return to zero be? In particular, to what extent do the simulation results just discussed, which are obtained from models in which the entire rate of return is treated as the normal returns to capital, overstate the efficiency gains from adopting a consumption tax? This is a difficult question to answer, because there is no simple way of extending the models to incorporate aggregate risk, in which the risky and safe rates of return are determined in equilibrium and the risk premium will change as the tax system and equilibrium change. We can get some idea of how the results might change, however, by considering a simpler experiment, in which the economy's capital intensity is held constant but the initial rate of return to capital is taken to be substantially lower than in the simulation results discussed earlier.

In Table 2.1 the summary statistics for simulations using the basic Auerbach-Kotlikoff model are reported. For the base case simulations, all of the preference and production parameters are the same as those used for the base case simulations in Auerbach and Kotlikoff (1987) and Auerbach (1996), except that costs of adjustment are assumed to exist for investment. A 25 percent proportional income tax is assumed, with no other taxes or government debt. For each simulation of a transition to a new tax system, the table presents three summary statistics: the percentage increase in output in the long run; the percentage gain in welfare of the representative individual in the long run (expressed relative to full lifetime resources—the present value of the individual's labor endowment, out of which consumption and leisure are financed); and the percentage gain in economic efficiency, calculated as the long-run gain in welfare when generations born prior to the beginning of the transition are compensated for gains or losses in welfare and all subsequent generations share equally the gains (or losses) from the change in tax policy.[21]

The results of a simulation of an immediate shift from the income tax to a proportional consumption tax are shown in the first row of Table 2.1. The long-run output gain is nearly 8 percent and the long-run gain in welfare is nearly 4 percent. The efficiency gain is considerably smaller, just over 0.5 percent, because a large share of the long-run gains comes from intergenerational redistribution. The second row of the table shows the results for a simulation of an immediate switch to a wage tax, revealing a drop in long-run output and long-run welfare, and an efficiency loss that is smaller in absolute value than the long-run welfare loss once the capital bonuses of early generations are neutralized. These results are consistent with those simulation results discussed earlier, in particular the efficiency gain under the consumption tax and the efficiency loss under the wage tax.

Consider now the effects of reducing the rate of return. For these alternative simulations, I reduce two parameters, the capital intensity of pro-

Table 2.1. The Long-Run and Efficiency Gains from Adopting a Consumption Tax: Simple Model Simulations

	Percentage Gain in		
Simulation[a]	Long-Run Output	Long-Run Welfare[b]	Efficiency[b]
Consumption Tax, Base Case	7.94	3.95	0.55
Wage Tax, Base Case	−2.63	−2.78	−1.35
Consumption Tax, Low Interest Rate	2.77	0.76	0.03
Wage Tax, Low Interest Rate	−0.91	−0.42	−0.14
Consumption Tax, Low Interest Rate, Rent[c]	6.42	1.53	0.15

a. All simulations based on the standard Auerbach-Kotlikoff (1987) closed-economy model, starting with an income tax of 25%, except where specified, and no other taxes or national debt. For the base case, preference and production parameters follow the original model's base case assumptions, except that adjustment costs in investment are assumed. For low interest rate simulations, the production share of capital is reduced from 0.25 to 0.09, and the rate of time preference is adjusted to hold the initial capital-output ratio fixed while reducing the interest rate to 0.4 times its base case value.

b. Gains expressed as a percentage of lifetime resources. *Long-run welfare gain* is gain of generations after the transition is complete. *Efficiency gain* is the gain of all generations born post-reform, when lump-sum taxes and transfers are used to neutralize welfare effects of all pre-reform generations.

c. The presence of rent is simulated by increasing the implicit capital levy, combining a higher rate of consumption tax with a wage subsidy.

duction and the rate of time preference, so that the capital-output ratio remains constant in the initial steady state while the interest rate in the initial steady state is reduced to 40 percent of its original value, from 7.90 percent to 3.16 percent.[22]

Before discussing the results of this experiment, it is useful to go through the intuition regarding the effects that this change in assumptions should have. For the transition to a wage tax, we should expect all the effects to be smaller in absolute value, for as capital income becomes smaller as a share of total income, the differences between a wage tax and an income tax become less significant; the capital bonus provided to earlier generations is reduced, as is the efficiency gain from removing the intertemporal distortion. Although these effects work in opposite directions, we know that as the rate of return converges to zero, the wage tax and the income tax become identical and hence the net change in all summary statistics converges to zero. As there is no reason to suspect that one of these effects should phase out more quickly than the other as the initial interest rate goes down, we would expect that a partial reduction in the initial interest rate would also reduce the impact of a transition to a wage tax.

For a consumption tax, the intuition is not quite as clear. Again, as the initial interest rate falls, the efficiency gain from eliminating the intertemporal distortion falls. But, even at a very low interest rate, the consumption tax's capital levy seems, at least at first, to remain fully in place. That is, consumption of existing assets will still be fully taxed under a consumption tax, even if these assets generate a low rate of return. However, the value of the capital levy to the government in terms of reducing distortionary taxes will still be reduced. If one thinks of the capital levy as a government asset providing an infinite stream of future returns that can be used to reduce wage taxes in future years, these returns will be lower, given the size of the capital levy, if the rate of return is lower. Hence, under the consumption tax we should also expect smaller efficiency gains for a lower initial interest rate.

The results shown in the third and fourth rows of Table 2.1 confirm the intuition of the previous two paragraphs. All measures move substantially closer to zero, particularly the efficiency effects of the two tax policies; yet there may be more to the story.

First, recall that a consumption tax alleviates the tax on the safe return to capital, but not on economic rents. To the extent that the higher observed return to capital in the economy, which the original parameter choices of the Auerbach-Kotlikoff model aimed to match, represents economic rents rather than returns to risk taking, the capital levy of the consumption tax will provide a larger stream over time than those generated by the previous consumption tax simulation. That is, even though the normal rate of return to new investment may be low, the capital levy will capture both the normal returns and the rents from existing capital. If the assumption of perfect competition still holds, then these rents are simply returns to fixed factors and provide an efficient tax base.

To explore how much larger the efficiency gain could be in the presence of economic rents, I consider the extreme case in which the entire gap between the observed return to capital in the economy and the safe rate of return is attributable to economic rents; that is, the flow from the capital levy is as large as in the base case simulations, but the efficiency gain from eliminating the intertemporal distortion is still smaller because of the lower return to new saving.[23] The result of this simulation is given in the fifth row of Table 2.1. As expected, the gains in output and efficiency are now much larger, although still smaller than those under the base case (high-interest-rate simulation). That a gap remains makes sense, because even with the restoration of the capital levy's value, getting rid of the intertemporal distortion is still less important. Recall, too, that this simulation reflects the extreme assumption that the entire return to the existing capital stock is either rent or a normal return to capital. If rent accounts for a smaller share of observed returns, the effects will be muted.

3.3. Caveats in the Interpretation of Simulation Evidence

There are two additional considerations that point toward higher potential gains from reducing taxation on capital income, relative to the low-interest-rate simulations in Table 2.1.

First, if economic rents are present, there may be more to take into account than just the capital levy on such rents. One should also reconsider the standard assumption of perfect competition. Rents could be generated in a competitive environment, but they also may be the result of imperfect competition. If firms are restricting production to levels at which price exceeds marginal cost, then to the distortions of taxation we must add the additional noncompetitive mark-up. Assuming that capital goods markets are among those in which noncompetitive distortions exist, moreover, means that the departure from perfect competition will not simply distort consumption by raising consumer prices, but will also discourage the use of capital in production by raising capital goods prices.

This additional wedge in the capital goods market has two implications for polices that reduce capital income taxation: the efficiency gains will be larger, because the reduction is starting from a more distorted initial point; and the optimal capital income tax will be lower, because even a zero capital income tax will leave the non-tax distortion of capital use in place. Starting from an infinite horizon model in which the optimal long-run capital income tax would be zero under perfect competition, Judd (1997) finds that the optimal capital income tax is quite negative in a noncompetitive environment calibrated to U.S. evidence. While the qualitative implications of this analysis are clear—the efficiency gains from eliminating capital income taxes are bigger than otherwise estimated—the quantitative implications for the life-cycle simulation results discussed here are not clear without further efforts at simulation modeling that incorporates different types of imperfect competition.

Second, one should remember that capital income taxes are not simply symmetric, proportional taxes on capital income. If they were, then the effective tax rate on capital income would not vary with the division of the observed rate of return into its components of safe return, rent, and excess return to risk-taking—the tax base would be capital income, and all components of the tax base would have the same tax rate applied. But the tax system is much more complicated, and different factors suggest that as we take risk into account and recognize that the safe rate of return is lower than the observed return to capital, our estimated effective tax rate on that safe rate of return will be higher.

Asymmetries in the tax system increase the tax burden on risky assets, a point understood since the work of Domar and Musgrave (1944). That is, the tax burden on the excess return is not zero, so for risky assets this must be added to the burden that the capital income tax imposes on the safe rate of return. Because depreciation schedules are not based on actual, *ex post* economic depreciation, the effective tax rate, even under a symmetric tax system, will vary with the safe discount rate and the extent to which depreciation itself is risky. As shown in the Appendix, reducing the assumed discount rate and taking risky depreciation into account will both tend to increase our estimate of the effective tax rate on investment.

Thus, the rate of return relevant in calculating the intertemporal distortion may be lower than has been assumed in simulation models, but the tax rate applicable to that lower rate of return is likely to be higher. How much higher is difficult to know, because it depends on an asset's riskiness, the extent to which the firm is able to offset one asset's losses with another asset's gains, and how tax asymmetries interact with adjustments for risk.[24]

3.4. A Further Consideration of Taxation and Risk

Until now, the discussion of risk has maintained the assumption of market efficiency—that taxation provides no insurance function because the private market has already efficiently pooled risks and that the remaining aggregate risk has been allocated among individuals in an efficient manner. While this may be a reasonably accurate assumption for securities markets, it is more problematic for some assets, such as small businesses, and for the returns to human capital as well. As has long been understood, taxation can serve as a means of pooling risks if markets to pool risks are incomplete. Even distortionary taxes might improve welfare by also improving the efficiency of risk pooling and risk bearing.

Taking this market failure into account can change ones conclusions regarding the desirability of certain tax policies. For example, Nishiyama and Smetters (2005) extend the Auerbach-Kotlikoff model to include idiosyncratic risks to labor income and longevity, and find that the transition from a progressive income tax to a proportional consumption tax would induce an efficiency loss by reducing marginal tax rates on labor income and hence the tax system's implicit provision of insurance. Presumably, the same type of analysis would apply to reductions in capital income taxes to the extent that individuals have idiosyncratic capital risks. In this case, the consumption tax would diverge from the wage tax in its treatment of the return to risk-taking, because the assumption that investors can scale up or down their risky asset positions would no longer apply. The consumption tax, like the income tax, would provide insurance of risky capital income, although, as in the Nishiyama-Smetters analysis, any reduction in marginal tax rates would also reduce the tax system's insurance function.

One needs to exercise some care, though, in thinking about the role of the tax system when markets for risk are incomplete. An analysis needs to also consider why market failure has occurred in the first place. As Weisbach (2004) points out, there are different reasons why individuals might hold undiversified positions. One reason might be adverse selection; for example, a small business whose owner seeks to lay off some of its ownership risk might be perceived as a lemon. In this case, the tax system's mandatory participation would provide a benefit, as the analysis above suggested. On the other hand, some of the lack of diversification might be due to moral hazard; for example, individuals who insure their human capital risk would have little incentive to work if there is no way to separate the effects on observed income of effort and stochastic shocks. A tax system that provided such insurance would have the same disincentive effects, making the insurance function unattractive.

3.5. Other Behavioral Issues

Until now, I have said nothing about inheritances and bequests. There are many potential explanations for bequests, and they differ in how they would affect the previous analysis. A strong altruistic bequest motive, as in Barro

(1974), turns the decisions of a life-cycle individual into the infinite horizon calculations of a dynasty, thereby increasing the deadweight loss from capital income taxation. On the other hand, accidental bequests that occur because of incomplete annuity markets do not imply any extension of an individual's planning horizon. As confirmed by simulations presented in Altig et al. (2001), even planned bequests, if they are motivated by the benefits of giving rather than the ultimate consumption of one's heirs, need have little impact on the desirability of consumption taxes. Moreover, as already discussed above, the distortions of future consumption resulting from capital income taxation are already significant within the long-horizon life-cycle context, so the potential lengthening of the horizon beyond one's own lifetime doesn't make the efficiency argument for eliminating capital income taxes that much stronger.

Perhaps a more important behavioral realm is the various departures from unconstrained life-cycle saving behavior. As many recent authors have suggested, observed saving behavior, at least on the part of a significant share of the population, seems at odds with fully informed optimization. The implications for capital income taxes are not clear, however, even if individuals fail to save adequately. Depending on the nature of the departure from the standard rational choice assumptions, one might wish to increase tax incentives to save or, alternatively, to tax capital income (Bernheim and Rangel, 2005). Yet the institutional arrangements associated with saving, such as the default options of employer-sponsored pension plans, may be quite important, even though such arrangements are of minor consequence in the standard model.

Thus, the efficiency effects of a consumption tax may turn on how the change in taxation influences the nature of institutional arrangements. For example, if a shift from targeted saving incentives to a broad-based favorable treatment of saving reduces the appeal of coordinated saving through employer-sponsored plans, saving might actually fall. This effect is by no means certain, for tax reforms could be structured to maintain some advantages for coordinated saving. But there is increasing appreciation that this developing line of research may be of central importance in thinking about tax reform.

4. The Progressivity of Consumption Taxes

One of the common concerns about shifting from an income tax to a consumption tax is that a consumption tax would be less progressive than the income tax. There is little of a general nature that can be said about this without reference to the consumption tax under consideration. There is little doubt that a national retail sales tax would shift burdens away from groups with high earnings, or that an X-tax, with progressive rates on labor income, would be less likely to do so. Indeed, the simulations in Altig et al. (2001) find that, in the long run, the distributional effects of a switch from the income tax to the X-tax would be quite neutral, with very similar percentage increases in lifetime welfare for all lifetime-income classes; the slight differences among the groups would favor those with lower lifetime income.[25] Rather than comment on the progressivity of the consumption tax per se, it is more useful to touch on a few issues regarding how this progressivity should be judged.

First, the conclusions of Altig et al. (2001) are based on lifetime tax burdens, not the taxes paid in a single year. It is a simple implication of consumption smoothing that consumption will fluctuate less than income, so that the consumption tax base will appear less progressive when evaluated on an annual basis than on a lifetime basis. But it is not clear why one would wish to evaluate progressivity on an annual basis.

Second, in the presence of bequests, the form of consumption taxation and the nature of the bequest motive matter for incidence calculations. The model used by Altig et al. (2001) included a realistic level and pattern of bequests, modeled as resulting from a "utility of bequests" motive, but also found that the long-run welfare consequences, including the roughly equal percentage welfare gains by lifetime income groups, were not significantly affected by whether the bequest motive was present. This finding may seem surprising, given that bequests are concentrated among the highest lifetime income groups. One might think, for example, that with bequests not being taxed as consumption, the most affluent would fare much better once bequests were taken into account. Indeed, it has been a concern among many that it would be hard to replicate even lifetime progressivity under a consumption tax, given how large a share of their lifetime resources the rich *do not* consume. Altig et al. likely did not encounter this problem because the cash flow component of the X-tax is collected at the business level. As discussed above, this means that the tax is capitalized into the value of assets.[26] Thus it hits not just lifetime consumption, but also bequests.

Under a personal consumption tax like the consumed income tax, the same treatment of bequests would require taxing bequests as consumption instead of taxing them upon eventual consumption by heirs. But this shift in the timing of taxation would have no impact on heirs' consumption and hence no impact on the lifetime welfare of donors unless the utility of bequests was based on gross bequests, rather than on the level of consumption that bequests could finance.

Third, long-run calculations do not take into account the incidence of transition provisions. If a consumption tax is implemented without transition relief, for example, the effects of the capital levy on initial generations could be quite progressive. This would be even more relevant to the extent that the assets are inherited, given the concentration of bequests and inheritances.

Fourth, it is difficult to analyze consistently the distributional effects of different consumption tax proposals using an annual frame of reference because, as discussed above, the timing of tax payments differs among approaches. For example, a consumption tax with transition relief may impose the same burdens on all individuals as a wage tax, but consumption tax payments will be aligned with consumption, not wages. This difference will wash out of calculations done on a lifetime basis, but will be misleading on an annual basis, regardless of whether individuals are grouped by current income, lifetime income, or some other measure of ability to pay.

Finally, as is always the case in incidence analysis, one needs to distinguish between tax burdens and tax payments. For instance, to the extent that capital income taxes, or consumption taxes, fall on the excess returns to risky assets, the theory discussed above suggests that these taxes impose no burden. Thus, these taxes should be left out when assessing the tax burdens of the respective tax systems.

5. Conclusions

One can draw several conclusions from this chapter's analysis. I mention four here.

First, there are several attributes that define a consumption tax and distinguish it from an income tax, although not all of these attributes are found in every variant of the consumption tax. Most versions of the consumption tax would impose a zero effective tax rate on the normal returns to capital but a progressive annual consumption tax might not. Most would tax economic rent and the excess return to risk-taking, but a wage tax would not. Most would be imposed on a destination basis, but a flat tax would not. Most would eliminate any consideration of asset basis, but an X-tax in which undepreciated basis is carried forward with interest would not.

Second, several of the supposed key advantages in adopting some form of consumption tax do not stand simple scrutiny, notably its purported ability to improve the trade balance through border adjustments and to reach economic activities that escape the income tax.

Third, evaluations of consumption taxes need to control for differences in their application; for example, with respect to the timing of tax payments, whether or not taxes are structured so as to be capitalized into observed market values of assets, and whether excess returns to risk-taking are included in the tax base. These differences are especially a problem when one attempts to evaluate the distributional impact of a tax system using annual tax payments as a measure.

Fourth, the efficiency gains from adopting a consumption tax depend on how the tax is implemented, particularly on how assets are treated during transition. Simulation evidence to date has not taken into account a variety of issues that could significantly affect the estimated efficiency gains from adopting a consumption tax. Some of these issues point toward smaller potential gains, while others point toward larger gains. Recent contributions in behavioral economics suggest that a variety of institutional characteristics beyond the effective tax rate on capital income may be very important in determining the effects of adopting a consumption tax.

Appendix: Effective Tax Rates and the Safe Rate of Return

The standard formula for the effective tax rate, based on the user cost of capital (see, e.g., Auerbach 1983) is

$$\tau = \frac{(r+\delta)(1-uz)-(r+\delta)(1-u)}{(r+\delta)(1-uz)-\delta(1-u)} \tag{2.A.1}$$

where r is the real required return, δ is the rate of economic depreciation, u is the statutory tax rate, and z is the present value of depreciation allowances.

Suppose τ has been calculated using the observed after-tax rate of return, and we now wish to change the calculation to take into account the fact that the observed return is risky. As discussed in Auerbach (1983), there are two changes necessary. First, the value of r that appears in (2.A.1) and in the calculation of z must be reduced to the safe rate of return. Second, as uncertain depreciation is effectively equivalent to a faster rate of deprecation (a point first noted by Bulow and Summers 1984), the value of δ must be increased. If we assume that τ equals u in the original calculation, meaning that the acceleration of depreciation allowances just offsets the effect of inflation at the original values of r and δ, then it may be shown that $d\tau/dr < 0$ and $d\tau/d\delta > 0$, so both adjustments (reducing r and increasing δ) initially increase the estimated effective tax rate.

NOTES

This chapter was presented at a conference, "Key Issues in Public Finance: A Conference in Honor of David Bradford " held at New York University in May 2006. I am grateful to Dan Shaviro, my discussants Glenn Hubbard and Al Warren, and other conference participants for comments on earlier drafts.

1. The right-hand side of expression (2.1) is referred to as gross national income, differing from GNP only by the statistical discrepancy that arises in measuring the same aggregate on the product and income sides.
2. The notation used for net foreign income reflects the fact that most such income is capital income.
3. For simplicity, expression (2.3) omits international transfer payments from the current account balance. Such transfer payments include government and private foreign aid as well as tax payments to foreign governments.
4. *Blueprints* referred to assets included under the cash flow tax as "qualified" assets, while the Meade Committee distinguished between registered assets (those subject to the cash flow tax) and unregistered assets.
5. See Auerbach (1997) for further discussion.
6. Note that this reasoning does not require perfect competition on the part of domestic firms. As an exchange rate appreciation is equivalent to an ad valorem tax on exports from the point of view of domestic producers, a border adjustment combined with an offsetting exchange rate appreciation leaves marginal revenue conditions unaffected. The same argument holds on the input side with respect to the impact of a tax on imports combined with exchange rate appreciation. Thus, regardless of whether firms are price-takers or not, there should be no change in their behavior.
7. Net income from abroad, R^f, remained positive through 2005 for the United States, even though the U.S. net international investment position has been negative for several years. This indicates that U.S. assets abroad have been earning a higher rate of return than foreign assets in the United States. However, with the increasingly negative U.S. international investment position, net income from abroad is still trending downward, virtually hitting zero in 2005 and falling below zero in the final quarter of that year.
8. Ironically, another current argument favoring the U.S. adoption of a destination-based VAT is that, given large current U.S. trade deficits, it would raise more

money than an origin-based version. This highlights the distinction between short-run and long-run revenue consequences.

9. Indeed, the incidence of these taxes and subsidies does not require full adjustment of the nominal exchange rate; for example, if the domestic price level rose to offset the border adjustment in reaction to the shift from origin to destination basis, no change in the exchange rate would be necessary to maintain equilibrium, but domestic assets would rise in nominal value and hence still appreciate in units of the foreign currency, and U.S.-held foreign assets would have their real values reduced when deflated by the U.S. price level.
10. http://www.bea.gov/bea/newsrelarchive/2005/intinv04_fax.pdf.
11. See, e.g., Graetz (1979).
12. The story is more complicated under the current system in which IRAs provide a higher rate of return than fully taxed assets. If the alternative investment is subject to income taxes but not subject to taxes on withdrawal, then there are offsetting effects on the value of the IRA, the relative impact of deferred taxes declining with respect to the length of the holding period as the advantage of tax-free investment grows. See Poterba (2004) for further discussion.
13. The same distinction will apply to the domestic prices of foreign assets. Recall that, under a VAT, border adjustments will cause the home currency to appreciate against foreign currencies in proportion to the border adjustment. As border adjustments effectively apply cash flow taxation to net foreign investment, this reduction in the domestic value of existing foreign assets is analogous to the reduction in value of domestic assets under a VAT. Under a consumed income tax, extending cash flow treatment to the purchases and sales of foreign assets would impose the same tax treatment as would border adjustments under a VAT, but would not induce a change in the exchange rate. Investors would be in the same after-tax positions under both systems, but the taxes would be collected at the company level and hence capitalized under the border-adjusted VAT.
14. See the simulations in Auerbach (1996) or Altig et al. (2001).
15. See, e.g., Auerbach (1983).
16. One might argue that the borrowed funds still must come from somewhere and therefore require additional saving, but even this is not necessarily true because the funds can come from one's own sheltered investments. For example, an individual's pension fund saving can be used to purchase that same individual's new interest-deductible mortgage. In this example, there would be no net saving, as the increased borrowing would exactly equal the increased pension assets.
17. For a good recent survey of much of this literature, see Zodrow (2005).
18. See, e.g., Kremer (2001).
19. This is distinct from the incentive that a government will have to deviate from a previously announced policy; for example, to announce a capital subsidy but then implement a capital income tax once capital has been accumulated.
20. As is discussed in the recent report of the President's Advisory Panel on Tax Reform (2005, p. 174), how the transition relief is provided can determine whether the long-run output gain from a consumption tax is reduced. In

Auerbach (1996) and Altig et al. (2001), the cost of transition relief was spread smoothly over the indefinite future and thus permanently raised taxes and reduced output. If, instead, the cost of transition relief were paid for entirely during a short transition period, the long-run impact on output and tax rates would be nil—the tax system would be identical to the case without transition relief, and so the economy would look the same as well. But long-run output gains and efficiency gains are distinct, and it is likely that concentrating the cost of transition relief would reduce the efficiency gains from tax reform even more than paying for such relief smoothly over time, because of the nonlinear relationship between deadweight loss and marginal tax rates.

21. Further details of the simulation methodology and parameter assumptions may be found in Auerbach and Kotlikoff (1987) or Auerbach (1996).
22. In the model's Cobb-Douglas production function, the capital intensity parameter in the production function, β, equals capital's share of output, $r\kappa$, where r is the before-tax interest rate and κ is the capital-output ratio. In the base case, $\beta = 0.25$, consistent with capital's observed income share of about one quarter. I reduce β to 0.10 and then reduce the pure rate of time preference from its original value of 0.015 so that enough saving is generated to maintain κ at its original value in the initial steady state. (The new value of the pure rate of discount is -0.009.) Since κ stays the same, r must drop by the same percentage that β does, i.e., from 0.25 to 0.10, or by 60 percent.
23. To simulate this scenario, given that the model itself has no economic rents, I combine a higher consumption tax with a wage subsidy, letting the consumption tax account for 250 percent of required revenue and using the excess revenue for the wage subsidy. Because a consumption tax plus a wage subsidy is simply a capital levy, this policy multiplies the capital levy in the transition to a consumption tax by 2.5. This magnification just offsets the lower rate of return that the capital levy generates because the safe interest rate is 0.4 times its original value.
24. Auerbach (1983) calculates effective tax rates for different assets taking asymmetric taxation into account, and performs separate calculations of the impact of risk adjustment on effective tax rates. But these calculations are done separately and are not integrated.
25. It is, of course, conceivable that the percentage of welfare gains under the X-tax would have been higher for the very highest lifetime income groups, had Altig et al. (2001) broken down the top 2 percent of the population, their highest group, into still smaller groups.
26. Altig et al. (2001, Table 4) find that the long-run value of Tobin's q, the ratio of market value to capital, is reduced by 12 percent by the X-tax.

REFERENCES

Altig, David, Alan J. Auerbach, Laurence J. Kotlikoff, Kent A. Smetters, and Jan Walliser. 2001. "Simulating Fundamental Tax Reform in the United States." *American Economic Review* 91(3): 574–595.

Andrews, William D. 1974. "A Consumption-Type or Cash Flow Personal Income Tax." *Harvard Law Review* 87(6): 1113–1188.

Atkinson, Anthony B., and Joseph E. Stiglitz. 1976. "The Design of Tax Structure: Direct versus Indirect Taxation." *Journal of Public Economics* 6(1–2): pp. 55–75.

Auerbach, Alan J. 1983. "Corporate Taxation in the United States." *Brookings Papers on Economic Activity* 14(2): 1451–1505.

Auerbach, Alan J. 1996. "Tax Reform, Capital Allocation, Efficiency and Growth." In Henry Aaron and William Gale, (eds.), *Economic Effects of Fundamental Tax Reform* (pp.29–81). Washington: Brookings.

Auerbach, Alan J. 1997. "The Future of Fundamental Tax Reform." *American Economic Review* 87(2): 143–146.

Auerbach, Alan J., and David F. Bradford. 2004. "Generalized Cash-Flow Taxation." *Journal of Public Economics* 88(5): 957–980.

Auerbach, Alan J., and Laurence J. Kotlikoff. 1987. *Dynamic Fiscal Policy.* Cambridge: Cambridge University Press.

Barro, Robert J. 1974. "Are Government Bonds Net Wealth?" *Journal of Political Economy* 82(6): 1095–1117.

Bernheim, B. Douglas, and Antonio Rangel. 2005. "Behavioral Public Economics: Welfare and Policy Analysis with Non-Standard Decision Makers." NBER Working Paper 11518, July.

Bradford, David F. 1986. *Untangling the Income Tax.* Cambridge, MA: Harvard University Press.

Bradford, David F. 1998. "Transition to and Tax Rate Flexibility in a Cash-Flow Type Tax." In James M. Poterba (ed.), *Tax Policy and the Economy* (vol. 12, pp. 151–172). Cambridge, MA: MIT Press.

Bradford, David F., and the U.S. Treasury Tax Policy Staff. 1984. *Blueprints for Basic Tax Reform* (2nd ed.). Arlington, VA: Tax Analysts.

Bulow Jeremy I., and Lawrence H. Summers. 1984. "The Taxation of Risky Assets." *Journal of Political Economy* 92(1): 20–39.

Chamley, Christophe. 1986. "Optimal Taxation of Capital Income in General Equilibrium with Infinite Lives." *Econometrica* 54(3): 607–622.

Domar, Evsey D., and Richard A. Musgrave. 1944. "Proportional Income Taxation and Risk-Taking." *Quarterly Journal of Economics* 58(3): 388–422.

Economic Report of the President. 2006. Washington, DC: U.S. Government Printing Office.

Fisher, Irving. 1939. "The Double Taxation of Savings." *American Economic Review* 29(1): 16–33.

Golosov, Mikhail, Narayana Kocherlakota, and Aleh Tsyvinski. 2003. "Optimal Indirect and Capital Taxation." *Review of Economic Studies* 70(3): 569–587.

Gordon, Roger H. 1985. "Taxation of Corporate Capital Income: Tax Revenues versus Tax Distortions." *Quarterly Journal of Economics* 100(1): 1–27.

Graetz, Michael J. 1979. "Implementing a Progressive Consumption Tax." *Harvard Law Review* 92(8): 1575–1661.

Hall, Robert, and Alvin Rabushka. 1985. *The Flat Tax.* Stanford, CA: Hoover Institution Press.

Hines, James R., Jr. 2004. "Might Fundamental Tax Reform Increase Criminal Activity?" *Economica* 71 (August): 483–492.

Hubbard, R. Glenn. 1997. "How Different Are Income and Consumption Taxes?" *American Economic Review* 87(2): 138–142.

Institute for Fiscal Studies. 1978. *The Structure and Reform of Direct Taxation.* London: Allen and Unwin.

Judd, Kenneth L. 1985. "Redistributive Taxation in a Simple Perfect Foresight Model." *Journal of Public Economics* 28(1): 59–83.

Judd, Kenneth L. 1997. "The Optimal Tax Rate for Capital Income is Negative." NBER Working Paper 6004, April.

Kaldor, Nicholas. 1955. *An Expenditure Tax.* London: Allen and Unwin.

Kaplow, Louis. 1994. "Taxation and Risk Taking: A General Equilibrium Perspective." *National Tax Journal* 47(4): 789–798.

Kremer, Michael. 2001. "Should Taxes be Independent of Age?" Unpublished manuscript, Harvard University.

Nishiyama, Shinichi, and Kent Smetters. 2005. "Consumption Taxes and Economic Efficiency with Idiosyncratic Wage Shocks." *Journal of Political Economy* 113(5): 1088–1115.

Poterba, James M. 2004. "Valuing Assets in Retirement Saving Accounts." *National Tax Journal* 75(2): 489–512.

President's Advisory Panel on Federal Tax Reform. 2005. *Simple, Fair, and Pro-Growth.* Washington, DC: U.S. Government Printing Office.

U.S. Department of the Treasury. 1977. *Blueprints for Basic Tax Reform.* Washington, DC: U.S. Government Printing Office.

Warren, Alvin C., Jr. 1996. "How Much Capital Income Taxed under an Income Tax Would Be Exempt under a Cash-Flow Tax?" *Tax Law Review* 52(1): 1–16.

Weisbach, David A. 2004. "The (Non)Taxation of Risk." *Tax Law Review* 58(1): 1–57.

Zodrow, George R. 2005, September. "Should Capital Income Be Subject to Consumption-Based Taxation?" Paper presented at the American Tax Policy Institute Conference on Taxing Capital Income.

CHAPTER 2

Comment 1

R. GLENN HUBBARD

Alan Auerbach's chapter provides an excellent primer on consumption taxation, with both a useful review and instructive new insights. The choice between an income tax and a consumption tax is often discussed in policy circles in terms of stark differences but, as Auerbach reminds us, conceptual differences between textbook income and consumption taxes are, in many respects, modest. In any event, most actual tax systems in industrial economies (including the United States) are a hybrid of income and consumption taxation.

This essay was an important one to include in the conference that led to this book, as the topic was near and dear to David Bradford's heart. Bradford, a master thinker and teacher, probed the distinction between income and consumption taxation with his customary intellectual passion. Recent U.S. policy changes to reduce capital income taxation owe an enormous debt to Bradford. And my own work in the area benefited tremendously from Bradford's probing questions and advice, with conversations stretching back to the late 1970s at the Summer Institute Program of the National Bureau of Economic Research. Bradford's interest in consumption taxation reflected conventional economic concerns about efficiency consequences of taxation and about costs of complexity. But his take on "fairness" comparisons of income and consumption taxation was a signature question: Why should the tax code penalize an individual who chooses to save for the future as opposed to consuming all of his or her, current resources?

Auerbach's chapter provides three things: (1) a primer on the definition of consumption taxes, (2) caution against simple extrapolation of intuitive ideas about consumption taxes, and (3) challenges for economic analysis. His punch lines are three. First, defining a consumption tax is simple . . . *or not.* (Where lies the devil in the details?) Second, delineating efficiency gains is straightforward . . . *or not.* (How much of the gain from reform reflects consequences of transition-period reallocations? How different are income and consumption taxes anyway?) Third, understanding businesspeople's occasional enthusiasm for consumption taxes is easy . . . *or not.* (Or, as I describe below, is the attraction for businesspeople to no capital taxation or to border-tax adjustments?)

1. What Is a Consumption Tax?

To put Auerbach's primer in context, a brief history of economic thought is in order. Early contributions by economists and legal academics emphasized direct individual consumption taxation (as opposed to European-style value-added taxes [VAT]); see especially Fisher (1939), Kaldor (1955), and Andrews (1974). This approach was embodied in policy analysis, including the *Blueprints* work Bradford supervised at the U.S. Treasury Department (U.S. Department of the Treasury, 1977) as well as the Meade Committee Report in the United Kingdom (Institute for Fiscal Studies, 1978). More recent contributions by Bradford and others embraced hybrid approaches of direct and indirect taxation (see, e.g., the X-tax of Bradford, 1986; the flat tax, Hall and Rabushka, 1985; and, in the context of the income tax, the Comprehensive Business Income Tax described in U.S. Department of the Treasury, 1992).

While these strands of policy analysis have made substantial progress in describing how a consumption tax might be implemented in practice, many open economic questions remain about the distinctions between consumption and income taxation, as Auerbach notes. Since the late 1970s, theoretical and empirical research by economists has sharpened our knowledge of the effects of tax policy on saving (sensitivity to the net return), investment (sensitivity to the user cost of capital), portfolio risk-taking, and entrepreneurial risk-taking, as well as implications for capital income taxation of imperfect competition.

2. What Does a "Consumption Tax" Tax?

One can think of a consumption tax as being equivalent to a tax on wages plus taxes on net cash flows (i.e., gross income less gross investment) from domestic and foreign activities. (By *consumption tax,* I mean a broad-based tax on consumption, as opposed to consumption taxes, like many value-added taxes, which exempt some categories of consumption from taxation.) Expressed this way, a switch to a broad-based consumption tax is often characterized by a move to a wage tax plus a one-time capital levy (i.e., a tax on net cash flows on existing assets). From the standpoint of efficiency, revenue from this capital levy can be used to keep distorting taxes on wages low. From the standpoint of fairness, the consumption tax is said to exempt capital income from taxation, so that the question of the distribution of capital income becomes important.

Including net cash flows in the definition of the consumption tax base raises the question of what is capital income. *Capital income* is really the sum of the safe rate of interest, the risk premium (compensation for *ex ante* risk bearing), inframarginal returns (tracing to market power on entrepreneurial skill), and luck (*ex post* realizations). If one contrasts, say, the base of the Hall-Rabushka flat tax or the Bradford X-tax with the Treasury Department's Comprehensive Business Income Tax, one can conclude that the taxation of the risk premium, inframarginal returns, and luck is equivalent under the income and consumption tax prototypes; the difference lies in the taxation of the safe rate of interest (see the analysis and review in Hubbard, 1997; Gentry and Hubbard, 1997, 1998). This difference is not large, as the safe rate of interest is small. Such a conclusion does not imply gains from tax reform are small; the move from the present tax system to either a broad-based income tax or consumption tax is likely to generate substantial efficiency gains. But the observation does raise questions about models of efficiency or distributional consequences of fundamental tax reform that assume a single rate of return on capital.

The inclusion of net cash flows from foreign activities in the consumption tax base is of particular interest to businesspeople, as Auerbach notes. Some implementations of consumption taxes (e.g., a conventional VAT) would be allowed under present international conventions to impose border-tax adjustments on imports and exports, while others (such as the flat tax) would not. Do border adjustments matter? I sometimes hear from business friends that the world can be divided into "economists" and "real people." If so, border tax adjustments are a wedge issue! Economists observe that the present value of a country's imports and exports must be equivalent, so that a tax on net imports (i.e., a border-tax adjustment) has a zero present value. Business leaders are seldom persuaded by this argument, and believe that a border-tax adjustment will increase the competitiveness of domestic firms. Now, it is true that economists abstract from how long current account imbalances persist before they are corrected and tax rates may change over time, but one can design examples under which border-tax adjustment could help or harm domestic competitiveness in the near term. To a first approximation, the question of a border-tax adjustment should not be an important one for the choice of consumption taxation or even for the prototype for consumption taxation. And, as Auerbach points out, even systematic intervention in foreign-exchange markets by a foreign government (as in the case of China today) offers no support of the border-tax-adjustment-promotes-competitiveness view so long as the foreign government looks to the real exchange rate as its measure of competitiveness.

Both domestic and foreign net cash flows raise interesting questions about equivalences in the present value of taxes collected under alternative prototypes of consumption taxation. Under constant tax rates, tax-exempt treatment for returns to saving imposes no tax, and the present value of deductions and taxes under cash flow treatment is also zero. That is, thinking of a consumption tax as a front-loaded IRA or a back-loaded IRA makes no difference. Varying tax rates complicate matters, though Bradford (1988) offered an alternative (though somewhat difficult) method to maintain a zero effective tax rate on capital accumulation—carrying the basis of capital investment forward with interest and using economic depreciation. The other departure from the IRA equivalence occurs in the policy process—the use of narrower time windows for revenue calculations in which front-loaded and back-loaded IRA treatment appears to be different, possibly distorting policy choices.

3. How Important Are Transition Costs?

The shift to a consumption tax is often described as including a tax on old capital because the tax falls in part on net cash flows on existing assets. Some care is in order in interpreting this observation, though, as a shift to a consumption tax can lead to multiple effects on asset prices (and the value of old capital). Because a consumption tax incorporates expensing of new capital assets, the shift to a consumption tax should reduce the value of existing capital and asset prices. But there are reasons to believe these asset price effects are not as large as many conventional models suggest. First, costs of adjusting the capital stock bid up the value of existing capital in the near term. Second, and more important, consumption tax reforms that eliminate investor-level taxes on dividends and capital gains raise equity prices to the extent that dividend and capital gains taxes are at least partially capitalized (see Harris, Hubbard, and Kemsley, 2001; and the papers in Hassett and Hubbard, 2001).

4. Topics for Economic Analysis and Concluding Thoughts

There has been substantial theoretical and empirical research by economists in recent years in evaluating efficiency costs of capital income taxation. A relatively strong consensus has emerged that the optimal tax on capital income should be zero in the long run (see Judd, 1985) or, with consideration of imperfect competition, at most zero (see, e.g., Judd, 2001).[1]

Empirical estimates of efficiency gains highlight the distinction between a shift to a consumption tax and a wage tax and the importance of analyzing the extent of transition relief (see, e.g., Auerbach, 1996; Altig et al., 2001). But most models do not explicitly incorporate risk or economic rents (see, e.g., the instructive discussion in Judd, 2001). Auerbach offers interesting and suggestive estimates of incorporating economic rents, although additional research is surely warranted. Understanding these issues will be important to the discussion of both efficiency and fairness in tax policy.

Alan Auerbach's chapter offers a useful primer for consumption taxation and a roadmap to areas for future theoretical and empirical research. Looking through the mirror of economics, efficiency consequences may be larger or smaller than they first appear, and distributional analysis is almost certainly harder than it may seem.

A shift to a consumption tax remains a bold experiment. Many years ago, as a young assistant professor, I asked Bradford (then the head of the Public Economics Program of the National Bureau of Economic Research) why he recommended so much economic study and policy analysis of consumption taxation when such a fundamental tax reform seemed so unlikely. Bradford's work has made fundamental tax reform more achievable (recently enshrined in the report of the President's Advisory Panel on Federal Tax Reform, 2005). And I still remember his answer to my question: "Why not the best?"

Why not, indeed?

NOTE

1. More recently, some economists have suggested that one might wish to implement a tax system in future periods in which tax policy is conditioned on current decisions. In one such setting, Golosov et al. (2003, 2006) conclude that a positive capital income tax is efficient (specifically, private insurance markets are assumed to be absent, so that the government must both raise revenue and correct this capital-market imperfection). But, with a richer set of capital markets, the capital

income taxes become privately enforced distortions arising from asymmetric information, with a more limited role for government intervention. While implications of incentive and informational problems for analysis of corporate taxation are an interesting topic research, the zero tax on capital efficiency benchmark still strikes me as reasonable.

REFERENCES

Altig, David, Alan J. Auerbach, Laurence J. Kotlikoff, Kent A. Smetters, and Jan Walliser. 2001. "Simulating Fundamental Tax Reform in the Unites States." *American Economic Review* 91(3): 574–595.

Andrews, William D. 1974. "A Consumption-Type or Cash Flow Personal Income Tax." *Harvard Law Review* 87(6): 1113–1188.

Auerbach, Alan J. 1996. "Tax Reform, Capital Allocation, Efficiency, and Growth." In Henry Aaron and William Gale, (eds.), *Economic Effects of Fundamental Tax Reform.* (pp. 29–81). Washington, DC: Brookings Institution.

Bradford, David F. 1986. *Untangling the Income Tax.* Cambridge, MA: Harvard University Press.

Bradford, David F. 1998. "Transition to and Tax Rate Flexibility in a Cash-Flow Type Tax." In James M. Poterba (ed.), *Tax Policy and the Economy* (vol. 12). Cambridge, MA: MIT Press.

Fisher, Irving. 1939. "The Double Taxation of Savings." *American Economic Review* 29(1): 16–33.

Gentry, William M., and R. Glenn Hubbard. 1997. "Distributional Implications of Introducing a Broad-Based Consumption Tax." In James M. Poterba (ed.), *Tax Policy and the Economy* (vol. 11). Cambridge, MA: MIT Press.

Gentry, William M., and R. Glenn Hubbard. 1998. "Fundamental Tax Reform and Corporate Financial Policy." In James M. Poterba (ed.), *Tax Policy and the Economy* (vol. 12). Cambridge, MA: MIT Press.

Golosov, Mikhail, Narayana Kockerlakota, and Aleh Tsyvinski. 2003. "Optimal Indirect and Capital Taxation." *Review of Economic Studies* 70(3): 569–587.

Golosov, Mikhail, Aleh Tsyvinski, and Ivan Werning. 2006. "New Dynamic Public Finance: A User's Guide." Working Paper, MIT.

Hall, Robert E., and Alvin Rabushka. 1985. *The Flat Tax.* Stanford, CA: Hoover Institution Press.

Harris, Trevor S., R. Glenn Hubbard, and Deen Kemsley. 2001. "Are Dividend Taxes and Imputation Credits Capitalized in Share Values?" *Journal of Public Economics* 79(2): 569–596.

Hassett, Kevin, and R. Glenn Hubbard. 2001. *Transition Costs of Fundamental Tax Reform.* Washington, DC: AEI Press.

Hubbard, R. Glenn. 1997. "How Different Are Income and Consumption Taxes?" *American Economic Review* 87(2): 138–142.

Institute for Fiscal Studies. (1978). *The Structure and Reform of Direct Taxation.* London: Allen and Unwin.

Judd, Kenneth L. 1985. "Redistributive Taxation in a Simple Perfect Foresight Model." *Journal of Public Economics* 28(1): 59–83.

Judd, Kenneth L. 2001. "The Impact of Tax Reform in Modern Dynamic Economies." In Kevin A. Hassett and R. Glenn Hubbard (eds.), *Transition Costs of Fundamental Tax Reform* (pp. 5–53.) Washington, DC: AEI Press.

Judd, Kenneth L. 2006. "Corporate Income Taxation in a Modern Economy." Working Paper, Hoover Institution, Stanford University.

Kaldor, Nicholas. 1955. *An Expenditure Tax.* London: Allen and Unwin.

President's Advisory Panel on Federal Tax Reform. 2005. *Simple, Fair, and Pro-Growth.* Washington, DC: U.S. Government Printing Office.

U.S. Department of the Treasury. 1977. *Blueprints for Basic Tax Reform.* Washington, DC: U.S. Government Printing Office.

U.S. Department of the Treasury. 1992. *Integrating the Corporate and Individual Income Taxes: Taxing Business Income Once.* Washington, DC: U.S. Government Printing Office.

CHAPTER **2**

Comment 2

ALVIN C. WARREN, JR.

It is always a pleasure to comment on an essay by Alan Auerbach because he is such a gentleman and a scholar. A gentleman, because he refers in his chapter to discussions of income and consumption taxation that are confusing, logically flawed, and do not stand simple scrutiny, but he graciously provides not a single citation to the authors.

A scholar, because he has produced a careful and useful primer for tax specialists on what is known and unknown about some of the key economic issues involved in the choice between income and consumption taxes. As usual, Auerbach scrupulously states the assumptions underlying each of his conclusions, a step that is often omitted in writing on this subject. (In the spirit of his chapter, I will provide no citations.)

As Auerbach laments, much of what appears in his primer, even ideas of long date, has not been incorporated into the general policy discussion of these issues. Like Auerbach, David Bradford devoted considerable time to educating non-economists whose voices are important in the formulation of tax policy, including presidential appointees, members of Congress, and their staffs. Auerbach's essay thus led me to reflect on why so few of the ideas he examines have passed into the general policy discussion of consumption versus income taxation.

I want to suggest two explanations for that failure. First, understanding the ideas described by Auerbach involves three analytic moves that may not be natural for many transactional lawyers, corporate executives, and journalists: disaggregation of financial flows, tracing market responses, and seeing financial or economic equivalences. Second, opinion leaders who do come to understand these ideas are often deeply skeptical about the underlying assumptions. I want to illustrate these two explanations by looking at nine of Auerbach's key propositions, and then I have a suggestion for a different sort of primer that he might write.

Consider first the well-known relationship of income and consumption taxation under certain assumptions:

1. Assuming that tax rates are constant, that taxation of gains and losses is symmetric, and that investors can scale up holdings, a consumption tax differs from an income tax only in the failure to tax the safe return on assets. (Auerbach, Section 2.1)

What would it take to communicate this idea to an opinion leader who has no or little background in tax policy? The first step would be to disaggregate capital income into its components; the second to show that scaling up (a market reaction) under a consumption tax would eliminate the tax on riskless and risky returns, but not on inframarginal returns and luck; and the third would be to show that the result of portfolio shifting under the income tax would differ only in preserving a tax on riskless return.

Communicating those three steps seems straightforward, but there is, of course, always a danger that having understood the argument, a nonspecialist would propagate the conclusion without making the assumptions explicit. Alas, much of the discussion of these issues in the legal literature has this fault.

On the other hand, nonspecialists who do follow the standard analysis and recognize the assumptions might respond by asking for the evidence that investors could (or would) shift their portfolio allocations in response to taxation. Opinion leaders are usually familiar with diversification and life-cycle asset allocation strategies, but their investment advisors have probably never spoken to them about adjusting the riskiness of their portfolio in response to changes in tax base or rates. An opinion leader skeptical about such portfolio shifting might well conclude that the difference between income and consumption taxation is greater than that stated in proposition 1.

Now consider three of Auerbach's propositions regarding economic efficiency:

2. Much of the efficiency gains from substituting a particular consumption tax for an income tax can be due to an implicit capital levy on existing assets. (Auerbach, Section 2.1 and 3.1)
3. Partial steps toward consumption taxation, such as additional favorable treatment of some capital income, are not necessarily desirable, even if substitution of consumption taxation for income taxation is considered desirable. (Auerbach, Section 2.7)
4. If the only difference between income and consumption taxation is taxation of the riskless return, the efficiency gains from substituting

a consumption tax for an income tax may be much less than have been traditionally estimated. (Auerbach, Section 3.1)

Explaining the first of these propositions is a matter of disaggregating old and new capital, and then showing the equivalence with an explicit capital levy on old capital. Communicating the second would require showing that partial taxation of capital income coupled with full deductibility of interest creates an incentive not for saving, but for tax shelters, which is not the desired market response. The final proposition seems obvious, but would be worth recalling to our hypothetical opinion leader, because there are certainly participants in the policy debate who say *both* that there is not much difference between the two taxes *and* that it is urgent to make the switch to consumption taxation.

Next consider three of Auerbach's propositions on the relationship of origin- and destination-based taxes:

5. Exchange rates will adjust to eliminate any advantage to exporters and disadvantage to importers from adopting a destination-based VAT rather than an origin-based VAT. (Auerbach, Section 2.2)
6. Destination-based and origin-based taxes differ in that the former is equivalent to imposing a cash flow tax on net outgoing investment, thereby imposing a capital levy on net foreign assets, which in the case of the United States is negative. (Auerbach, Section 2.2)
7. Adoption of a destination-based VAT would substantially reduce the value of U.S. assets held abroad and increase those held here by foreigners. (Auerbach, Section 2.2)

Proposition 5 has certainly been widely explained in policy discussions, and Auerbach understandably expresses considerable frustration that currency market reactions are often ignored or simply denied by participants in those discussions. The real puzzle here is not that many policy makers are skeptical of such adjustments, but that the managers of major U.S. corporations are often skeptical. As in the case of proposition 1, such managers often ask for evidence that the hypothesized currency adjustments will actually come about in the financial markets they know.

Communicating proposition 6 to an opinion leader would involve two steps: recalling proposition 2 (the capital levy implicit in some forms of consumption tax) and using the basic balance-of-payments identity to show that the effect of a destination-based tax (including imports and excluding exports) is equivalent to including cash inflows from abroad and deducting cash outflows. Understanding proposition 7 requires two further steps: the equivalence with cash flow taxation in proposition 6 indicates that cash flows from assets abroad will effectively be subject to tax; and a currency adjustment, such as that in proposition 5, indicates that such a tax would result in lower values for the foreign assets.

Finally, consider two relationships that depend directly on market reactions, one of which is fairly intuitive, the other of which may not be:

8. A VAT or retail sales tax, when added to factor incomes, would have a higher measured price level than a consumed income tax levied on individuals. (Auerbach, Section 2.5)
9. Substitution of a VAT for an income tax would not necessarily improve tax collections from activities that illegally escape income taxation. Indeed, if more labor intensive than activity in other sectors, illegal activity might actually increase. (Auerbach, Section 2.6)

Communicating the first would simply be a matter of showing the different price level adjustments that would follow from whether the tax was placed on consumers or businesses. Communicating the second to an opinion leader would require more steps. The chapter's strategy is to return to the difference between income and consumption taxation in proposition 1, which is the taxation of capital income (the components of which are not disaggregated for these purposes). From this perspective, neither labor nor capital income is taxed in the illegal sector under the income tax, while both are taxed in another sector. The effect of substituting a consumption tax for the income tax would then be to exempt capital income in the taxed sector. This change would be followed by a market adjustment, under which there would be a shift from labor to capital in production in that sector, lowering the relative costs in whichever activity is more labor intensive—which could easily be the illegal sector.

To recapitulate, I have suggested two explanations for the failure of much of what we know to penetrate the general policy discussion. First, these nine propositions (and others in Auerbach's primer) involve three analytic moves that may not come naturally to many opinion leaders not trained in economics: disaggregation of financial flows, tracing market adjustments, and seeing financial or economic equivalents. Second, even when understood, these propositions often depend on behavioral assumptions about which nonspecialists are skeptical.

The good news is that the ideas Auerbach discusses are not particularly difficult to explain to intelligent nonspecialists, particularly if care is taken with unfamiliar analytic moves. I would therefore encourage Auerbach (or other interested specialists) to write a second primer on the choice between income and consumption taxation, which would be aimed at opinion leaders, rather than tax policy analysts. Such a project would have to respond directly to doubts about the validity of the assumptions in the standard models.

A skeptic of the value of such an enterprise might point to the failure of the present-value equivalence of origin- and destination-based taxes, which has certainly been explained in nontechnical terms, to have much impact on the public debate. A skeptic might also be appalled by the repetition by some writers of the proposition that consumption taxation differs from income taxation only in the exclusion of riskless return, without disclosure of the required assumptions. On the other hand, it is worth recalling that this is a book dedicated to the memory of David Bradford, who was steadfast in his belief in the value of educating government officials and other opinion leaders about taxation.

CHAPTER 3

Implementing Income and Consumption Taxes

DAVID A. WEISBACH

My purpose in this chapter is to explore the parallels in implementation methods between income taxes and consumption taxes. The economic difference between the two taxes is thought to be the taxation of pure time value returns under an income tax but not under a consumption tax. In theory, therefore, *all* differences in implementation should be traceable to the measurement of time value returns.

To explore the extent to which this is true, one must examine what I call the *parallel implementation hypothesis*: each method of implementing either an income or consumption tax has a corresponding method for implementing the other base, modified only with respect to the measurement of time value returns. To illustrate, there are cash flow consumption taxes and, modified to measure time value returns, cash flow income taxes. Traditional value-added taxes (VATs) measure consumption but can be modified to measure income. In this light, the U.S. Treasury's (1992) Comprehensive Business Income Tax (CBIT) can be seen as David Bradford's X–tax modified to measure time value returns. A Haig-Simons income tax can be modified to measure consumption by adjusting basis for the time value of money. For each implementation method for a consumption tax, one can find a parallel that taxes income and vice versa.

Bradford's work plays a key role in evaluating this hypothesis. To give but a few examples, Auerbach and Bradford (2004) showed how to modify a cash flow tax to measure income. Bradford (1998) illustrated how a consumption tax can be implemented using basis accounts traditionally associated with income taxation. In addition, Bradford (1996) revived Shoup's (1955, 1969) claim that both income and consumption taxes can implemented through a VAT, and his (Bradford, 1986) X-tax is parallel to CBIT. Understanding the equivalences and differences in these implementation methods is central to evaluating the parallel implementation hypothesis.

An underlying assumption is that implementation methods matter. Economists often assume that the side of the market that remits a tax is irrelevant. Moreover, while they assume that some items, such as ability, cannot be observed, they generally assume that most other items can be observed perfectly. As Bradford (2000) observed, all too often income is something "captured by the symbol *y*, the sum of a wage rate times the quantity of labor and an interest rate times the quantity of capital." Under these assumptions, it would not matter whether tax liability or remittance is imposed on firms or individuals and it would not matter what, other than ability, was used to measure it. The differences in the two taxes would relate purely to the efficiency and distributional effects of taxing time value returns. This is a vast simplification from the world of tax administration. Indeed, the opposite position, that implementation methods are the most important item in choosing the tax base, is plausible. As Slemrod (1990) emphasized, we must think about optimal tax systems rather than optimal taxes.

Implementation can matter because it affects tax administration and compliance costs. There may be economies of scale in tax auditing and in tax compliance; for example, taxing large entities, such as firms instead of individuals, might be desirable. In addition, firms might collect tax-relevant information for other reasons, making taxation of firms relatively less costly (Bird, 1996). On the other hand, there may be economies of scale in tax avoidance as well as collection, potentially making taxation of firms less desirable. Different types of transactions might also be more easily observable than others. Thus transfer prices among related entities cannot be taken to be correct, while prices in arm's length transactions usually can. Similarly, the value of many assets may not be observable, making a pure Haig-Simons tax infeasible. We do not yet have a general theory of tax implementation, but there can be no doubt that these choices matter. Understanding the extent to which implementation choices can be made equivalently under income and consumption taxes, therefore, is important.

My original goal for this chapter was to lay out all the major dimensions along which tax systems can vary and then compare income and consumption taxes along these dimensions. This turned out to be too ambitious given the space constraints. Instead, I explore here four basic decisions in tax system design: (1) the use of cash flow or basis systems to measure the tax base; (2) remittance of the tax by firms or individuals (or some combination); (3) whether the tax system is open or closed; and (4) how the tax system operates across borders. For each decision, I describe the similarities between income and consumption taxes by exploring the associated implementation details.

Examining only these four areas leaves out many issues, although I would argue that these four should be on anyone's list of the most important elements of tax design. Without attempting to be complete, a longer list would include such items as the use of a real or a real plus financial base, *ex ante* or *ex post* measurement, the rate structure, the filing unit, ability to incorporate tax expenditures, personal deductions, the length of the accounting period, the treatment of the poor (including how transfers are to be made), and the treatment of losses. These issues are interesting and important but will have to wait for another day.

In Section 1 the background on income and consumption taxes and how the two bases compare is discussed. A consideration of the measurement of the tax base using cash flow and basis mechanisms follows in Section 2. The next three sections consider taxation at the individual or firm level, whether the tax system is open or closed, and international issues. Section 6 concludes.

1. Definitions

A consumption tax consists of three parts: (1) a tax on labor earnings; (2) a tax on economic profits (sometimes called inframarginal returns); and, possibly, (3) a tax on existing wealth. Because it does not tax time value returns, the timing of consumption does not affect the present value of tax liability. One immediate implication is that the tax on labor earnings can be imposed either at the time they are earned or at the time of consumption (or some combination of the two). Thus, a 30 percent tax on labor earnings reduces all consumption, now or in the future, by 30 percent. A 30 percent uniform tax on consumption would have the same effect.

The taxes on profits and existing wealth are likely to be central to consumption tax design. Without these elements of the tax base, a labor income tax would suffice. If profits and existing wealth are to be part of the tax base, however, a tax on labor income would not be sufficient because it would omit these elements. Thus, for example, a tax directly on consumption (such as a VAT) differs from a labor income tax in that it would tax profits and (without special relief) all existing wealth.

The efficiency of a tax on existing wealth may be particularly sensitive to design choices. As discussed in Kaplow (this volume), the efficiency claim for a tax on existing wealth is that it would be a surprise and that it would be unlikely to be repeated. Wholesale switching of tax systems might meet these requirements, but this would depend on the method employed. For example, if consumption were measured using basis accounts similar to those of current law, a tax on existing wealth would require setting basis equal to zero at the time of transition. It is hard to imagine that setting basis accounts to zero would be viewed as a one-time change when similar accounts are used under both the old and new tax systems. Basis could easily be eliminated while retaining the income tax or retained within the consumption tax, making it hard to explain why it was being done only once, simultaneously with a change of the tax base. A switch to a traditional VAT or another type of cash flow system, however, might be viewed as unlikely to be repeated. Exactly how various taxes on existing wealth are perceived is as much a matter of psychology as economics, but it seems clear that tax system design would play a key role.

An income tax is a consumption tax plus a tax on the risk-free return to savings. This additional tax on time value returns will influence the choices available to implement an income tax. Note that an income tax includes within it a tax on consumption, and a consumption tax is thought to include a tax on existing wealth. An income tax, therefore, should also include a tax on existing wealth at the time it is imposed. Our current income tax, however, did not impose a tax on existing wealth when first imposed—only gains or losses accrued after 1913 were subject to taxation.

The returns to bearing risk are, in theory, not taxed under either system. There are two ways to think about this issue. The first, common in the economics literature (e.g., Gordon, 1985), is to note that the present value of any tax on risky returns is zero. The second, usually taken in the legal literature, is to argue that taxpayers can adjust their portfolios to offset the tax on risky returns (Warren, 1996). The difference between these approaches arises because the portfolio adjustment might be easier under some implementation methods than others. If one takes a portfolio adjustment approach, and a particular method of implementation makes adjustments difficult, risky returns are at least partially taxed. If one takes the present value approach, whether portfolio adjustments are easy makes no difference—the present value of the tax is zero regardless. My own inclination is to require that taxpayers be able to adjust their portfolios to offset the tax on risky returns rather than simply assuming that they are not subject to the tax. My reasoning is that taxpayers who would choose a level of risk without tax evidently want that level of risk and the resulting return, even if its present value is zero. Taking away that opportunity imposes costs. Under this view, whether risky returns are taxed might depend on implementation methods. If the relevant implementation methods for income and consumption taxes are similar, however, both systems will equally tax risky returns.

2. Cash Flow versus Basis

Both cash flow and basis, consumption and income taxes can be imposed at either the firm or individual level, or some combination of the two. This section focuses on individual-level taxes, while Section 3 will add the possibility of firm-level taxes.

2.1. Cash Flow Consumption Taxes

An individual-level cash flow consumption tax is based on the observation that receipts less investments must be equal to annual consumption (perhaps with additional rules for any non-investment, nonconsumption uses of money) (Fisher and Fisher, 1942; Andrews, 1974). A cash flow system does not burden the normal return to investments because the benefit of deducting an investment when made exactly offsets the tax cost imposed when the investment is sold. Thus, suppose that, under tax rate τ, a taxpayer invests α at time 0 and receives future value [$FV(\alpha)$] at time 1. A deduction when the investment is made is worth $\tau\alpha/(1-\tau)$ and the tax on the sale is $\tau FV(\alpha)/(1-\tau)$. These two have the same present value. If there are economic profits, the future return is greater than $FV(\alpha)$, so the future tax has a cost of more than $\tau FV(\alpha)/(1-\tau)$. Therefore, profits are taxed under 0a cash flow system.

Note that for this equivalence to hold under the portfolio adjustment version of the argument, the mere equality of present values is not sufficient. Instead, it would have to be the case that taxpayers can adjust their portfolios under a cash flow tax so that they end up with the same outcome as if the normal return were explicitly exempt. In the simple setting considered here, this is the case: if taxpayers invest the value of the deduction, $\tau\alpha/(1-\tau)$, in the same investment as the original α, taxpayers will have an additional $\tau FV(\alpha) / (1 - \tau)$ in the future, which is sufficient to pay the tax, leaving them with the original α to invest. Kaplow (1994) pointed out that this holds in general equilibrium only if the government makes offsetting portfolio adjustments. The portfolio adjustment view argues that profits are taxed because if an individual has a chance to make an investment that earns profits, he will do so to the full extent possible absent taxes. Having already made the largest possible investment, the individual would be unable to increase the investment because of taxes, resulting in a tax on the profits.

A cash flow tax is potentially a very simple tax. Only cash flows need to be observed. There would be no need to estimate depreciation or keep inventories. The timing of realization would not matter, potentially eliminating all the problems of current law associated with the realization rule. Because of its potential simplicity, cash flow consumption taxes have attracted significant attention, for example, by Andrews (1974), Bradford and the U.S. Treasury Tax Policy Staff (1984, hereafter *Blueprints*), Meade (1978), and Graetz (1979). These studies have revealed a number of significant complications and, perhaps because of these complications, individual-level cash flow taxes have rarely been seriously considered and never enacted by a major economy. (Firm-level cash flow taxes in the form of a VAT, however, are pervasive.) I will briefly consider three issues here: rate graduation, tax rate changes, and the treatment of loans.

2.1.1. Rate Graduation in an Individual Cash Flow Consumption Tax

As Graetz (1979) observed, the major reason for considering individual as opposed to firm-level taxes is to be able to impose graduated rates. Cash flow consumption taxes, however, do not work well with graduated rates. If rates are graduated, the pattern of consumption will affect the present value of tax liabilities, contrary to the basic idea of a consumption tax (which is that it should not affect the pattern of consumption over time). In particular, lumpy consumption will produce higher taxes than smoothed consumption. For example, if tax rates are zero below $20,000 and 50% above, an individual with consumption each year of $15,000 has a lower present value tax than an individual who varies between $0 and $30,000 every other year. Moreover, we tend to account for durable good purchases in a lumpy fashion even if they provide level consumption over time. Thus, if the $30,000 every other year represents the purchase of a durable good that provides $15,000 of consumption for each of two years, a cash flow system will tend to treat this as lumpy rather than smooth. This means that when there are purchased durable goods, rate graduation can affect the present value of tax liabilities even when consumption is level. (Note also that renting the durable good for $15,000 per year would produce a different tax result, thereby distorting the choice between renting and owning.)

A solution to this problem would be to have an explicit system of averaging so that higher or lower rates apply only to consistent, long-term patterns of higher or lower consumption. A Vickrey-type system (Vickrey, 1939), modified to be on a consumption base, would seem feasible, but the limited U.S. experience with averaging under an income tax was not good.

In *Blueprints*, the U.S. Treasury proposed an alternative system of accounts that would allow individuals to self-average. As noted, if tax rates are constant (and there are no profits), a cash flow system is equivalent to a zero rate of tax on capital income. *Blueprints* would have allowed individuals to invest in accounts that were treated alternatively as cash flow or simply not taxed at all ("yield exempt" or, in *Blueprints* terminology, "tax-prepaid" because there is no deduction when an investment is made). Strategic borrowing from one account to invest in the other would allow self-averaging even if consumption is lumpy. For example, if an individual was going to purchase an expensive item in a given year, say a wedding or a car, the individual might be thrown into a higher tax bracket. To avoid this, the individual could borrow from the tax prepaid account and invest the money in the cash flow account, generating a net deduction and reducing the measure of consumption for the year. In the example above, the individual who consumes $30,000 every other year, could, in the year he spends $30,000 borrow $15,000 from the prepaid account and invest it in the cash flow account. This would generate a $15,000 deduction with no net flows. In the year he spends $0, he could then withdraw the $15,000 from the cash flow account and repay the loan to the prepaid account. This generates $15,000 of gain, thereby leveling his tax base over time.

The self-averaging system potentially solves the problem of graduated rates but it requires a high degree of sophistication by taxpayers. Merely understanding the equivalence of the two accounts is difficult. Optimal allocation between the accounts would involve predictions about the future rate structure and where one is likely to fall within that structure because of future consumption patterns. The problem is akin to the choice between regular and Roth IRAs today.

A second and perhaps more serious problem with the dual account system is that by allowing investments in prepaid accounts, the dual account system potentially allows taxpayers to reduce or eliminate taxation of economic profits by simply putting likely profit-making assets in the tax prepaid account. Indeed, if prepaid accounts were available without limit, the tax could revert to a labor income tax. Limiting the amount or types of assets eligible for the accounts would be possible but would add complexity. (*Blueprints* itself would have prohibited putting nonfinancial business assets in the tax prepaid accounts.)

A final problem with the dual account system is that by simply making offsetting book entries in the different accounts, taxpayers could choose not to pay taxes at any given time (Meade, 1978, p. 178). The government would be, in effect, a lender for anyone who wished to borrow from it. If a proper rate of interest were required, this would not necessarily be a problem. Given however, that individuals could simply make perfectly offsetting entries in the accounts, interest rates could be set arbitrarily low, allowing individuals to borrow from the government at whatever rate they wanted. For example, imagine an individual facing a financial crisis with $100 of wage income and a 30 percent tax rate. By simply making offsetting book entries (showing that he borrowed $100 from the yield exempt account and invested it in the cash flow account), the individual could arrange to borrow $30 from the government. If the market would have charged the individual a 10 percent rate of interest, any rate on the offsetting book entries below 10 percent would mean that the government was lending at too low a rate.[1] The government could require some minimum interest rate in the accounts, but the rate could not be tailored to individual circumstances, creating an adverse selection problem.

The reverse transaction might also cause problems—by charging an arbitrarily high rate of interest when borrowing from the cash flow account, taxpayers can lend to the government at an arbitrarily high rate. For example, suppose that an individual borrowed $100 from the cash flow account, charging a 50 percent annual interest rate. If the tax rate is 30 percent, $30 of tax would be due. The $100 would be invested in the prepaid account. The prepaid account would use the funds to buy an asset, such as a loan held by the cash flow account that happens to pay a 50 percent rate of interest. At the end of one year, the two accounts could be offset against one another, closing the prepaid account and paying off the loan from the cash flow account. The receipt of the $150 from the prepaid account and payment of $150 to the cash flow account generates a deduction of $150. The government would owe the taxpayer a refund of $45. The individual thereby has caused the government to borrow at a 50 percent rate of interest, generating \$15 of gains. The government might try to police this by arguing that the prepaid account could not have earned such a return and, therefore, the cash flow loan was not paid off in the claimed amount. Such policing, however, would take resources and inevitably be imperfect.[2]

2.1.2. Tax Rate Changes under an Individual Cash Flow Consumption Tax

A second problem with cash flow systems is tax rate changes. Under a cash flow system, tax rate changes that occur between the time of investment and the time of sale create windfall gains and losses. If tax rates change from τ_0 to τ_1, the present value of $\tau_1 FV(\alpha)$ will not be equal to $\tau_0 \alpha$. Bradford (1998) has argued that the effect of tax rate changes is a significant disadvantage of a cash flow system. Every time tax rates change, capital holders would be subject to a levy or windfall. Unless rate changes are a complete surprise, this would produce inefficiencies as individuals sought to avoid levies or take advantage of windfalls. It is not clear that there is any way to fix this problem within a cash flow system.

2.1.3. Loans under an Individual Cash Flow Consumption Tax

A third and final problem with cash flow systems is the potential taxation of loan proceeds. Under a pure cash flow tax, loans are taxed like any other receipt. Birnbaum and Murray (1987, p. 52) have illustrated the problem with this treatment. According to the authors, the U.S. Treasury staff advised the Secretary, Donald Regan, on options for what would become the Treasury's *Tax Reform for Fairness Simplicity, and Economic Growth* (1984). The staff discussed a cash flow consumption tax and explained that borrowings would be taxed because they are inflows used to finance consumption. Regan's response was that this was infeasible. He is reported to have said, "I'll tell you what. The next time you go to a cocktail party, you ask people what they think of a tax system in which borrowings are treated like income. They're going to tell you you're crazy." The idea of an individual-level consumption tax was soon dropped.

Loans, however, do not have to be included in the tax base to measure consumption. Just like the cash flow treatment of assets results in a zero present value tax, the cash flow treatment of loans also results in a zero present value tax. Prepaid accounts can, therefore, be used for loans just like they can be used for assets. For example, the *Blueprints* averaging system explicitly allowed prepaid (as well as cash flow) treatment of loans—it had to in order to allow taxpayers to self-average.

The dual account system, as argued above, has significant problems. Purely elective treatment of loans would, for similar reasons, probably not work. Even if the dual account system were not used in general, however, one can imagine that within an otherwise pure cash flow system, many ordinary loans could be given mandatory tax prepaid treatment, in effect, taking them out of the tax system altogether. Thus, credit card loans (possibly below a certain size) and loans used to finance durable goods such as houses or cars could be on a prepaid system. Yet drawing lines and establishing categories would be complex. Moreover, tracing might be required to reduce the avoidance opportunities created by a dual account system.

2.2. Basis-Method Individual Consumption Taxes

An alternative to the cash flow system is to use basis accounts. As Bradford (1998) illustrated, a system that uses basis and traditional income tax accounting (i.e., depreciation and inventories) can measure consumption if basis is increased by inflation and the risk-free rate of return in each period. If the difference between income taxes and consumption taxes is the risk-free rate of return, increasing the basis of investments by this amount converts an income tax into a consumption tax. Or, in other words, recovery of the basis in the future has the same present value as a cash flow deduction today if the basis is increased by the interest rate. The difference between a basis system and a cash flow system is that the tax recovery for an investment occurs at the same time as the taxation of the receipts, which means that the same tax rate applies to both.

Basis-method, as opposed to cash flow, individual consumption taxes have received almost no attention in the literature. They deserve closer scrutiny than I can give them here, but the following are some initial observations.

Keeping basis accounts and adjusting them for interest is obviously more complicated than a pure cash flow system. Depreciation schedules would have to be maintained and inventory systems kept. Basis allocation rules would be needed for partial sales of assets. On top of this burden, which is familiar from our income tax, the basis adjustments themselves would be complex, particularly over long periods of time and for property that was inherited or received as a gift. Nevertheless, because the present value of basis recovery would be the same regardless of when it occurs, perfecting these systems would matter far less than in an income tax. For example, if depreciation is estimated to be too fast or too slow, the present value will remain constant (and equal to the value of a current deduction). Therefore, the pressure to make these systems accurate would be far lower than under an income tax. Moreover, one of the most important simplifications of a cash flow consumption tax, that the timing of realization would not matter, would also apply in a basis-method consumption tax.

Although some of the problems with cash flow systems would be eliminated or reduced, using basis might introduce new concerns. Bradford (1998) proposed the basis system to eliminate problems with tax rate changes. To the extent that basis is equal to the fair market value, it would do (see Samuelson, 1964). Any difference between basis and fair market value would produce effects similar to those under a cash flow system, although one would expect that they would be smaller than they are under a cash flow system because the basis system attempts to approximate fair market value.

Similarly, graduated rates would be less of a problem because outlays and receipts would be taxed at the same rate. For example, imagine an investor who makes small investments each year and then withdraws a large amount at a single point in time to fund consumption. Under a cash flow system with increasing marginal rates, the deductions for the investments might be at a lower rate than the tax on the withdrawal. Under a basis system, the two are automatically matched. Problems with graduated rates, however, are not eliminated. Durable goods would still likely be accounted for as lumpy consumption. In addition, if investments are risky, gains might be taxed at a higher rate than losses even under a basis system. For example, imagine investing $100 in an asset that will be worth either $0 or $200 in the future. The bet breaks even without taxes. If, however, gains are taxed at a higher rate than losses, the bet becomes a losing bet after taxes.

Finally, under a basis system, borrowings would not generate immediate tax, reducing the "Secretary Regan" problem, but their treatment would be very complex. The treatment of the initial borrowing would look much like their treatment under a conventional income tax, which is that it would basically be ignored and taxpayers would keep track of the amount borrowed (the principal amount). Under a conventional income tax, payment back of more than the principal amount generates interest deductions and payment back of less than the principal amount generates gain (known as cancellation of indebtedness income). Under a consumption tax, the only difference is that like basis for assets, the principal amount of the loan would have to be increased (or interest deductions decreased) for the time value of money. For example, suppose an individual borrows $100 and buys an asset for $100. If the individual sells the asset for $105 next year when the risk-free rate is 5 percent, the basis of the asset will have increased to $105 and there will be no gain or loss on the asset. If the loan is repaid for $105, there should be no gain or loss on the loan either. This is achieved by having the loan basis increase to $105. Any repayment for more or for less than this amount would generate loss or gain, respectively.

The consumption tax rules for loans just described would be complex—they are closely analogous to inflation adjustments sometimes considered (and rejected) for loans under a conventional income tax. An alternative would be to use the tax prepaid system for some loans (i.e., ignore them). As in a cash flow system, credit card loans and mortgages might be ignored. If loans used to purchase investment assets were ignored, however, we might end up with a different "Secretary Regan" problem. Imagine an individual borrowing $100 at a 10 percent rate and investing it in an asset that earns 10 percent. At the end of the year, the individual sells the asset and pays off the borrowing. If the risk-free rate is 3 percent, the individual would have $7 of gain on the asset. If the loan were ignored, the individual would have to pay tax on this transaction notwithstanding that there was no net gain and no increase in consumption. No amount of explanation would convince anyone at a cocktail party that this makes sense. Thus, at a minimum, including some loans in the tax base would seem necessary.

While possibly solving some of the problems with cash flow systems, basis accounts might introduce new ones. In particular, the manipulation of basis is a central element in tax shelters under current law and many of the same manipulations might be possible under a consumption tax structure. To know more, we would have to know more about the details of the system, such as whether it is open or closed (see Section 4 below). Rules to properly measure investment (and therefore, basis) and rules to prevent shifting of basis among taxpayers would be needed.

Two final points are worth making on basis-method consumption taxes. Bradford (1998) proposed a basis system in part to eliminate the tax on existing wealth on transition. This seems to work very well. It is difficult to imagine using a basis system and yet imposing a tax on existing wealth. Basis accounts would have to be set to zero, which seems implausible. Depending on your view of such a tax, this can be a virtue or benefit. Finally, portfolio adjustments under a basis system look different than under a cash flow system. The reason is that there is no immediate deduction to generate cash with which to make the adjustment. Instead, individuals would have to borrow. Many legal academics are skeptical that these adjustments occur in a conventional income tax because of the need for borrowing. They might likewise be skeptical in a basis-method consumption tax.

2.3. Individual Income Taxes

Income taxes are conventionally thought of as using basis. The Haig-Simons system, for example, uses basis to track investments, as does the current law realization system. Unlike in a consumption tax, the timing of basis recovery matters because an income tax taxes time value returns. The Haig-Simons system, therefore, requires valuation of assets at the end of each taxable period, which many think to be infeasible. The realization alternative has well-known and serious problems. There is little need to rehash these issues here.

Auerbach and Bradford (2004) showed that an income tax can be implemented using a cash flow system, potentially solving the problems with basis systems under an income tax. They observed that under a cash flow system, if the future tax rate is just the right amount higher than the rate at the time when an investment is made, the tax burden on an investment can exactly equal the tax burden were the risk-free return taxed directly. To illustrate, under a pure Haig-Simons income tax, if the pretax return in one period is $1 + r$, the after-tax return is $1 + (1 - t)r$ where t is the tax rate. Suppose in a cash flow tax, an individual invests \$1 at time zero and the tax rate at time zero is t_0. Because of the immediate deduction, the individual will be able to invest $\$1/(1 - t_0)$, which will grow to $(1 + r) / (1 - t_0)$ before taxes. If the tax rate at time 1 is t_1, the individual will have $(1 - t_1)(1 + r) / (1 - t_0)$ after taxes. To mimic a Haig-Simons tax, this amount has to be equal to $1 + (1 - t)r$. Therefore, t_0 and t_1 must be set such that $(1 - t_1) / (1 - t_0) = [1 + (1 - t)r]/(1 + r)$. The right hand side is less than 1, so t_1 has to be greater than t_0. The same analysis holds for t_1 and t_2, t_2 and t_3, and so forth, creating a pattern of increasing tax rates over time. Auerbach and Bradford solve for the unique rate schedule that evolves according to this pattern. The conclusion is that by imposing increasing rates using this pattern, an income tax can be imposed on a cash flow basis.[3]

The advantage of this system over a Haig-Simons tax is that it avoids valuation issues and the timing of realization would no longer be important. Moreover, all the issues associated with basis, such as estimating depreciation, allocating basis for partial sales, and keeping accounts would be eliminated. All that is needed to compute tax liability is the cash flows at a given point in time. A tax rate schedule of increasing rates over time would be applied to the cash flows.

There are, however, a number of significant disadvantages. All the problems with cash flow consumption taxes would be problems under a cash flow income tax. Thus, rate graduation, tax rate changes, and loans all present problems. Auerbach and Bradford proposed a self-averaging system based on the *Blueprints* system, but it might actually work better than the *Blueprints* proposal. The two accounts would be a cash flow income tax account and a mark-to-market account. Only a limited set of assets, say publicly traded assets, could be put into the mark-to-market account. Unlike the prepaid account in *Blueprints,* the mark-to-market account would tax profits and the obvious abuses of the prepaid account system are not present. (One possibility of improving the *Blueprints* account system, therefore, might be use to use a mark-to-market account with basis adjustments instead of the prepaid account.)

The obvious problem with a cash flow income tax is its complexity. If the Secretary Regan cocktail party standard is relevant, it is hard to see how a cash flow income tax could pass.

Moreover, even aside from its complexity, the Auerbach-Bradford system creates problems because tax rates increase continuously. Rates would rise toward 100 percent over time. In theory, because it is a cash flow system, the nominal rate is not relevant. Instead, only the difference in rates between the time of investment and the time of withdrawal results in a tax. Deducting at 99 percent and including at 99.03 percent should produce the same effect as deducting at 10 percent and including at a corresponding higher rate.[4] In practice, the portfolio adjustments necessary to offset the tax on risky return become arbitrarily large as rates get high. At some point, portfolio adjustments would cease to be feasible.

To avoid this problem, Auerbach and Bradford set rates for each individual rather than for the economy as a whole. For example, rates for an individual can be set at birth or set to be equal to the appropriate number for a person of age 40. Because the rates would be linked to individual life spans, they would never get too high. Note, however, that this solution limits their system to individuals—it is not likely to be feasible to set rates separately for each business or corporation, given that businesses can merge or split up in ways that individuals cannot. Whether a cash flow income tax can be made to work at the business level remains to be worked out.

A more difficult problem is that if the wage tax rate is set equal to the nominal rate on investments, the taxes on wages would quickly become inefficiently high. It might be possible to set the wage rate lower than the rate on investments, but this would create administrative problems because of the need to differentiate types of cash flows. Absent a way to distinguish the two, one could invest, deducting at a high rate, and receive the proceeds as wages, taxed at a low rate. Auerbach and Bradford argue that increasing wage tax rates may be desirable. If this is the case, a unified system would be possible. It is far from clear, however, that increasing wage rates over time would be desirable.

My own view of the Auerbach-Bradford system is that it is useful for understanding the economics of income taxation but not feasible for implementing an actual tax. This means that individual-level income taxes are forced to choose between the problems of valuation and the problems of realization.

2.4. Summary

The parallel implementation process holds in broad theory: both consumption and income taxes can, in theory, be implemented using either cash flow or basis mechanisms. Most of the purely individual-level systems have problems, however. Cash flow consumption taxes create problems with respect to graduated rates, rate changes, and loans. Cash flow income taxes add to these the problem of increasing rates over time. Basis-method income taxes have the familiar problems with either valuation under a mark-to-market method or realization under a realization method. Basis-method consumption taxes have not been explored in the literature and are worth further research.

3. Individual versus Business Level

We can now consider an additional choice in designing the tax system: allowing businesses to be subject to taxation as well as individuals. The choice between business-level taxation and individual-level taxation is primarily seen as a trade-off between ease of collection (favoring business-level taxes) and tailoring the tax to individual circumstances (favoring individual-level taxation). Yet business-level taxation is important for two additional reasons. First, it allows expansion of the tax base because it allows taxation of tax-exempts and foreigners that cannot be taxed in a purely individual-level system. Second, it is important for taxing time value returns under an income tax in the absence of an individual-level mark-to-market regime.

Before turning to the details, Joel Slemrod has emphasized (in comments on this paper and elsewhere) that it is important to be clear about what one means by a business-level tax. Firms cannot bear the burden of a tax. At most firms can remit taxes. They can be legally liable for taxes in the sense that sanctions will be imposed for failure to remit. They can also be mere withholding agents, remitting taxes on behalf of individuals, with the individuals ultimately liable for the tax. Withholding taxes can alternatively be final or they can be subject to reconciliation on an individual's return. Withholding can be based on various levels of information provided to firms and, therefore, can be variously tailored to the circumstances of the individual. The difference between these systems is not particularly clear. For example, it is not clear whether taxes paid by firms in a credit imputation system (in which dividend recipients get tax credits for firm-level taxes) are business-level taxes. Firms are legally liable for the taxes and the amounts are based purely on attributes of the firm not the owners, but there is a reconciliation of taxes on owners' returns and the tax ultimately imposed on the business earnings depends on the attributes of the owners.

What I mean here by a business- or firm-level tax is a tax remitted by firms that is based on the characteristics of the firms, not the owners, contractors, or employees. A withholding system differs in that the remittance is based on characteristics of a taxpayer other than the firm. Withholding systems are worth substantial study. They may offer some of the advantages of business-level taxes, such as economies of scale in compliance and audit, with some of the advantages of individual-level taxes, such as tailoring liability to individual circumstances. Space constraints, however, prevent me from considering them here.[5] It seems unlikely that withholding systems differ systematically for income and consumption taxes, which is the focus here.

A review of the existing literature shows that both income and consumption taxes can, in theory, be implemented at the individual level, business level, or a mix, in roughly parallel fashion. Thus, VATs are normally consumption taxes because they allow immediate deductions for capital expenditures (or an equivalent credit). As Shoup (1955, 1969) and Bradford

(1996) pointed out, substituting income tax accounting (i.e., traditional income tax basis-method accounting) for cash flow accounting converts a VAT into a business-level income tax. We can also shift between cash flow and basis accounting within a VAT for each of the tax bases. For example, by adjusting basis for inflation and time value, a VAT could measure consumption while using otherwise conventional income tax accounting. In theory, Auerbach and Bradford's (2004) cash flow accounting could be applied at the business level to create a cash flow income tax at the business level. As noted, however, increasing tax rates over time would create problems not easily dealt with in a business-level tax.

We can shift various pieces of the tax to the individual level by allowing businesses to deduct the relevant financial flows and requiring individuals to include those flows. The most important piece to shift to the individual level is likely to be labor income because labor income is thought to be a signal of ability (and, therefore, we might want to adjust the tax on labor income for individual attributes). The X-tax and similar systems take this approach by allowing businesses to deduct wages and taxing individuals on wage income using graduated rates. Hall and Rabushka (1995), Bradford (1986), and Zodrow and McLure (1991) all had variations on this theme. Exactly the same shift can occur within an income tax structure. The U.S. Treasury's (1992) CBIT is the most prominent illustration. CBIT computes tax at the firm level just like an income-type VAT would but allows a deduction for wages and taxes wages at the individual level using graduated marginal rates. Note also that we might want to shift only a portion of labor income taxation to individuals. For example, fringe benefits might more easily be taxed at the firm level, and, therefore, could be nondeductible to the firm and not taxed to wage earners.

Interest or other financial returns can also be shifted from firm-level taxation to individual-level taxation. VATs of both the consumption and income type generally ignore financial flows—they are neither included when received nor deducted when paid. For example, firms might be allowed to deduct interest and other non-stock financial payments and to tax the receipt of those payments to individuals. The Treasury's (1992) dividend exclusion system follows this pattern. It is the same as CBIT except that it allows firms to deduct interest and other financial payments (other than those with respect to stock) and taxes those payments to individuals. The X-tax could use a similar structure, taxing financial inflows and allowing a deduction for financial payments. Such a structure is often called an $R + F$

base (where R is domestic gross capital income, F is net flows from financial assets), following the Meade (1978) terminology. Firms could also be allowed to deduct both dividends and interest. This turns a dividend exclusion system into a dividend deduction system. In each case, we shift part of the base out of firms and to the individual level.

As noted, the central trade-off between firm-level taxation and individual-level taxation is the trade-off between compliance costs and tailoring the tax to individual circumstances. The X-tax and CBIT have an attractive structure under this trade-off because they allow tailoring of the tax on labor income while retaining firm-level taxation for everything else. As noted, the theory behind this structure is that labor income is a signal of ability and should be tailored to individual circumstances. Other types of returns (depending on the tax base, profits, existing wealth, or time value returns) are best taxed at a flat rate. The other important element of the X-tax/CBIT structure is that there are few incentives for relabeling cash flows. The business tax rate is set equal to the highest wage tax rate. This means that relabeling wages as capital income cannot reduce taxes. Moreover, all capital income is taxed at the business level—there is no debt/equity or similar distinction.[6] The dividend exclusion and similar systems retain the debt/equity distinction, which means that simple relabeling can change tax liabilities.

A different reason for taxing at the firm level is that there is considerably more flexibility with respect to tax-exempts and foreigners with a firm-level tax than with a purely individual-level tax. Consider tax-exempts first. The treatment of exempt entities in a firm-level tax is familiar because existing consumption-type VATs face these issues. Income-type VATs are likely to be similar, although if time value returns of endowments are to be taxed, there might be some additional considerations.

The treatment of production by a tax-exempt depends on whether it is operating at the retail or wholesale level. If it is operating at the retail level, value added by the tax-exempt would not be taxed because of the exemption of the firm. Value added at prior levels of production, however, can either be taxed or not, depending on the treatment of purchases by the tax-exempt. To illustrate, if a tax-exempt hospital purchases supplies for \$90 and sells health care services for \$100, the \$10 of value added is not taxed because of the hospital's tax exemption. If the hospital is completely out of the tax system (it does not file returns, claim deductions, etc.), it cannot claim a deduction for the cost of its supplies. Therefore, the \$90 cost of the supplies includes the VAT paid at prior levels and so will the \$100 retail sale. Our current income tax works like this—tax-exempts are not taxed on their gains but purchase inputs at after-tax prices. Alternatively, the tax-exempt could be allowed to deduct its costs. (The deduction would have to be refundable because the tax-exempt would not be generating gains to use against the deduction.) The deduction would remove the tax paid at prior levels of production, which means that goods or services sold by the tax-exempt would be entirely free of tax. This is, in effect, the pattern followed by a retail sales tax.

The effects are different if the firm sells at the wholesale level. Suppose a business purchased the $100 of health care services from the hospital. If the business cannot deduct the cost of the services, there will be a tax on the services because it will go into value added by the business. For VAT cognoscenti, it is the same as purchasing a good from a nonregistered business. Moreover, if the hospital cannot deduct its $90 of inputs, there would be a double tax on the $90, making tax-exemption worse than being taxed. If the hospital can claim a deduction for its inputs, then tax-exemption is merely the same as being taxed.

Alternatively, businesses could be allowed to deduct purchases from tax-exempts. If the $100 cost is deductible, there will be no tax on the value added by the hospital. Whether the $90 of inputs is taxed depends on whether the hospital can deduct its costs. If the hospital cannot deduct its costs, its value added remains untaxed but value added at prior levels of production is taxed. This is how our current system works—purchasers from tax-exempts are allowed to recover the costs of their purchase but tax-exempts themselves are not. If the hospital could deduct the cost of its inputs, taxes at all prior levels of production would be eliminated. This approach (allowing a deduction by purchasers from tax-exempts and a deduction by the tax-exempt for its costs), however, might lead to massive abuses because businesses could simply pass products through tax-exempts to eliminate prior levels of taxation.

There is far less flexibility with a purely individual-level tax because all the tax system observes is the ultimate consumption (usually at the point of sale). Tax-exemption in an individual-level tax has meaning only if individuals can exclude from the tax base purchases from tax-exempts. Otherwise, a purchase from a university, church, or hospital is treated the same as a purchase from any other producer. Thus, for example, in a cash flow system, individuals would deduct the cost of purchases from tax-exempts. If, however, purchases from tax-exempts are not included in the tax base, inputs used by the tax-exempt would also not be taxed. The choice of taxing inputs but not value added by the tax-exempt (the choice found in current law) is not available. An individual-level tax, therefore, has less flexibility than a firm-level tax. An analysis of endowments of tax-exempts would produce similar conclusions—firm-level taxes give tax policy makers many more options than individual-level taxes with respect to taxing the returns to endowments.[7]

Taxing the labor income of employees of tax-exempts becomes more difficult, however, when there is only a firm-level tax as opposed to an individual-level tax. With an individual-level tax, no special rules are needed to tax these wages. With a firm-level tax, labor earnings of employees would go untaxed unless a special rule is provided to tax them (at either the firm level or the individual level). For example, compare a country that imposed a VAT (of either the income or consumption type) as its only tax with a country that imposed an individual-level tax. If there were no special rule, the country that imposed the VAT would not tax the wage income of individuals who work for tax-exempts while the country that imposed the individual-level tax would.

The treatment of transactions with foreigners will be analyzed extensively in Section 5 below. Briefly, firm-level taxes (traditionally in the consumption context and, I will argue, also in the income tax context) are normally thought to offer the choice between origin and destination bases. The two bases differ in how they tax profits and transition gains with respect to inbound and outbound investments. They also differ on how they tax tourism. An individual-level tax does not match either the destination or origin bases and, therefore, is a third, independent choice. Therefore, the introduction of firm-level taxes expands the set of options with respect to cross-border transactions.

None of the discussion so far of business-level taxes has distinguished income from consumption taxes, because the two are very closely parallel with respect to the issues that have been raised. I think, however, that there are some special considerations with respect to income taxes. The primary issue relates, as expected, to measuring time value returns.

If asset valuation is feasible, a firm-level tax can mimic an individual Haig-Simons tax. Firms rather than individuals would be taxed on their change in value. One could accomplish this by direct valuation of the firm's assets or, where shares of the firm are traded, through observing the value of those shares. Bankman (1995) and Knoll (1996) discuss some details of such a system.

Absent valuation (or an alternative anti-deferral regime), the calculus changes. Purely individual-level income taxes would no longer be feasible, and firm-level income taxes (either on their own or as an addition to an individual-level income tax) become very complex. Consider first a pure individual-level income tax that does not have an anti-deferral mechanism. Suppose, for example, that individuals are taxed on wages and realized gains and losses but there is no business-level tax. Individuals could simply leave assets in businesses until they were ready to consume. If the individual wants to adjust his portfolio, the business could do so without tax. The tax on the risk-free return could be avoided at will, and the system would not be effective. One can imagine having personal holding company rules, accumulated earnings taxes, or similar regimes in an attempt to salvage the system, but these taxes have never been thought to work well.[8]

Firm-level taxes that rely on realization would also have problems. Consider an income VAT. VATs do not normally tax stock sales because they ignore all financial flows which would include dividends and gains from the sale of stock. CBIT has a similar structure. Without a tax on stock sales, however, businesses could simply transfer assets by incorporating them and selling the stock. Assets would not have to leave their protective shell corporations until they are consumed, which means that this strategy would convert an income VAT or CBIT into a consumption tax. For example, each widget or group of widgets could be put into its own corporate shell. When an early stage of production wants to sell the widget to the next stage of production, it would simply sell the stock of the shell corporation and pay no tax. The widget would thus move through its chain of production entirely without tax. Eventually, when the widget is consumed, it must leave the shell corporation and at that point, firm-level taxes would be due, but this effectively converts the tax into a tax on consumption.

The obvious solution to this problem is to tax stock sales (and have anti-shell corporation rules and other messy and incomplete provisions). Taxing stock sales, however, creates problems because gain and loss on assets and stock are duplicative—appreciation in the assets creates gain in the stock. If a corporation sells assets, the gain would have to be reflected in the stock basis. Similarly, gain or loss on the sale of stock would have to be reflected in asset basis. Mechanisms to conform inside and outside basis exist in current law but they are fabulously complex and imperfect. Weisbach (2007) explores this in some detail.

There is little or no work exploring the details of whether or how firm-level income taxes such as CBIT would work. My initial conclusion is that they would be very difficult to implement. Absent mark-to-market or some other anti-deferral rule, purely individual income taxes would not work at all. The inevitable firm-level back-up taxes, however, will be highly complex because of the difficulty in coordinating asset and stock sales. This is not the case with consumption taxes. We have little experience with individual consumption taxes but we know from long experience that firm-level consumption taxes such as VATs work reasonably well.

4. Open versus Closed

The idea that a tax system can be open or closed was described in Weisbach (2000). McLure (1987) used the same idea using the terms "naive" (open) and "sophisticated" (closed). Both Weisbach and McLure were using these terms in the context of a consumption tax and argued that it was important for a consumption tax to be closed. In particular, subtraction-method VATs, as opposed to credit-method VATs, are usually thought not to require invoices but Weisbach and McLure argued that this is naive. Without invoices, purchasers would be able to claim deductions even if sellers were not taxed. This creates serious abuse potential. Numerous examples are illustrated in Weisbach.

If income and consumption taxes are truly parallel, these ideas should translate to income taxes, and problems with open income taxes should be similar to problems with open consumption taxes. We can define *open* and *closed* in the income tax context the same way we do in the consumption tax context, which is whether a buyer gets tax credit (a deduction in the case of a consumption tax, basis in the case of an income tax) for purchases from nontaxpayers. Current law is open to some degree because the tax treatment to one party to a transaction is often not explicitly conditioned on the tax treatment of the other side. For example, interest is deductible when paid to a tax-exempt lender and purchasers may get basis or deductions for imports. The possible mismatch of the two sides to a transaction and the resulting rules to prevent abuse is one of the major reasons for the complexity of current law. That is, under the current law income tax is open, and depending on views about the problems of current law, opinions about the problems of open consumption taxes claimed by McLure (1987) and Weisbach (2000) may be strengthened or weakened.

We can alternatively imagine a closed income tax, in which buyers do not get basis or deductions for purchases from or payments to nontaxpayers. What this system would look like is beyond the scope of this chapter, but it is easy to imagine that the avoidance opportunities of current law would be significantly lessened—shifting income to nontaxpayers would be much more difficult.

5. International

The treatment of international transactions under both income and consumption taxes has been the subject of an extensive literature. The goal of this section is to investigate the parallel implementation hypothesis; that is, whether the various implementation methods for cross-border cash flows can be used equally under both income and consumption taxes. In particular, both the economics and the implementation of consumption taxes, with their alternative destination and origin bases, is well understood and comparatively straightforward. Income taxes are typically described using entirely different language and implementation is very complex. The questions are whether we can understand income taxes using the consumption tax terminology and whether the complexity of international income tax regimes is inherent. I begin by describing the well-known results for consumption taxes and then turn to income taxes.

5.1. Consumption Taxes

5.1.1. In General

The basic choice for cross-border flows for consumption taxation is usually phrased as the choice between destination- and origin-basis taxes. A destination-based tax attempts to tax domestic consumption. It does not tax exports (because the export is not consumed domestically). Thus, a broad-based retail sales tax is a destination-based tax because it taxes all domestic consumption (whether by U.S. residents or foreigners) but does not tax foreign consumption by U.S. residents. If the tax is imposed at each layer of production, like in a VAT, the tax on prior layers must be refunded when a good is exported, leading to so-called border rebates. Tourists taking products out of the country should also get a rebate of taxes because the consumption does not occur domestically. Imports must be fully taxed, because the imported good is consumed here. Therefore, under a destination-based VAT, no credit or deduction is allowed for the import but a tax is imposed when it is sold domestically.

An origin-based tax is on domestic production, regardless of where consumed. Thus, sales abroad are taxed (in an amount equal to the value at the border because this is the amount of domestic production). Imports are not taxed (except to the extent of value added domestically). Thus, under a VAT, the importer may deduct the cost of the imported good (and is taxed on the domestic sale). Tourists, both domestic tourists visiting other countries and foreigners visiting domestically, get no special treatment because it is the location of production that matters, not consumption.

The comparison between origin- and destination-based consumption taxes is well-known (e.g., Grubert and Newlon, 1995), and is summarized in Table 3.1. In particular, origin-and destination-based taxes impose equal burdens for marginal investments but tax inbound and outbound profits, transition wealth, tax rate changes, and tourism differently.

To see the equivalence on the margin, note that domestic production (the origin base) and domestic consumption (the destination base) have to be the same in present value terms. Leaving aside foreign aid, you can only consume what you make. The two taxes can vary in any given year because we may borrow or save, but the present values must be equal.

Another way to think about the equality is as a parallel to the equivalence between cash flow and yield exempt taxes. Consider a U.S. firm engaging in

Table 3.1. A Comparison of Origin-Basis and Destination-Basis Taxation

	Origin-Basis	Destination-Basis
On the Margin	No tax	No tax
Profits		
Inbound	Yes	No
Outbound	No	Yes
Transition and Tax Rate Changes		
Inbound	Yes	No
Outbound	No	Yes
Tourism		
Inbound	No	Yes
Outbound	Yes	No

outbound investment. An outbound investment involves an up-front export and a future import. Under a destination-basis tax, there is the equivalent of a deduction on export because of the rebate. When the investment yields future imports, consumed in the United States, these are taxed (because a destination-basis tax taxes all domestic consumption). Under an origin-basis tax, there is no up-front deduction for the export; exports are taxed like any other sale. There is also no tax on the future import because we do not tax foreign production even if consumed here. Thus, for exports, an origin-basis tax looks like a yield-exempt tax (no deduction up front, no tax on the back end) and a destination-basis tax looks like a cash flow tax (deduction up front, tax on the back end). As is well-known, cash flow and yield-exempt taxes are equivalent at the margin when tax rates stay the same.

From the perspective of a foreign importer, the two systems switch. Suppose that a foreigner makes a domestic investment. This is equivalent, from the domestic perspective, to an import today followed by a future export. Under a destination-based tax, there is a tax on the import and no tax on the future export. This looks like a yield-exempt system. Under an origin-based tax, there is no tax on the import but there is a tax on the export, which looks like a cash flow system. Again, they are equal on the margin.

To see how profits are taxed, note that under a destination-based tax, a U.S. investor in a foreign country gets cash flow-like treatment, which means that profits are taxed. In real terms, the present value of the future imports exceeds the cost of the current export and this difference is taxed. A foreign investor in the United States gets yield-exempt treatment, which means that profits are not taxed. Under an origin-based tax, a U.S. investor in a foreign country gets yield-exempt treatment, which means that profits are not taxed, while the profits of a foreign investor in the United States would be taxed.

Tax rate changes and transition effects are similar. Under a destination-based tax, a U.S. investor in a foreign country is subject to windfall gains and losses because of the effective cash flow treatment of the investment. A foreign investment in the United States is not subject to this because of the yield-exempt treatment. Under an origin-based tax, the opposite is true: outbound investments are not subject to the transition tax while inbound investments are.[9]

Finally, with respect to tourism, consider a tourist who leaves a destination-basis tax system for a foreign country. If the tourist consumes in the foreign country, there is no domestic tax (the foreign country might impose a tax). If the tourist brings consumption items back to the home country, there should be a tax imposed at the border. If a foreign tourist consumes in a destination-basis country, a tax is imposed. If the foreigner purchases something in a destination-basis country and brings it home, there should be no tax imposed (and any tax imposed at prior levels of production should be rebated). Therefore, a destination-basis system taxes inbound but not outbound tourism. This makes sense because a destination-basis tax taxes domestic consumption. An origin-basis system works the opposite way, taxing outbound but not inbound tourism.

5.1.2 Individual-Level Taxes

Analyses of origin- and destination-basis systems are almost always done assuming that the tax is collected at the business level. The context is usually one of comparing different types of VATs. Consumption taxes can also be imposed at the individual level, which leads to the question of whether there are individual-level analogues of destination and origin bases.

Consider a cash flow personal consumption tax. This tax is similar to a destination-based tax because investments abroad generate a deduction and imports from abroad generate a tax. This means that profits earned abroad are taxed as with a destination-based tax. Foreign investment in the United States is not taxed at all, also consistent with a destination-based tax. Transition also follows the destination pattern: assets of U.S. taxpayers held abroad are taxed and assets of foreign taxpayers held here are not. Consumption abroad by U.S. taxpayers, however, is taxed and consumption of foreigners here is not taxed. This is the origin-basis pattern. Therefore, a personal cash flow tax is not on either the destination or origin basis. It does not tax domestic consumption nor domestic production. Instead, it taxes consumption by domestic taxpayers.

There is only limited flexibility with a purely individual-level tax to change these choices to something more closely resembling the origin base. We could give transition relief for assets held abroad, although doing so but not for domestic assets may not make sense. We could also not tax profits earned abroad, but again, the rationale is not clear. I do not see how we could tax profits of foreign firms earned here or impose a transition tax on foreign capital invested here without a business-level tax. Thus, the individual-level tax, as a practical matter, seems to be a third choice, independent of origin- and destination-basis systems.

5.1.3. Transfer Pricing, Policing the Borders

There are significant administrative issues in the choice between the two systems. An origin-basis system is open and introduces transfer pricing problems. We might think of transfer pricing manipulation as fraudulently locating economic profits abroad. Because origin-based taxes do not tax profits earned abroad, fraudulently moving profits abroad takes them out of the tax base. Destination-based taxes are not subject to the same manipulation because they tax foreign-earned profits when they are eventually repatriated for consumption.

Bradford (2001) proposed an interesting solution to the transfer pricing problem. His diagnoses of the problem was that the X-tax, the VAT, or similar business-level taxes tax only real flows and not financial flows. To illustrate, suppose that a U.S. parent sells $1 million of goods to a foreign subsidiary for only $700,000. In an origin-based system, the $700,000 is subject to tax. This transaction reduces the U.S. tax base by $300,000 relative to a fair market value sale. But, says Bradford, it increases the future dividends from the foreign subsidiary by a present value of $300,000. It is the failure to tax these future financial flows that creates the problem. By switching (for related parties) from a system that looks only at real flows to one that measures both real and financial flows, the tax base will be back where it should be.

I do not think this solution works. Suppose we recast the transaction as an exchange of goods. The U.S. company transfers $1 million of goods to a foreign subsidiary and puts down $700,000 of gross receipts on its tax return. The foreign subsidiary exchanges the goods for other goods, also worth $1 million, and ships the new goods back to the U.S. parent. At the border, the U.S. parent claims a deduction of $1 million. The transaction balances in the sense that there are no future dividends or payments to be made and it involves only real goods, yet the tax base is reduced by $300,000.

One possibility is that the transfer of the goods to the foreign subsidiary creates a deemed stock issuance, which is a financial transaction, taken into account under the new system. In this case, there would be a $700,000 receipt from the transfer of the goods abroad and a $700,000 deduction for the purchase of the stock, netting to zero. There would be a $1 million deduction on the transfer of the foreign goods here and an offsetting $1 million tax on the deemed redemption of stock, again netting to zero. This is merely a destination-based system, at least for related parties. Thus, Bradford's solution to the problems of an origin-based system is to switch (partially) to a destination-based system.

Using destination-basis for related parties and origin-basis for other transactions might create odd results. For example, profits of U.S. companies earned abroad would be taxed if earned through a related party but not if earned through unrelated parties, and vice versa for profits of foreign companies earned here. It is not clear that taxing profits based on ownership structure would make sense. Because different sectors of the economy may have different optimal ownership structures, different sectors would be taxed differently. There would also be transition issues when companies change status, from related to unrelated or unrelated to related. At the time that status changes, from related to unrelated or vice versa, there could be non-zero balances (i.e., the foreign entity owes the U.S. or vice versa), creating transition effects.

Destination-based taxes, on the other hand, have to measure all domestic consumption. An invoice system can be used to prevent taxpayers from claiming deductions for imports—deductions would be allowed only for purchases from registered taxpayers and foreigners would not be able to register. It would be somewhat more difficult to exclude from tax only sales abroad because goods could be trans-shipped—passed through a port as if exported and then shipped to another domestic port. A more serious problem is the taxation of services. Computerized transactions allow foreign firms to sell services directly to U.S. consumers. For example, gambling, financial services, tax preparation, and information provision (newspapers, magazine, etc.) can all be provided online. These services would have to be taxed domestically under a destination-based system.

5.2. Income Taxes

The language used to describe the international aspects of income taxes is quite different from that used to describe consumption taxes and is not nearly as simple. Common questions include the primacy of source and residence, whether the taxes should be worldwide or territorial, the difference between passive and active investments, and how foreign tax credits should be allocated. None of these concepts are discussed in the consumption tax context. In contrast to how a typical VAT works, the international rules for income taxes are breathtakingly complex. The question here is why this is so. In particular, is it possible to describe income taxes using the typical consumption tax language? Why does income taxation become so complex? Not surprisingly, the problem arises from the challenge of measuring time value returns.

Begin by noting that an individual-level Haig-Simons tax would not require any special rules for international transactions. Individuals would be taxed on wages and time value returns regardless of where they invest. There would be no source or crediting rules. Instead, the tax would be based solely on where the individuals are located—it would be residence-based. If all countries adopted such a system, coordination would be automatic—no treaties, credits, source rules, and the like would be needed. The tax would be capital export neutral in that investments would bear the same tax burden regardless of where they are made. It would not be capital import neutral because the tax burden on an investment in a given country would depend on the residence of the investor. It is parallel to an individual cash flow consumption tax. It looks mostly destination-based except for tourism, where it follows the origin pattern. This makes sense—the only difference between the Haig-Simons system and a cash flow system is cost recovery. Their treatment of cross-border investments should be the same. Similarly, like with consumption taxes, there does not appear to be a feasible individual-level origin-based income tax. Thus, the parallel implementation hypothesis holds for individual-level taxes on cross-border flows.

Imagine now a pure firm-level income tax, like an income-type VAT. If sales to abroad are taxed and purchases from abroad produce cost recovery (i.e., the purchase price produces basis which is recovered at the appropriate time), the tax is origin-based. The only difference between this tax and an origin-based consumption tax is the cost recovery system. Because of the use of income tax accounting, time value returns to domestic investments would be taxed in those countries.

To illustrate, consider foreign direct investment by a U.S. parent company, operating through a foreign subsidiary. The initial setup of the foreign subsidiary involves, in real terms, an export. In the future, there will be imports in an amount equal to the future value of the export. Under an origin-based system, these flows, the export and import, are given yield-exempt treatment. (Imagine the U.S. parent using after-tax cash to purchase a good and then sell it to its foreign subsidiary, producing no tax. On import, the U.S. purchases goods from the subsidiary and sells them in the United States. Other than possible appreciation while held in the United States there would be no U.S. tax.) The operations of the foreign subsidiary, however, would be taxed in its home country on the time value returns to its capital and also on any profits. A similar analysis applies to inbound foreign direct investment. The time value returns and profits would be taxed in the United States, where the capital is employed. Finally, portfolio investments are normally done through financial instruments which are not in the VAT base. Instead, any time value returns and profits would be taxed through the firm-level tax imposed in the country where the capital is invested, just like in the foreign direct investment case.

The major difference between an origin-based income tax and an origin-based consumption tax is the need to have detailed source rules under the income tax. The reason they are needed for an income tax is to capture time value returns. That is, to implement an income tax, we have to have a notion of which time value returns are attributable to which country. This idea, the source of capital income, unlike the place of consumption, is not well defined, and if countries have differing tax rates, even consistent source rules can matter. Inconsistent source rules create obvious opportunities for mischief. Note, however, that origin-based consumption taxes tax profits based on their source, and, therefore, might face similar problems, although to a lesser extent.

A pure origin-based income tax would meet capital import neutrality but not capital export neutrality. There is some question as to whether either of these is an appropriate goal of taxation (Graetz, 2001; Desai and Hines, 2003). To the extent it matters, a pure origin-based income tax imposes a tax at the rate of the country where the capital is invested, which means that it is capital import neutral.

The third version of an income tax is a firm-level destination-based income tax. Following the consumption tax pattern, sales to abroad would not be taxed (but basis would be recovered, generating a border rebate). Purchases from abroad would not generate basis, creating a tax at the border.

The results (with respect to time value returns) would be effectively the same as in the origin-based system. Imagine a U.S. parent company engaging in foreign direct investment through a foreign subsidiary. The initial export to fund the subsidiary would produce a rebate to the U.S. parent and the future import, a corresponding tax with equal present value (unless there are profits). Any time value returns to the foreign investment would be taxed by the foreign country. This is the same as in the origin-based income tax. In essence, pure business-level income taxes (i.e., *R*-based systems) are source-based because they tax returns to capital where it is being used. Both origin- and destination-based income business-level taxes are capital import neutral but not capital export neutral.

Note that neither the origin- nor the destination-based income tax needs treaties, rules giving priority to source over residence, or many of the other complications we normally associate with international aspects of income taxes. Both systems likely need careful source rules and the origin-based system needs transfer pricing rules. Neither pure system, however, would approach the complexity of current law nor, arguably, would they be significantly more complex than pure consumption taxes.

Furthermore, mixed systems, such as systems that measure both real and financial flows, can shift the location of the taxation of time value returns. For example, if interest is taxed (and deducted), time value returns attributable to borrowing are taxed in the country where the capital originates rather than where it is invested. The effect is similar to how taking financial flows into account for domestic income shifts the location of the tax to the investor and away from the firm. Less than pure systems, however, create the potential for arbitrage. For example, a system that allows deductions for interest but not dividends creates an artificial distinction depending on the form of the financial payment. Taxpayers can take advantage of this by, say, using stock to transfer an asset to a tax haven and then debt to transfer the asset from the tax haven to the operating company in the country of the investment.

So why do international income tax regimes tend to be such a complex mixture of approaches? One possibility is the adoption of capital export neutrality as a policy goal while trying to impose taxes at the business level. This combination requires a complex mix of approaches. Another possible reason is the attempt to tax income at both the individual and business level. I argued earlier that this was inevitable for income taxes because of problems with deferral. In the international context, it creates a mix of residence and source taxation. Note that neither of these explanations attempts to be historical in the sense of explaining what went on in the creation of current law. Instead, the goal is to understand what features of taxing income tends to lead to the types of complexities we see.

Consider the first argument—that the combination of business-level taxes and capital export neutrality produces complexities. Business-level taxes tend to produce source-based or capital import neutrality. To make them capital export neutral, we need a method of taxing time value returns in the home country. Only by doing so can we ensure that capital invested by a resident faces the same rate regardless of where it is invested. In the international context, this has translated into anti-deferral rules. Generally, these rules apply when time value returns are not taxed at a sufficient rate in the country where capital is invested, thereby providing a rough form of capital export neutrality. Under a business-level tax, however, the country where the investment is made is also taxing time value returns. This creates the need for a priority system, which under current law takes the form of the foreign tax credit. Combine the source rules and transfer pricing rules implicit in an origin-based tax with anti-deferral rules and a crediting system, and we have come close to recreating the complexity of current law.

The second reason I posit for the complexity is that income taxes tend to tax both individuals and businesses for good reasons, independent of the international tax rules. If this is correct, the coordination problems once again become serious. For example, countries would be attempting to tax based both on residence and source, requiring a priority system, which under current law takes the form of credits.

My initial conclusion is that there is a rough parallel between income and consumption taxes in the international context, but that income taxes have a tendency to become very complex in a way that consumption taxes do not. The primary reason for this is the taxation of time value returns, the attendant measurement problems, and the related concerns about efficiency (i.e., the conflict between capital import and capital export neutrality).

6. Conclusion

The parallel implementation hypothesis substantially holds. One can describe essentially parallel systems for income and consumption taxes: for each method of implementing an income tax, there is a corresponding consumption tax and vice versa. The differences in implementation in each case can be traced to the measurement of time value returns in an income tax and not a consumption tax.

David Bradford's work is central to our understanding of these implementation issues. It would be fair to say that he was the deepest thinker in the late twentieth century about how to implement consumption taxes. Much of his work harkens back to work by economists such as Shoup (1955, 1969) and Meade (1978), in which economists with a thorough knowledge of the economics of taxation focused on implementation. This, in my view, is all too rare.

NOTES

I would like to thank Ed McCaffery, Joel Slemrod, and the participants at the "Key Issues in Public Finance" conference.

1. Banks or other entities keeping the accounts would not independently care about the interest rate because, if the two accounts are kept at the same bank, they perfectly offset. Meade (1978, p. 178) argued that banks might not be willing to do so because of the implicit tax liability on the cash flow account. Details of the bankruptcy rules might affect these issues.
2. A similar yet subtly different problem with the use of yield-exempt accounts is illustrated by several examples found in Graetz (1979, p. 1604). Suppose that the taxable period is the calendar year. On January 1, a taxpayer borrows $1,000 from a cash flow account at a 10 percent rate of interest and invests it in an asset yielding a 10 percent rate of return in a yield-exempt account. On December 31, the asset is sold for $1,100 and the borrowing paid off for $1,100. The tax return for the year shows a net of a $100 deduction even though there has been no change in wealth, risk, or consumption. This result arises because the taxable period is too long. If the interest rate were correct and the taxpayer had to pay tax on the initial borrowing immediately and did not get the deduction for the repayment until it was made, there would be no net benefit. The deduction of $1,100 would be exactly offset by the earlier payment of tax on the $1,000 receipt. Because the tax on the $1,000 receipt is deferred, however, there is a net benefit. Weisbach (2000) points out similar problems in the context of the flat tax.
3. Their formula is actually more general than implied in the text. They also impose a tax on risky returns at a rate *G*.
4. If the pretax return is 10 percent and the desired tax on capital is 30 percent, a nominal cash flow rate of 99 percent at time zero translates into a rate of 99.03 at time one. If the nominal cash flow tax rate is 10 percent at time zero, the corresponding time one rate is 12.45 percent.
5. Note that this approach pushes in the direction of a mixed system. Firm-level remittance is likely to be less costly than individual-level remittance but cannot, under the approach taken here, be tailored. A mixed system, such as the X-tax, tries to take advantage of both. (Recall that the X-tax is exactly like a VAT except that firms deduct wages and individuals are taxed on wages based on individual characteristics.) A withholding system might be an alternative method of bridging this gap, allowing both firm-level remittance and tailoring. The question would be whether firms could obtain the relevant information necessary to withhold taxes precisely.
6. The major relabeling opportunity is that if an owner does not have sufficient wage income to push him into the highest wage bracket, relabeling some capital flows as wages can reduce taxation. This, however, is capped by the size of the rate brackets.

7. A potential difference between income and consumption taxes is that to tax time value returns of endowments there must be a firm-level tax.
8. Correspondingly, businesses would also have an incentive to retain earnings. Distributing earnings that will be reinvested would result in a tax on time value returns.
9. Bradford (2004) does not agree with this analysis. He claims that under a switch to a destination-basis tax, net investments in the United States are subject to the transition tax. Suppose, for example, that a French company invested $100 in the United States and a U.S. company invested $100 in France, with no other cross-border flows. Bradford would say that the switch to a destination-basis tax would have no net effect, while the above analysis, following Grubert and Newlon (1995), would say that there is. The intuition that there would be a transition effect is that a destination tax falls in domestic consumption. Domestic consumption has not changed because of the crossing cash flow, so the two cannot be netted. If they were netted, the transition tax could be avoided at will by simply exchanging assets with foreigners immediately before the transition.

REFERENCES

Andrews, William D. 1974. "A Consumption-Type or Cash Flow Personal Income Tax." *Harvard Law Review* 87: 1113–1188.

Auerbach, Alan J., and David F. Bradford. 2004. "Generalized Cash-Flow Taxation." *Journal of Public Economics* 88: 957–980.

Bankman, Joseph. 1995. "A Market-Value Based Corporate Income Tax." *Tax Notes* 68: 1347.

Bird, Richard. 1996. "Why Tax Corporations?" International Centre for Tax Studies, University of Toronto, Working Paper 96–2.

Birnbaum, Jeffrey, and Alan Murray. 1987. *Showdown at Gucci Gulch*. New York: Vintage.

Bradford, David F. 1986. *Untangling the Income Tax*. Cambridge, MA: Harvard University Press.

Bradford, David F. 1996. *Fundamental Issues in Consumption Taxation*. Washington, DC: AEI Press.

Bradford, David F. 1998. "Transition to and Tax Rate Flexibility in a Cash-Flow Type Tax." In James Poterba (ed.), *Tax Policy and the Economy* (vol. 12 pp. 151–172). Cambridge, MA: MIT Press.

Bradford, David F. 2000. *Taxation, Wealth, and Saving*. Cambridge, MA: MIT Press.

Bradford, David F. 2001. "Blueprint for International Tax Reform." *Brooklyn Journal of International Law* 26 (4): 1449–1463.

Bradford, David F. 2004. *The X-Tax in the World Economy: Going Global with a Simple, Progressive Tax*. Washington, DC: American Enterprise Institute.

Bradford, David F., and U.S. Treasury Tax Policy Staff. 1984. *Blueprints for Basic Tax Reform* (2d ed.). Arlington, VA: Tax Analysts.

Desai, Mihir A., and James R. Hines, Jr. 2003. "Evaluating International Tax Reform." *National Tax Journal* 56(3): 487–502.

Fisher, Irving, and Herbert W. Fisher. 1942. *Constructive Income Taxation*. New York: Harper & Row.

Gordon, Roger H. 1985. "Taxation of Corporate Capital Income: Tax Revenues Versus Tax Distortions." *Quarterly Journal of Economics* 100: 1–27.

Graetz, Michael. 1979. "Implementing a Progressive Consumption Tax." *Harvard Law Review* 92: 1575–1661.

Graetz, Michael. 2001. "Taxing International Income: Inadequate Principles, Outdated Concepts, and Unsatisfactory Policies." *Tax Law Review* 54: 261–336.

Grubert, Harry, and T. Scott Newlon. 1995. "The International Implications of Consumption Tax Proposals." *National Tax Journal* 48: 619–647.

Hall, Robert E., and Alvin Rabushka. 1995. *The Flat Tax* (2d ed.). Palo Atto, CA: Hoover Institution Press.

Kaplow, Louis. 1994. "Taxation and Risk Taking: A General Equilibrium Perspective." *National Tax Journal* 47: 789–798.

Knoll, Michael. 1996. "An Accretion Corporate Income Tax." *Stanford Law Review* 49: 1–43.

McLure, Charles E., Jr. 1987. "The Value-Added Tax Key to Deficit Reduction." Washington, DC: American Enterprise Institute.

Meade J. E. 1978. *The Structure and Reform of Direct Taxation*. London: Institute for Fiscal Studies.

Samuelson, Paul A. 1964. "Tax Deductibility of Economic Depreciation to Insure Invariant Valuations." *Journal of Political Economy* 72(6): 604–606.

Shoup, Carl S. 1955. "Theory and Background of the Value-Added Tax." Proceedings, Forty-Eighth National Tax Conference.

Shoup, Carl S. 1969. *Public Finance*. Chicago: Aldine.

Slemrod, Joel. 1990. "Optimal Taxation and Optimal Tax Systems." *Journal of Economic Perspectives* 4(1): 157–178.

U.S. Department of Treasury. 1984. *Tax Reform for Fairness, Simplicity, and Economic Growth*. Washington DC: Department of the Treasury.

U.S. Department of Treasury. 1992. *Integration of the Individual and Corporate Tax Systems: Taxing Business Income Once*. Washington, DC: U.S. GPO.

Vickrey, William. 1939. "Averaging of Income for Income Tax Purposes." *Journal of Political Economy* 72: 604–606.

Warren, Alvin C. Jr. 1996. "How Much Capital Income Taxed under an Income Tax Is Exempt under a Cash Flow Tax." *Tax Law Review* 52: 1–16.

Weisbach, David. 2000. "Ironing Out the Flat Tax." *Stanford Law Review* 52(3): 599–664.

Weisbach, David. 2007. "The Irreducible Complexity of Firm-Level Income Taxes: Theory and Doctrine in the Corporate Tax." *Tax Law Review* 60(4): 215–262.

Zodrow, George R., and Charles E. McLure, Jr. 1991. "Implementing Direct Consumption Taxes in Developing Countries." *Tax Law Review* 46(4): 405–487.

CHAPTER 3

Comment 1

A Tale of Two Davids

EDWARD J. MCCAFFERY

David Weisbach has given us a work that would have made David Bradford proud. I can think of no higher compliment than that, and it is well warranted.

Bradford devoted much of his considerable intellectual gifts to figuring out analytic equivalences among various, seemingly divergent, tax systems, and attempting to carefully explain them to participants in the political process (as in *Blueprints for Tax Reform,* with the U.S. Treasury Tax Policy Staff, 1977 and 1984) and even to a wider general public (as in *Untangling the Income Tax,* 1986). Bradford's earlier work, most prominently *Blueprints,* used the equivalence of "prepaid" and "postpaid" consumption taxes to mix and match in coming up with a practicable, comprehensive plan for tax reform. In his later work, Bradford went several steps further, developing the X-tax as a prominent alternative to the income tax; the X-tax combined an individual-level progressive wage (or, equivalently, prepaid consumption) tax with a business-level tax measured by receipts minus wages (Bradford, 2004). Both sets of ideas have had significant influence on real-world policy proposals and outcomes: a variant of the X-tax, for example, featured in the recent President's Advisory Panel on Federal Tax Reform (2005).

In his chapter in this volume, Weisbach, following in Bradford's impressive footsteps, has bored down on some rather precise details, flirting with a general theorem of equivalence between income and consumption tax "implementation methods," demonstrating that "for every income tax implementation method, there should be an equivalent consumption tax method" (Weisbach, this volume). I shall call this idea the "Equivalence Theorem." In other work (e.g., Weisbach, 2000), Weisbach has similarly analyzed the precise implementation details of popular tax reform proposals, most notably the flat tax, and he has also examined closely the differences between income and consumption taxes (Weisbach, 2004). Weisbach, like Bradford before him, pushed the analysis out far enough to see that the only difference between the two major comprehensive tax bases, at least in a Coasean-like world of no transactions costs and fully informed and rational agents (more on this, anon), lies in the taxation of the "pure, riskless return" to savings: an income tax includes this; a consumption tax does not. There is, of course, normative work to be done in deciding whether or not this aspect of material value *should* be taxed. But, first, note that this core difference between income and consumption taxes means that the Equivalence Theorem cannot precisely hold, as Weisbach well knows. It must, rather, be the case that any implementation method, not affecting the taxation of "time value returns"—as Weisbach calls the riskless return to savings—has an equivalent in the other major type of tax (i.e., every income tax method has a consumption tax equivalent, and vice versa).

Stated thus, the Equivalence Theorem is almost surely correct, because it follows from definitions—if the only real difference between an income and a consumption tax is the inclusion *vel non* of the riskless return to savings, then there are no other differences between an income tax and a consumption tax. But to say that the Equivalence Theorem is obvious once suitably stated is not to say that it is not surprising, or valuable, to see it laid out. After all, the Coase Theorem—which I simplify to my students by telling them that it stands for the basic proposition that "efficiency happens"—is also obvious enough, once Coase got around to setting it out and making most (if not quite all) of us see it, work for which he rightfully received a Nobel Prize (Coase, 1960). There is no such prize in tax scholarship, alas, or Bradford surely would have received it long ago, proudly, and Weisbach would be on his way to taking his own turn on the pedestal.

Thus Weisbach works out his basic ambition, and the Equivalence Theorem, with four specific examples, among many possible others:

1. Cash flow versus basis accounting;
2. Individual- versus business-level taxation (or, perhaps better put, as Joel Slemrod notes in his commentary, because of incidence, individual versus business remission of taxes);
3. *Open* versus *closed*, terms used somewhat idiosyncratically by Weisbach, following his 2000 treatment, by which he means whether or not the tax system features transactional symmetry—that is, whether or not the tax treatment on one side of a transaction *dictates* the tax treatment on the other (buyer versus seller, say); and
4. International, such as destination- versus origin-based taxes.

This is all good and important work, rich in detail and thoughtful analysis. Weisbach's chapter rewards a close reading, and indeed, rereading.

In this brief commentary, I have three more humble goals. One, to take a step back, and situate the Equivalence Theorem in a wider intellectual history of tax policy, using slightly different terms, picking up, perhaps, the aspect of Bradford's life and work wherein he (sometimes) took pains to explain his analysis to a general readership. Two, I offer some comments on the normative foundations of this work, exploring the role of normativity within the analyticity of tax. Three, I offer some near final thoughts on, when all is said and done, how we should go about thinking about equivalent implementation methods in tax.

1. Laying Out the Analytics of Tax

Both Davids follow in a distinguished line of tax policy analysts, stretching back at least to John Stuart Mill (1848), who famously laid out the case against the income tax as a "double tax" on wealth that is saved or not immediately consumed, and in favor of a consumption tax as a single tax on wealth. The line continued through Henry Simons (1938, 1950), Nicholas Kaldor (1955), William Andrews (1972, 1974, 1975), Alvin Warren (1975, 1980), and beyond. We can discern four distinct waves.

The first wave, beginning with Mill and culminating in Simons, was concerned with laying out the essential difference between income and consumption taxes. Income = Consumption + Savings, to simplify Simons' precise language a bit (Simons, 1938; McCaffery, 2002). Rearranging terms, we can see that Consumption = Income − Savings (Fisher and Fisher, 1942; Andrews, 1974). Thus an income tax includes, and a consumption tax excludes, savings from its base. This leads to Mill's (1848) critique of the income tax as a double tax on wealth that is not immediately consumed, because the wealth is taxed first, when it enters the household, and again when, not having been consumed, it generates a yield.

The second wave, which certainly had its roots in prior writings, reached full flower in the writings of Andrews (1974) and Bradford et al. (1977, 1984). Whereas income taxes are double taxes on wealth, consumption taxes are single ones. This led to the observation that, holding tax rates constant, it does not matter when the single tax gets levied: it could come up-front, when money is earned, as in a wage or prepaid consumption tax, and never again; *or*, it could come later, when money is spent, as in a sales or value-added or postpaid consumption tax. Algebra alone tells us the two forms are equivalent. Let P equal principal or present value, r the rate of return, n the compound period, t the tax rate, and $(1 - t)$ the value left after-taxes in a taxpayer's hands. Then the commutative principle of multiplication, which holds that ab = ba, tells us that: $(1 - t)P(1 + r)^{n} = P(1 + r)^{n}(1 - t)$. In simpler terms, under a flat rate structure, wage taxes and sales taxes are equivalent.

The third wave challenged the equivalence, given "inframarginal returns" or the return to risk, noting that a postpaid consumption tax reached such windfalls, whereas a prepaid consumption tax did not (Graetz, 1980; McCaffery, 1992, and 2005).

The fourth wave (Bankman and Griffith, 1992; Warren, 1996), of which Weisbach is a prominent representative, has come around to see that the difference between an income and a postpaid consumption tax may not be so great, turning only on the taxation of the pure riskless return (Weisbach, 2004), which Bankman and Griffith first considered at length in the legal literature at a time when a case could be made that this pivotal rate was close to zero. Other aspects of this fourth and contemporary wave concern a debate as to whether the portfolio adjustments needed to eliminate the taxation of risk under various regimes in fact get made; one hears echoes of all this in Weisbach's chapter.

Weisbach's chapter, like much of Bradford's work, grows out of this background; it assumes some knowledge of a conversation long running. Interestingly, for Weisbach and many others writing in this tradition (e.g., Auerbach, 2006), *prepaid* consumption taxes have dropped out of the analysis, as an obviously inferior choice that does not even reach inframarginal returns. The difference between an income and a prepaid consumption tax is the taxation of any and all returns to savings: pure riskless, inframarginal, and otherwise (Weisbach, 2006). As I shall explore further in the next section, Weisbach's (implicit) acceptance of the norm of taxing at least the inframarginal returns leads him to define *consumption taxes* as only including postpaid models: the equivalence of the second phase of tax policy analysis has altogether gone by the boards. This is a bit curious because, as I have argued at some length elsewhere (McCaffery, 2005), practical tax policy has been heading relentlessly, and seemingly inexorably, toward a prepaid consumption or wage tax for some decades now. In other words, somehow, some way, tax policy analytics have gotten away from the people and practice of tax.

2. The Normativity of the Analytics

David Hume (1739) (to bring another David to bear) famously cautioned that one cannot derive an *ought* from an *is:* that a simple statement of fact or analytic truth cannot dictate a moral, normative position. Although there are subtle ways in which facts can indeed have normative significance—the postmodern turn in philosophy and language having long ago attempted to implode the fact-value distinction behind the Humean position—it nonetheless takes argument to get from a truth to a principle, especially with analytic truths. Yet it is surprising how often analytics lead to apparent norms without pause or reflection. The most famous and damaging example in tax policy is the Haig-Simons definition of income, which holds: "Income may be defined as the algebraic sum of the market value of rights exercised in consumption plus the change in value of the store of property rights between the beginning and end of the period in question" (Simons, 1938). Or, more simply, as noted above, that Income = Consumption + Savings. This definition is no more or less than a tautology, which can be restated as the truism that all income is either spent (consumption) or not (savings) (McCaffery, 2002). Yet this definition has led to many a tree being felled in pursuit of the "comprehensive tax base as an ideal," a concept that Boris Bittker (1967) most heroically attempted to lay to rest, without total success. Part of the brilliance of Andrews' work (e.g., Andrews, 1972) was to see that not all consumption—such as medical expenses and casualty losses—stood on the same normative footing, in terms of ordinary moral intuitions. I have attempted to argue that we had best extend Andrews' insight that "uses matter" to the uses of savings as well as consumption (McCaffery, 1992, 2005); just as Ralph Waldo Emerson (1841) cautioned against an at least "foolish consistency," comprehensiveness, without argument, is not an ideal.

Similar moves and mistakes have haunted other aspects of tax policy. There is a danger in going far, as both Davids, Bradford and Weisbach, were inclined to go, with the analytics of tax policy, without first getting the normative foundations and commitments down right. One can get blinded by the analytics, making equivalents into arguments without justification or broad-based appeal to ordinary moral intuitions. I had a long-running conversation with Bradford, which, tragically, was never resolved in our lifetimes. Bradford, like others in the line of tax policy he pursued, through the "fourth wave" and beyond, seemed to believe—rather passionately—that the analytics, beginning with Mill, led to a normative position. The ideal was that the timing of a person's consumption patterns should be irrelevant to the ultimate imposition of taxes (Bradford, 1980, 1998). This norm was also central to Andrews (1974) (see also Andrews and Bradford, 1988), which led him, in the face of a critique from Warren (1975, 1980), to be troubled by progressive rates, which destroy the equivalence of prepaid and postpaid consumption taxes, as noted in the equation above (Andrews, 1975). Bradford kept pushing out the analysis, and so *Blueprints* featured an elaborate plan for income and consumption averaging, and his later work (e.g., Bradford, 1998) explored the "problem" of varying tax rates in even greater detail. Such analytics haunt Weisbach as well: he frets over "consumption lumpiness" and seems to assume that the only debate worth having is whether tax should include time value returns or not. Once we have made this central choice, the Equivalence Theorem gives us a menu of practical implementation details to consider, which can be left to technocrats to sort through (who else could understand them?). This pattern of thinking leads to, among other things, the out-of-hand dismissal of prepaid consumption tax models—which just so happen to be dominating the real world of tax politics.

Now I find this way of going about answering the "ought" questions of tax puzzling and unhelpful. First off, I have always found it odd that many tax policy theorists, with the notable exception of William Vickrey (1939, 1947), have not been all that bothered by *income* lumpiness, although the pattern of labor and even capital market returns seems more morally arbitrary than the pattern of consumption or spending. Further, as I have argued at some length, the problem of consumption lumpiness seems wildly overstated as a criticism of my preferred tax policy outcome, a progressive postpaid consumption tax (McCaffery, 2005). But most fundamentally, while the norm of consumption neutrality, or imposing equal burdens on aggregate consumption paths equivalent in present value terms, strikes me as an elegant touch, it is hardly the kind of foundational, "all the way down" norm that can drive a practicable and politically acceptable tax policy. The normative commitment of a progressive cash flow consumption tax is to tax people when, as, and only when, they spend. At the moment of spending, or "private preclusive use" as Andrews (1974) called it, society can make the inevitable judgments of the appropriate level of taxation. Those who are living well, in some objective sense of the term, pay more taxes than those who are living more modestly, and so on. People who work hard and save well, and pass on wealth to their heirs, need not envision death-bed taxation: the heirs, having inherited the assets with a carryover basis of zero, will pay taxes when and as they spend, at progressive marginal rates triggered by their lifestyles. The analytics of the progressive postpaid consumption tax follow from its normative commitments, which in turn reflect an interpretation of reasonable ordinary moral intuitions, rather than analytic equivalences.

Back to Weisbach's effort, I am even more skeptical that his equivalents can be normative all the way down, as a philosopher might write. I find it implausible, that is, that anyone could have a foundational commitment to basis-method accounting, such that one would cling to an income tax, until or unless a basis-method consumption tax could be worked out. What Weisbach has shown us, in a project that would have done Bradford proud, is that it is possible to pose a quite general Equivalence Theorem; indeed, my statement in this commentary goes beyond the strength of the statement Weisbach made in his chapter. But this follows, as I have said, from definitions: if the only real difference between an income and a consumption tax is the taxation of time value returns, then the Equivalence Theorem, à la Coase, must hold. What does not follow from definitions is any kind of normative position. We are still waiting for that, as for Godot.

3. Thinking about Equivalents

If, as I have argued, equivalent implementation methods are not themselves normative, all the way down, and if, in fact, running with the analytics before walking with the moral commitments has interfered with the development of compelling tax policy in sync with ordinary moral intuitions, what then, are equivalent implementation methods all about? Here I think there are three very important sets of answers, reminiscent of post-Coasean developments in economics: transactions costs, politics, and perceptions.

Transactions costs are a familiar subject of post-Coasean economics (Williamson and Masten, 1998), well known to destroy the theoretical equivalence of different allocations of rights. It is worth noting, as Weisbach does, that there might be very wide divergences among various equivalent implementation methods, such that, as Slemrod (1990) has argued, "optimal tax systems" may mean something very different from "optimal taxes." Here, "equivalent" implementation methods may not be equivalent at all because of their different transactions costs, and so it helps very much to have the menu of "equivalents" that Bradford and Weisbach have started to provide.

Politics clearly matter, because tax reform is a quintessentially political act. As Dan Shaviro (2008) has persuasively shown, politics can interact with "ideal" tax policy in ways that will make certain reforms, *ex ante*, more or less attractive, because of how they are likely to look, *ex post*. Whether businesses or individuals remit taxes may not matter to the ultimate output of material well-being, but politicians may be more or less likely to raise, or have more or less political will to enforce, taxes remitted at different levels. So too with basis versus cash flow accounting, as Weisbach (this volume) notes: given a mechanism for keeping track of basis, politicians may be tempted to alter it. And so on.

Finally, to get back to some of my own work, this time in a different key, perceptions matter. Politicians and citizens will not always perceive "equivalent" mechanisms as being equally attractive, because of their framing and other psychological properties (McCaffery and Baron, 2005, 2006; McCaffery and Slemrod, 2006). The most ready example of this is business-versus individual-level remission of taxes. Economists and other readers of this volume may understand that it does not matter where the nominal or statutory incidence of a tax lies, but try explaining that to any citizen—or politician dependent on the votes of citizens—at your own peril. Broad-based, welfare-enhancing tax reform cannot obtain without broad-based understanding and popular support, so it behooves those of us living in the real world to figure out the most attractive ways to package good ideas (McCaffery and Baron, 2005). Of course, those on the other side will be using parallel techniques to package their "bad" ideas, so there is not, alas, an easy answer as yet. Hard questions persist.

For all these reasons, the Equivalence Theorem is a very important advance in our knowledge of theoretical and practical tax policy. David Weisbach, following in a tradition most ably serviced by David Bradford, has given all of us a dizzying array of choices to implement the tax policy we really want and deserve. If none of this is actually helpful in figuring out what, in the first instance, we really do want and need, that is, in the end, our shortcoming and our responsibility, not theirs. Meanwhile, we can thank the two Davids, and hope for more like them.

REFERENCES

Andrews, William D. 1972. "Personal Deductions in an Ideal Income Tax." *Harvard Law Review* 86: 309, 331–337.

Andrews, William D. 1974. "A Consumption-Type or Cash Flow Personal Income Tax." *Harvard Law Review* 87: 1113.

Andrews, William D. 1975. "Fairness and the Personal Income Tax: A Reply to Professor Warren." *Harvard Law Review* 88: 947, 954.

Andrews, William D., and David F. Bradford. 1988. "Savings Incentives in a Hybrid Income Tax." In Henry J. Aaron et al. (eds.), *Uneasy Compromise: Problems of a Hybrid Income-Consumption Tax.* Washington, DC: Brookings Institute.

Auerbach, Alan J. 2006. "Tax Reform in the 21st Century." *Baker Institute Essay.* Available at http://www.econ.berkeley.edu/~auerbach/reform.pdf.

Bankman, Joseph, and Thomas Griffith. 1992. "Is the Debate between an Income Tax and a Consumption Tax a Debate about Risk? Does it Matter?" *Tax Law Review* 47: 377.

Bittker, Boris I. 1967. "A 'Comprehensive Tax Base' as a Goal of Income Tax Reform." *Harvard Law Review* 80: 925.

Bradford, David F. 1980. "The Case for a Personal Consumption Tax." In Joseph A. Pechman (ed.), *What Should Be Taxed: Income or Expenditure?* Washington, DC: Brookings Institute.

Bradford, David F. 1986. *Untangling the Income Tax.* Cambridge, MA: Harvard Univ. Press.

Bradford, David F. 1998. "Transition to and Tax Rate Flexibility in a Cash-Flow Type Tax." In James Poterba (ed.), *Tax Policy and the Economy* (vol. 12, pp. 151–172). Cambridge, MA: MIT Press.

Bradford, David F. 2004. *The X-Tax in the World Economy: Going Global with a Simple, Progressive Tax.* Washington, DC: AEI Press.

Bradford, David F., and U.S. Treasury Tax Policy Staff. 1977. *Blueprints for Basic Tax Reform.* Washington, DC: U.S. Department of Treasury.

Bradford David F., and the U.S. Treasury Tax Policy Staff. 1984. *Blueprints for Basic Tax Reform* (2d ed.). Arlington, Va: Tax Analysts.

Coase, Ronald H. 1960. "The Problem of Social Cost." *Journal of Law & Economics* 3: 1–23.

Emerson, Ralph Waldo. [1841] 1909–14. "Self-Reliance." *Essays and English Traits.* New York: P.F. Collier & Son.

Fisher, Irving, and Herbert W. Fisher. 1942. *Constructive Income Taxation: A Proposal for Reform.* New York: Harper & Brothers.

Graetz, Michael J. 1980. "Expenditure Tax Design." In Joseph A. Pechman (ed.), *What Should Be Taxed: Income or Expenditure?* Washington, DC: Brookings Institute.

Hume, David. [1739] 1978. *Treatise on Human Nature* (2d ed.). L. A. Selby-Bigge, ed. Oxford: Clarendon Press.

Kaldor, Nicholas. 1955. *An Expenditure Tax.* London: Allen & Unwin.

McCaffery, Edward J. 1992. "Tax Policy Under a Hybrid Income-Consumption Tax." *Texas Law Review* 70: 145.

McCaffery, Edward J. 2002. *Fair Not Flat: How to Make the Tax System Better and Simpler.* Chicago: University of Chicago Press.

McCaffery, Edward J. 2005. "A New Understanding of Tax." *Michigan Law Review* 103: 807–938.

McCaffery, Edward J., and Joel Slemrod (eds.). 2006. *Behavioral Public Finance.* New York: Russell Sage Publications.

McCaffery, Edward J., and Jonathan Baron. 2005. "The Political Psychology of Redistribution." *UCLA Law Review* 52 (6): 1745–1792.

McCaffery, Edward J., and Jonathan Baron. 2006. "Thinking About Tax." *Psychology, Public Policy, and Law* 12 (1): 106–135.

Mill, John Stuart. 1848. *Principles of Political Economy* (vol. 5, ch. II, § 4:179–180).

President's Advisory Panel of Federal Tax Reform. 2005. *Simple, Fair, and Pro-Growth: Proposals to Fix America's Tax System.* Washington, DC: U.S. Government Printing Office.

Shaviro, Daniel. 2008. "Simplifying Assumptions: How Might the Politics of Consumption Tax Reform Affect (Impair) the End Product?" In John W. Diamond and George R. Zodrow (eds.), *Fundamental Tax Reform: Issues, Choices, and Implications.* Cambridge, MA: MIT Press.

Simons, Henry C. 1938. *Personal Income Taxation: The Definition of Income as Problem of Fiscal Policy.* Chicago: University of Chicago Press.

Simons, Henry C. 1950. *Federal Tax Reform.* Chicago: University of Chicago Press.

Slemrod, Joel. 1990. "Optimal Tax and Optimal Tax Systems." *Journal of Economic Perspectives* 4(1):157–178.

Vickrey, William Spencer. 1939. "Averaging of Income for Income Tax Purposes." *Journal of Political Economy* 72: 604–606.

Vickrey, William Spencer. 1947. *Agenda for Progressive Taxation.* New York: Ronald Press.

Warren, Alvin C. 1975. "Fairness and a Consumption-Type or Cash Flow Personal Income Tax." *Harvard Law Review* 88: 931, 933—936.

Warren, Alvin C. 1980. "Would a Consumption Tax Be Fairer Than an Income Tax?" *Yale Law Journal* 89: 1081.

Warren, Alvin C. 1996. "How Much Capital Income Taxes under an Income Tax Is Exempt under a Cash Flow Tax? *Tax Law Review* 52: 1.

Weisbach, David A. 2000. "Ironing Out the Flat Tax." *Stanford Law Review* 52: 599.

Weisbach, David A. 2004. "The (Non) Taxation of Risk." *University of Chicago Law & Economics, Olin Working Paper* No. 203. Available at SSRN: http://ssrn.com/abstract=488846 or DOI: 10.2139/ssrn.488846

Williamson, Oliver E., and Scott E. Masten (eds.). 1998. *The Economics of Transactions Costs.* New York: Edward Elgar Publishing.

CHAPTER 3

Comment 2

JOEL SLEMROD

By focusing on differences in implementation methods between income and consumption taxes, David Weisbach's thoughtful and thought-provoking paper lies outside the standard economic model of taxation, where the only thing that matters for the consequences of taxation is what actions or states of the world *trigger* a present-value tax liability. In this standard framework, who or what entity remits a present-value liability,[1] and when they remit it—what one might call the implementation method—is irrelevant.

Put another way, inquiring about implementation methods is tantamount to accepting that who remits tax, and when they remit it, matters.[2] Weisbach does not provide a list of what remittance factors are important, although he sprinkles through the chapter allusions to his views on this matter. He suggests early on that implementation matters because it affects tax administration and compliance costs, and gives some examples of why that might be so. Economies of scale in tax auditing and in tax compliance may favor remittance by large entities, such as firms, instead of by individuals, especially because firms might collect tax-relevant information for other reasons; offsetting that is the fact that there may be economies of scale in tax avoidance as well as collection, potentially making taxation of firms less desirable. Different types of transactions might also be more easily observable, and verifiable, than others; for example, transfer prices among related entities cannot be taken to be correct, while prices in arm's length transactions usually can. Similarly, it may be very costly to ascertain and verify the value of many assets.

An excellent example of the importance of implementation issues is the debate about whether a retail sales tax or a value-added tax (VAT) would be a better replacement for U.S. income taxes. Although the retail sales tax is (to an American, at least), the more familiar consumption tax, one levied by 45 American states and thousands of local governments, the nearly unanimous view of tax administrators and academics is that a retail sales tax levied at a rate high enough to replace the U.S. income tax (over 30 percent) would be very expensive to administer and, even with considerable expense, would end up generating widespread avoidance and evasion, which costs resources and produces a capricious distribution of the tax burden.

Why is that? After all, a retail sales tax is a cash flow tax in the sense that it adheres to the principle that no distinction is made between expenditure on current items and expenditure on capital goods, and a cash flow base is widely touted as being relatively simple and monitorable.[3] But under a retail sales tax the entire remittance responsibility rests on one sector, retail businesses, who sell to a multitude of individuals who are not in the habit of keeping detailed records of their purchases, and who not only have no incentive to monitor the tax compliance behavior of the retailers, but may benefit from their noncompliance. It is very difficult to harness the consumer side of the market to even encourage compliance, such as treating sales receipts as lottery tickets, in the hope of encouraging monitorable cash register transactions as opposed to difficult-to-trace cash payments. Furthermore, under a retail sales tax the retail establishments need to distinguish between taxed sales to consumers and exempt sales to other businesses, in the face of a clear incentive for consumers to masquerade as businesses. These implementation problems are different from the implementation problems that arise in other textbook-equivalent consumption taxes, most notably a VAT. Under a value-added tax, the remittance responsibility is shouldered by all businesses, and no business need distinguish sales to consumers and sales to businesses. Furthermore, there is an element of self-enforcement in the usual invoice-credit method of implementing a VAT, in that purchasing businesses may claim a tax credit for purchases only if there is evidence that the seller has paid its VAT liability on the sales.[4]

Without any claim to comprehensiveness or prioritization, I would offer the following general rules regarding tax implementation that may be useful in minimizing administrative and compliance costs and the capriciousness of tax burden which can follow from avoidance and evasion:

- Maximize reliance on transactions between arm's-length parties, where information from one side can be easily checked against information from the other;
- Maximize reliance on financially sophisticated entities (i.e., large firms);
- Minimize the number of entities dealt with;
- Minimize reliance on nonmarket valuations; and
- Minimize reliance on easily changed labels (i.e., wage versus capital income).

Weisbach addresses the implementation issues that arise in the choice between an income and consumption tax, and focuses on four implementation dimensions along which tax systems can vary: (1) cash flow versus basis systems, (2) remittance by firms or individuals, (3) whether the tax system is open or closed, and (4) how the tax system operates across borders—and compares income and consumption taxes along these dimensions. In my comments I will focus on the second topic.

1. Income versus Consumption Taxes

Weisbach emphasizes that, in terms of an individual's lifetime budget set, an income tax is equivalent to a consumption tax that has rates that rise over time. Of course, this is not at all what supporters of the income tax have in mind now, nor had in mind when the modern income tax was introduced. Indeed, the origins of the income tax are instructive. Under the pressure of revenue needs of the Napoleonic wars, the British government first ratcheted up sundry excise taxes—such as the famous window tax—and then in 1798 introduced the Triple Assessment, which extended and consolidated the excise taxes and stipulated that the total levy could not exceed 10 percent of income.[5] It was a short step from an expenditure tax capped at 10 percent of income to a 10 percent tax on income and that, essentially, is what Prime Minister William Pitt instituted in 1799, with a generous level of exempt income.[6]

The idea that wages, but not property income, would be taxed would have been laughable in that context, because focusing on the not-particularly-affluent wage earners of the time would have run counter to the objective of achieving a progressive distribution of the tax burden. Moreover, eliminating the consumption tax in favor of a wage income tax would have delivered a subsidy to those affluent wealth-owners who were considered to be the most appropriate to bear the burden of the war expenditures. The same issue arose at the institution of the modern U.S. income tax, in 1913, which was meant to replace to some extent the more regressive tariffs and excise taxes the federal government had been relying on. Although Weisbach claims that the introduction of the income tax did not impose a tax on existing wealth when first imposed—because only gains or losses after 1913 were subject to taxation—it certainly did not attempt to shield existing wealth from taxation because the returns from capital put in place before 1913 were taxed.

The expansion of tax levies that occurred during the Napoleonic, and occurs during most, wars is an example of the issues that arise when tax rates change. As Weisbach discusses, the implementation details of a given tax become critical in a transition. For example, when making a real investment triggers changes in required tax remittances over the life of the investment, changes in the tax rate affect the ultimate *ex post* present value of the levy, in a way that would not occur if all the tax remittance implications occurred at the time of the investment. Another current example is the choice of a traditional versus a Roth IRA: the attractiveness of cashing in a traditional IRA, and paying tax on the proceeds, in order to purchase a Roth IRA depends critically on one's forecast of future tax rates. This is true even if the two kinds of savings vehicles have the same present-value tax consequences in a world of unchanging tax rates.

A key difference between an income tax and a consumption tax is clear even in a very simple model in which a representative individual lives for two periods, works only in the first period, but values both leisure in the first period as well as consumption in both the first and second periods. In order to consume in the second period, the representative individual must save some of the first-period wage income. There is no uncertainty, either about the return to saving or about second-period tax policy.

Under a consumption tax the only decision that affects the present value of tax liability is the labor-leisure choice. The present value of tax liability is the tax rate times the present value of consumption, which is equal to first-period wage income. Assuming perfect capital markets, as Weisbach does throughout (except perhaps when he talks about the portfolio method of argument), this tax can be implemented in an infinite number of ways, including a tax on wage income remitted in period one, a uniform tax on consumption remitted at the time of consumption, or a mixture of taxes based on wages and consumption at the same rate. Also irrelevant is whether the present value liability is remitted by the representative individual or by the retailer (not visible in the model), or by some combination of other firms or other individuals. In the standard model, the implicit assumption is that once the representative individual works some amount, some combination of individuals or business entities, at some point, will remit the appropriate present-value tax liability.

Under an income tax the present-value tax liability depends not only on the labor-leisure decision, but also on the consumption allocation decision. For any given value of labor income, the more the individual spends on future consumption, the higher is the present value of tax liability. In a world of perfect foresight and no uncertainty about the rate of return or future tax rates, this present value could be remitted all in the first period, when the income is earned, all in the final period, or any number of other combinations—as long as the present value is unaffected. Who or what entity remits this liability is also irrelevant.

2. The Role of Firms

Weisbach argues that the choice between individual-and business-level taxes is primarily a trade-off between ease of collection and tailoring the tax to individual circumstances. He applies the terms "business-level" or "firm-level" to taxes that are remitted by firms and where the present-value liability is based on the characteristics of the firm, but not on characteristics of the owners, contractors, or employees. That is critically different from what one might call a "business-based remittance system," which includes no-individual-return systems of the exact withholding type, under which employer remittances can depend on characteristics of their employees; such systems can implement a graduated tax schedule and personalization of the tax burden based on individual characteristics or decisions. Indeed, the United States is in the minority among developed countries in the Organisation for Economic Co-operation and Development (OECD) (9 out of 30) in requiring that individuals file tax returns. Half of the OECD operates a system in which most wage earners need not file due to exact, cumulative employer withholding.[7]

Like the United States, all but two OECD countries rely on withholding at source arrangements for the collection of the bulk of personal tax revenue on wage and salary income. However, unlike most OECD countries, the United States does not utilize withholding at source for the collection of personal income tax for dividends or interest nor, unlike many OECD countries, on independent personal services or royalties and rents. However, the United States maintains the most substantial program of information reporting of any OECD country. An extremely wide variety of transactions must be reported to the IRS, including interest, dividends, real estate transactions, rents, sales of securities, and wages.

Because of withholding, the implementation difference between taxes, such as between a VAT and a Hall-Rabushka flat tax, can be overstated. If employers remit tax to the government based on the wages they pay, the flat tax has an equivalent remittance system to a VAT plus a subsidy to labor income paid directly to individuals. A personalized version of the flat tax can be implemented as long as the requisite information about employees is transmitted to employers, either via the government as in the United Kingdom, or directly. In this way a VAT could be made consistent with a progressive tax on labor income. It could also be made compatible with a progressive comprehensive income tax, by substituting depreciation, or a present-value equivalent of depreciation, for expensing of capital assets.

Withholding, and in theory differential withholding, could be extended to capital suppliers. The United States already has a form of differentiated withholding on dividend and interest payments through its system of backup withholding, under which withholding (and remittance) is waived upon the provision to the IRS of information about the receiver. Credit imputation corporation integration systems allow shareholders to essentially treat the corporation tax as a withholding tax, as the shareholders can credit some or all of these payments against their individual tax liability, but also must treat some or all of the corporate income earned on their behalf as individual taxable income; the withholding could be more exact if shareholder information were transmitted to the corporation. Nonstandard and innovative remittance schemes have long been employed in developing countries, where administrative resources are scarce. For example, Soos (1990) discusses a system of "reverse withholding" for income tax that has been used in Indonesia, Pakistan, and Egypt under which sellers of goods to firms outside the income tax net withhold and remit tax based on the value of the sales.[8]

3. Language

Weisbach's paper adopts a style common to legal scholarship, in that it eschews the use of mathematical shorthand, and relies on prose. In contrast, economic argument has, at least since the early 1970s, tended to use a mathematical language, the trade-off often being a precision of meaning versus a sacrifice of nuance. With prose, using precise language becomes even more important. Weisbach deserves high praise for being careful about language. Without any claim to having optimized the vocabulary of tax systems, I would recommend the term *remit* tax to denote the act of writing a check or otherwise transmitting funds to the tax authority. The *statutory* bearer of a tax is the agent that is ultimately liable to remit tax. When an agent other than the statutory bearer must remit some tax, we call this remittance *withholding Final withholding* occurs when the withholding remittance equals the actual liability—no adjustment need be made by the statutory bearer. The tax authority *collects* tax from those in the private sector that remit taxes. Businesses do not collect tax in any meaningful sense,[9] although they remit the majority of taxes in most tax systems.

4. Conclusion

I commend David for making a substantial contribution to the nascent but important literature that is attempting to formalize and analyze the alternative ways that textbook-equivalent taxes can be implemented. Understanding these issues better should inform the choice between income and consumption taxes, as well as many other aspects of tax system design.

NOTES

1. The proposition about the irrelevance of the remitter is usually stated within the context of a tax in a single market, where the two possible remitters are the supplier and demander of the good. Presumably, for the irrelevance to hold, the remitter must have some connection to the transaction, but exactly how close that connection needs to be has not been thought through.
2. It may also imply that who has the statutory responsibility for tax liability, as distinct from the remittance responsibility, matters.
3. This principle is articulated by Kay and King (1990, p. 175) in the context of describing a cash flow corporation tax.
4. The self-enforcing feature is not airtight, as fraud such as counterfeit tax invoices needs to be monitored by the tax agency. In addition, the VAT has its own implementation issues that do not arise under a retail sales tax.
5. Another notable feature is that the tax base was the previous year's expenditure taxes.
6. Both the Triple Assessment and the 1799 income tax were deemed to be failures, in the sense that their yield fell far short of what had been estimated. It was up to Pitt's successor, Addington, to reform the income tax in 1803, with two key implementation reforms: a schedular system, so that no one in the government could easily get a sense of an individual's total income, and, most important, a system of withholding at source. These two aspects of Addington's tax remain in force today in the British income tax.
7. In several other OECD countries individuals need not file a tax return, and the tax authority sends taxpayers a pre-populated tax return based on the information they receive from third parties; the individual need only verify the information on the return.

8. Soos (1990, p. 144) describes this system as one in which sellers "*collect* income tax by adding it to the amount billed to the payor" (italics added), a usage which, as I elaborate on below, I find confusing.
9. For example, what would it mean to say that a particular business "collected" retail sales tax, if it failed to remit those funds to the tax authority?

REFERENCES

Kay, J. A., and M. A. King. 1990. *The British Tax System* (5th ed.). Oxford: Oxford University Press.

Soos, Piroska. 1990. "Self-Employed Evasion and Tax Withholding: A Comparative Study and Analysis of the Issues." *University of California Davis Law Review* 24: 107–193.

CHAPTER 4

Capital Levies and Transition to a Consumption Tax

LOUIS KAPLOW

1. Introduction

Transitions from one regime to another, whether involving taxation or other government policies, often result in substantial gains and losses to individuals on account of their preexisting investments.[1] The extent of such gains and losses, in turn, depends on the manner in which transitions are implemented, including whether they are accompanied by explicit forms of mitigation, ranging from windfall taxation and compensation to grandfathering and phase-ins.

The transition from an income tax to a consumption tax raises a broad spectrum of transition questions, many of which have been illuminated by David Bradford's (1996a, 1996b, 1998, 2004) incisive and discerning mind. One issue that is especially important and somewhat distinctive is whether a consumption tax should be designed and enacted in a manner that results in a significant levy on preexisting capital. This particular aspect of the transition to a consumption tax is the focus of this chapter. Furthermore, the focus here is conceptual, being limited to the central question regarding the desirability of a consumption tax transition capital levy and thus abstracting from different forms of consumption taxation, interactions with other taxes, the treatment of businesses, aspects of implementation, effects on different types of assets and liabilities, transactions involving other taxing jurisdictions, the effects of inflation, the relevance of graduated rates, and many other issues.[2] Likewise, no attempt is made to provide a careful analysis or empirical assessment of political economy questions, even though they are central to capital levies.

Section 2 elaborates three key features that determine the merits of capital levies. First is the likelihood of repetition, that is, whether a government's imposition of a capital levy will create the expectation of additional future levies, which would impose a large efficiency toll. Second is the extent to which a contemplated capital levy will be anticipated, for even if there would be no future repetition, a well-anticipated levy may be highly inefficient as well as ineffectual. Third is the distributive effect of the levy, which is pertinent to a full assessment of the welfare consequences and, relatedly, to comparisons with other means of raising revenue. In varying degrees, these elements are not fully understood and appreciated, so explicit attention is warranted.

Section 3 provides a brief overview of the general problem of transitions. Its central purpose is to differentiate among the various transition issues raised by moving to a consumption tax. Specifically, intended incentive effects—incentives attributable to living in the long run under a consumption tax rather than an income tax—are distinguished from accounting effects, the latter of which give rise to the possibility of a capital levy as part of a consumption tax transition.

Section 4 examines the transition to a consumption tax. Considered first is the relationship between transition to a consumption tax and imposition of a capital levy, which discussion draws on section 3's examination of accounting effects. Next, the three features of capital levies elaborated in section 2 are examined with regard to a consumption tax transition capital levy. Additional topics include: what would constitute full relief for such a capital levy, how the analysis extends to rate changes under a consumption tax, and whether owners of preexisting capital should be understood to be compensated for a consumption tax transition capital levy as a consequence of the higher net-of-tax return to capital that results when the transition also involves removal of an existing income tax.

Section 5 uses the present analysis to clarify the implications of prior literature that examines dynamic models of taxation. Discussed first is work that simulates the transition from an income tax to a consumption tax and contrasts the transition to a wage tax. As many are aware, the central difference is that the former is assumed to embody a capital levy that is taken to be absent in the latter. Second, the section explores models designed to determine the optimality of capital taxation in the long run. It is not widely recognized that these models are closely related to transition to a consumption or a wage tax and, in particular, that some of their features relate to capital levies.

2. Capital Levies

2.1. Repetition

The most familiar problem with capital levies is that of repetition. Supposing that a capital levy would be desirable today (notably, in light of the considerations to be raised in subsections 2.2 and 2.3), the same considerations may well indicate that it would also be desirable tomorrow, the next day, and so on. The prospect of such future levies, however, would be a substantial deterrent to subsequent capital accumulation, with highly deleterious efficiency consequences. In their seminal exposition of the time inconsistency problem, Kydland and Prescott (1977) explain that, accordingly, a majority group of workers may rationally choose a constitution that limits their power to expropriate capital.[3]

The relationship, however, between a present levy and future ones requires further specification. Why would a promise not to repeat the levy be credible? Supposing that it would not, why should prospective capital owners not expect a levy tomorrow even if no such levy is imposed today?

In the absence of an effective formal constitutional prohibition, the limitation on capital levies seems premised on social understandings.[4] Formally, one might suppose that society is engaged in a repeated game, with the status quo of no capital levies combined with robust private investment being maintained perhaps as a trigger-strategy equilibrium.[5] More loosely, there may exist social norms against capital levies. In either case, the repetition concern supposes that implementation of a capital levy would be followed by a substantial period during which individuals would behave as if another such levy was imminent. Deviations may be interpreted as defections that per se warrant punishment. Additionally, they may reveal pertinent information, including that social norms, promises, and political forces protecting existing capital are weaker than previously believed.

Eichengreen (1990), following related work by Grossman and Van Huyck (1988), has suggested the possibility that capital levies might be successfully employed in limited circumstances. In these models, the government in essence promises to levy on capital only in certain, circumscribed, states of nature—ones in which a levy would be particularly valuable. Allowing an exception to a flat no-levy promise provides a sort of insurance. As long as the probability of a levy is sufficiently low, the pertinent states can clearly be identified when they arise, and the government indeed abstains from a levy and fully pays its debt in all other states, it is possible to maintain an equilibrium in which there is little ex ante cost from discouraging investment. This formulation is concordant with Kydland and Prescott's (1977) concluding suggestion in favor of institutions that make deviations difficult in all but emergencies.

Eichengreen (1990) also presents a fascinating historical examination of capital levies, focusing particularly on extensive discussions of the possibility in the aftermath of World War I. Interestingly, the subject received (initially favorable) attention, even entire books, from leading economists of the day, including Dalton, Edgeworth, Hicks, and Pigou. Although offering various qualifications, Eichengreen (1990, p. 193) "finds virtually no examples of successful peacetime capital levies."[6] His explanation relates to the problem of repetition as well as that of anticipation, the subject of the next subsection.

2.2. Anticipation

Another difficulty with capital levies, one that is occasionally emphasized but often forgotten, is anticipation. Even assuming that the government can credibly commit never to repeat a capital levy, the initial levy will be inefficient and substantially ineffectual to the extent that individuals anticipate its imposition. Consider, for example, a government that was expected to impose a capital levy ten years in the future. The effect on investment in the interim period would be much like that after a capital levy if repetition were expected ten years later. Consumption would be accelerated, long-term investment would be avoided, and capital flight and other forms of avoidance would be encouraged. Moreover, to the extent that these means were successful, there would be little capital on which to levy when the imposition became effective. Society would bear all the costs but receive little of the benefits.

Anticipation is a matter of degree. First, the length of the interim period will vary depending on the clarity of the forces leading to the imposition of a capital levy, the nature of government processes, and the content of the enactment (e.g., a levy that is part of a substantive reform, such as the transition to a consumption tax, might be phased in over a period of time). Second and related, the probability of an impending levy may initially be low, generating limited avoidance, but subsequently rise. Some prospective levies may be largely ignored because they are believed to be overwhelmingly improbable, but as a levy becomes more realistic politically, a greater response would be expected.

Eichengreen's (1990) reading of history is that largely unanticipated capital levies are extremely difficult to enact, particularly in modern democracies, since major action follows open, prolonged deliberation and political activity. As will be discussed further in subsection 4.2.2, this point seems especially pertinent to a capital levy that is imposed not in response to an emergency but as a consciously chosen policy designed to raise revenue or redistribute income. If a capital levy were to accompany a major tax reform, there would be prolonged periods of academic analysis, public discourse, government contemplation, and political debate and compromise prior to enactment.[7] If one does not observe substantial reductions in investment during any of this period, the most plausible interpretation is that most individuals do not believe that reform—or, in particular, reform accompanied by a capital levy—is very likely.[8]

The exception that proves the rule is the actual imposition of a levy by the occupying authorities in Japan right after World War II: action was swift and unaccompanied by public discussion. Additionally, it may not have given rise to a fear of repetition since it was imposed by outsiders, soon to depart, and was apparently motivated by a desire to expropriate from those believed to have contributed to the outbreak of war and to have profited from its execution.

Eichengreen (1990) seems somewhat sympathetic to the aforementioned levies proposed in the aftermath of World War I, if they could have been enacted quickly (which he doubts), following the theory that levies carefully limited to certain emergency situations may be desirable. However, even if implemented swiftly at the conclusion of the war, there remains a substantial problem of anticipation. If it were accepted that governments could cancel their own debt after a successful war effort, individuals would be very reluctant to lend during wartime, which could be catastrophic. (And potential adversaries, knowing of such circumstances, would be more willing to attack.) For emergency exceptions of the sort described in subsection 2.1 to make sense, they must involve situations (say, a natural disaster) that investors do not anticipate with a high probability ex ante.

2.3. *Distribution*

The preceding two subsections focus on adverse effects due to the expectation of capital levies. If these problems are set to the side, it is ordinarily taken for granted that a capital levy would be desirable. Indeed, one-time capital levies are traditionally viewed as an ideal sort of tax because in principle they are nondistortionary. There is, however, a conceptual problem with this understanding because the distributive incidence of capital levies is also relevant to welfare.

To develop this point, observe that, in developed economies that have an income tax, one could raise sums distortion-free by reducing the grant component of the tax schedule, even making it negative (i.e., a uniform lump-sum levy). For example, in models with a linear income tax, one could raise the intercept and reduce the slope. The primary deterrent to using this approach is not inefficiency but dislike of the distributive consequences. If a capital levy is a mere substitute for lowering the uniform grant, and if the grant is already set optimally, then there is no benefit to a capital levy. And if the grant is not set optimally, one could simply adjust it.

A capital levy therefore is not appealing independently of its distributive consequences. Specifically, in a world in which all individuals were identical, a capital levy would raise problems of anticipation and repetition while offering no advantage over adjusting the uniform per capita grant. This point is especially striking because some work related to capital levies (see, e.g., that discussed in subsection 5.2) is undertaken in a Ramsey setting with identical individuals, in which it is arbitrarily assumed that an income tax is unavailable.[9]

It seems apparent, however, that a successful capital levy may nevertheless be welfare-increasing because of its indirect tendency to redistribute the fruits of labor effort without distorting labor supply. At any given point in time, ownership of the existing capital stock is distributed in a way that positively correlates with prior earnings and thus with underlying earning ability, for individuals' savings are the product of prior accumulations that ultimately derive from labor income. (And to the extent ownership derives from inheritance, there is a positive intergenerational relationship between earnings of donors and donees.) The correlation will be highly imperfect due to differences in life-cycle stage, preferences, and other factors, although such confounding effects could be addressed, such as by making the levy age dependent.[10] The point is that, although an optimal income tax can only redistribute at a distortionary cost, an idealized capital levy may accomplish some redistribution without distorting labor supply.[11]

Note that if capital levies are appealing because their incidence is correlated with labor earnings, there may be a better alternative: current taxation of prior labor earnings. Analogous to a capital levy—in particular with regard to problems of anticipation and repetition—suppose that a tax was suddenly imposed that was an increasing function of prior years' earnings, or that the upcoming year's income tax payments were unexpectedly announced to be a function of preceding rather than current earnings. Such a scheme might achieve a substantially higher correlation between tax obligations and underlying earning ability than would a capital levy, and thus be superior on distributive grounds (but equally nondistortionary). The possibility of making income tax payments explicitly a function of prior economic behavior has received some limited attention in the theoretical literature.[12]

3. Transitions: A Brief Conceptual Overview

Policy changes that are not fully anticipated tend to produce gains and losses regarding pre-enactment investments, raising the question whether some form of mitigation should be provided. The transition to a consumption tax was among the first to receive sustained attention by commentators. It was recognized that transition effects could arise in different ways and that losses from removal of a tax preference seemed distinguishable from losses due to the taxation of old capital that had previously been taxed under an income tax. Nevertheless, initially there was no framework delineating what sort of transition policy was optimal for various gains or losses, and no consensus existed regarding how much if any relief should be provided for different types of transition effects. Compare, for example, Bradford and the U.S. Treasury (1984) with Graetz (1979).

Kaplow (1986, 1987) formulated the question as determining what transition policy maximizes social welfare under a range of assumptions, including that the transition policy will be anticipated ex ante and implemented ex post—that is, with commitment rather than the time inconsistency problem.[13] In answering the question, two types of transition effects were distinguished: intended incentive effects and accounting changes. This approach was employed extensively in Shaviro (2000) and subsequently explicated in Kaplow (2003), who also surveys much of the literature. Portions of the pertinent work address transitions generally, but from the beginning the framework has been applied to tax transitions, including the transition to a consumption tax.

To illustrate the distinction and see its relevance to transition policy, consider two simple reforms involving Pigouvian taxes. In the first, an externality has recently been identified, leading ultimately to the enactment of a first-best Pigouvian tax on the activity. Should owners of preexisting investments be exempted (grandfathered) or compensated, or should the tax be gradually phased in? Grandfathering or a phase-in would result in uncorrected (or not fully corrected) post-enactment behavior. Moreover, the anticipation effect of all three forms of relief would be disadvantageous, assuming that there was a positive ex ante probability that the externality existed (which seems especially likely as evidence mounts during the period preceding enactment). One way to state the idea is to recall that it is generally efficient for market actors to bear changes in real resource costs on account of changes in technology or demand and also that the role of Pigouvian taxation is to induce actors to incorporate real social costs due to externalities into the same market calculus.

Second, suppose that a Pigouvian tax had previously been imposed on the purchase of inputs that produce the externality, but it is subsequently decided that it is administratively convenient to impose the tax instead at the time the inputs are utilized in production. Should the inputs in inventory be taxed twice—once under the preexisting regime and again under the new regime—or should already-taxed inventory be exempt from the reformulated tax? If anticipated ex ante, the prospect of double taxation would inefficiently discourage productivity during the pertinent period. Likewise, if the opposite reform were to be contemplated—moving from a tax at the time of production to a tax on input purchases—failure to tax inventory at the time of transition would produce an inefficient surge in pre-enactment activity.

To recapitulate, the first example is what might be referred to as an intended incentive effect and the latter might aptly be characterized as an accounting change. The transition to a consumption tax, as already suggested, clearly involves many effects in the former category, and, depending on the treatment of old capital, may have effects in the latter category as well.[14] Because this chapter is about the possibility of a levy on old capital, it is useful to offer some additional, tax-related examples of accounting changes.

The simplest example is the one initially presented in Kaplow (1986) to motivate the accounting change category. Suppose that tax was previously levied using an accounting year from July 1 to June 30, and it is decided that it would reduce bookkeeping costs to move tax years to January 1 to

December 31. Without a transition adjustment, a six-month period will be double-taxed or omitted, and the anticipation thereof would produce a large distortion in the timing of economic activity. To avoid this problem requires a transitional accounting "year" of six or eighteen months, as the case may be. Note that if one went with the double-taxation transition, one would have a sort of capital levy (or an additional levy on past earned income), which would have the desirable features described in subsection 2.3, if one could avoid the problems of anticipation and repetition.

To take another example, suppose that all retirement plans under the income tax were in the style of Roth IRAs, that is, tax prepaid, and it was decided to switch to taxation at the time of consumption. Failure to exempt pre-existing retirement accounts would again result in double taxation. (Note that this example has features virtually identical to those due to the transition from a wage tax to a consumption tax, on which more below.) Likewise, one could have the reverse transition (analogous to the transition from a consumption tax to a wage tax). One could similarly envision switches between income taxes due currently (withholding and estimated tax payments required) and income taxes due only at the end of the year. In these cases as well, the analysis is similar to that of the capital levies explored in section 2: distributive effects are likely to be desirable, but anticipation and repetition concerns may be serious.

Interestingly, in settings in which such accounting changes have occurred, it seems that single taxation is the norm. When fiscal years are changed, transitional accounting "years" are in fact employed to avoid double taxation or no taxation. When Roth IRAs were created, old IRAs could not freely (i.e., without prepayment) be converted. If Roth IRAs were to be repealed, one strongly suspects that existing accounts will not thereby become subject to tax upon withdrawal. As will be discussed momentarily, however, double taxation would arise in precisely this manner under some means of transition from income taxation to consumption taxation.

4. Transition to a Consumption Tax

4.1. Does a Consumption Tax Contain a Capital Levy?

4.1.1. Consumption Taxes, Wage Taxes, and Income Taxes

In a steady state, it is generally accepted that flat-rate wage and consumption taxes are equivalent.[15] A wage tax reduces one's earnings by a given fraction, which has the effect of reducing subsequent purchasing power by the same fraction regardless of how one chooses to allocate earnings over time. And this latter effect is precisely what consumption taxation does directly, whether it is implemented as a cash-flow tax (earnings are taxed, savings are deducted, and withdrawals are taxed) or as a sales tax or value-added tax (VAT). For convenience, subsequent discussion will focus on forms of cash-flow consumption taxation, but analogous schemes generally exist for other variants.

As background, two main arguments have been offered in support of moving from an income tax to a consumption tax or a wage tax (apart from considerations of a capital levy). First, an income tax—in addition to distorting labor supply, as do a consumption tax and a wage tax—also distorts the intertemporal allocation of consumption by taxing the return to savings.[16] As a consequence, individuals consume too much in early periods (save too little).[17] Second, moving to a consumption tax or perhaps a wage tax is believed by many to produce significant administrative benefits, including the important side effect of reducing inter-asset distortions that result from the difficulty of treating different types of capital uniformly under an income tax. This view was importantly advanced by Andrews (1974) and plays a substantial part in subsequent work by Bradford (e.g., 1986).

An important complication is that the present income tax is highly impure, really an awkward hybrid between an income tax and a consumption tax. Notably, retirement savings, consumer durables (including housing), human capital (in important respects), unrealized appreciation, and other assets are treated substantially as they would be under a consumption tax, although the lack of inflation adjustments and the existence of a corporate tax can increase the rate of taxation on capital. Furthermore, the continued deductibility of many types of interest produces an inconsistent system with opportunities for arbitrage. In aggregate, the actual system is probably a good distance toward a consumption tax already, although regarding administrative considerations many believe that the concomitant benefits of a consumption tax (or a purer income tax) would be particularly great. In any event, although these complications substantially affect the likely magnitude and distribution of any capital levy that might accompany a transition to a consumption tax, they do not affect its basic character and hence will be largely ignored hereafter.[18]

4.1.2. Capital Levies in the Transition to Wage versus Consumption Taxes

Return now to the statement that, in pure form, a wage tax and a consumption tax are equivalent in the steady state. Once one accounts for the transition, however, some define a consumption tax as equal to a wage tax plus a capital levy. Others dispute this definition, insisting that the two taxes should be viewed as equivalent regardless, because whether there is a capital levy is a separate question. Ultimately, this is a semantic dispute. It is helpful, nevertheless, to explain the various policy packages envisioned by the different approaches in order to understand the range of possibilities and clarify subsequent discussion.

Consider the following four schemes:[19]

1. *Consumption tax without capital levy:* For example, this scheme would tax all wages and withdrawals from qualified accounts and allow a deduction for all contributions into qualified accounts (one of the standard forms proposed for a consumption tax). Note that pre-enactment capital, under such a scheme, would effectively receive an immediate deduction when moved into one of the newly created qualified accounts.
2. *Consumption tax with capital levy:* For example, modify the prior scheme so that contributions to qualified accounts would only be deductible if from currently taxed wages (or from transfers from other qualified accounts) and, in addition, tax would be imposed on withdrawals from nonqualified accounts (including the use of proceeds from sales of assets not in qualified accounts or the use of cash not attributable to a withdrawal from a qualified account).
3. *Wage tax without capital levy:* For example, a wage tax could be levied on all post-enactment wages (period).
4. *Wage tax with capital levy:* For example, a wage tax could be supplemented by a tax on all spending not from qualified accounts, which would be accounts that could only receive deposits from previously taxed wages. (Such a scheme might back up a wage tax to deal with evasion problems.)

Clearly, the steady-state equivalence of wage and consumption taxation carries over to the transition if one compares schemes 1 and 3 or schemes 2 and 4. If one compares schemes 2 and 3, the result is that, in transition, the consumption tax equals a wage tax plus a capital levy, and if one compares schemes 1 and 4, in transition the wage tax equals a consumption tax plus a capital levy. Although some schemes may be easier to implement than others, or some may seem more "natural," it is clear that nothing in logic links a capital levy to a consumption tax or a wage tax and that, as a rough cut, the merits or demerits of a capital levy as such should determine whether it should be imposed.[20]

4.1.3. Transition to a Consumption Tax versus Elimination of an Income Tax

Although the motivation for consideration of the transition to a consumption tax is in substantial part that it might replace some or all of the existing income tax, the discussion of transition per se has thus far only referred to the implementation of a consumption or wage tax, each with or without a capital levy. Nevertheless, the idea that a transition capital levy would result in double taxation—taxing under a newly enacted consumption tax savings that (generally, to the extent of pre-enactment basis) had already been taxed under an income tax—links the capital levy to the fact that transition is *from* an income tax.[21]

One of the many lessons of Bradford's (1996a, 1996b, 1998) contributions, however, is that in important respects the capital levy should be associated with the imposition of a consumption tax of the type in scheme 2, without regard to repeal of a preexisting income tax.[22] This is most easily seen by the imposition of a consumption tax of the type in scheme 2 in an economy with no preexisting tax: the value of old capital would be reduced, and relatedly the prospect of the imposition of such a tax would have anticipatory effects, namely, increasing pre-enactment consumption, inducing capital flight, and encouraging other activities that reduced (at least apparent) capital holdings at the time of enactment. Bradford vividly illustrates the point with his familiar example of the retailer with an inventory of canned tomato juice. Under an operating cash-flow consumption tax, purchases of inventory would be deductible and sales out of inventory fully taxable. But inventory held at the moment of enactment would be subject to a capital levy under a type 2 scheme. (Note that this levy on inventory is identical to that described in section 3's second example of a Pigouvian tax that was previously levied on purchases of inputs but is reformed to be levied on the use of inputs.)

Another way to see the point, following Kaplow (1995), is to decompose the transition from an income tax to a consumption tax into two steps: (A) transition from an income tax to a wage tax (under scheme 3, with no capital levy), and (B) transition from a wage tax to a consumption tax (of type to be determined). Step (A), by construction, involves no capital levy. If the preexisting income tax was a pure, accrual income tax, then the net effect of step (A) is that all capital income would be taxed up until the moment of transition, after which it would no longer be subject to tax. The only anticipation effect would be to increase investment (savings) ex ante, since the future returns that are in the post-enactment period would be treated more favorably. (That is, the reduction of intertemporal distortion would to an extent precede enactment.)

Step (B), the move from a wage tax to a consumption tax, involves no steady-state difference. In the simple world depicted at the outset of this subsection, it is a pure accounting change. One could choose to have a capital levy, by moving to a consumption tax under scheme 2, or one could choose not to, using scheme 1. (One could also have a negative levy, by distributing funds to owners of preexisting capital, if one wished.) In addition, one could contemplate the move from a consumption tax to a wage tax and ask whether that transition should be the occasion for a capital levy or for bestowing a windfall.

4.2. Evaluation of a Consumption Tax Transition Capital Levy

4.2.1. Repetition

Even though the concern about repetition is the most discussed potential limitation of a capital levy, there has been little attention paid to whether the capital levy that might accompany transition to a consumption tax is one that would generate expectations of likely repetition. An exception is Weisbach (2003), who explains what is probably implicitly on the minds of many: that one would only replace the income tax with a consumption tax once, so repetition may be unlikely. An important caveat is that if, say, a consumption tax were implemented at a more modest level, merely to raise additional revenue or to replace only part of the income tax or payroll tax, there may well be an expectation of repetition. Another point is that rate increases under a consumption tax produce similar effects (a point elaborated in subsection 4.4); however, if most revenue were raised under a consumption tax, this problem may be limited, except to the extent taxes were generally rising over time (perhaps to fund continued growth in social insurance obligations).

However, the more it is recognized that a capital levy is optional under a consumption tax, the less sanguine one can be about the expectations of repetition that might accompany a consumption tax transition capital levy (see Shaviro, 2000). Consider, for example, that some economists, such as Auerbach (2005) and Kotlikoff (2005), have publicly advocated the virtues of the capital levy as an—perhaps the most—important reason to move to a consumption tax. Various consumption tax proposals, such as the plan in *Blueprints* (Bradford and the U.S. Treasury, 1984) and the USA tax proposal in the mid-1990s, have contained significant, even if incomplete, transition relief. Undoubtedly, there would be strong political pressure from those who stood to lose most by a capital levy to provide relief. If, in the end, a consumption tax with a transition capital levy were enacted, it would be widely understood that the capital levy was a major motivation for the policy change and that, when directly confronted with the prospect of a substantial capital levy, the balance of political forces and strength of anti-capital-levy social norms were such that a capital levy was on-balance politically attractive. In such circumstances, it is hardly clear why future prospective investors would believe that repetition (albeit under a different guise) was unlikely.[23]

4.2.2. Anticipation

Following the discussion in subsection 2.2, it seems that, in a modern democracy, substantial time would elapse from initial contemplation of a consumption tax transition capital levy to its ultimate enactment. The path from discussion by academics to broader public and political consideration to the formulation of proposals to lobbying, refinement, and ultimate enactment could not be expected to be brief. One possibility is that, until the very end, proposals could be in the form of scheme 1, without a capital levy, with a last-minute amendment shifting to scheme 2, with a capital levy. This approach—if truly unexpected, ultimately successful, and not altered shortly after, once the surprise had been discovered—would avoid the anticipation problem, but this chain of events seems unlikely.[24]

In addition, many consumption tax proposals, like other major tax reforms, contemplate a phase-in to ease the transition in various respects.

Although traditionally objected to on grounds of additional complexity and deferring the benefits of reform, in the present setting one must add the substantial interim distortion that would result.[25] See, for example, the simulations in Howitt and Sinn (1989) and also those in Auerbach and Kotlikoff (1987) on early announcement of reforms.

The forms of anticipatory activity would obviously depend on the length of time and various particulars of the consumption tax transition capital levy. Regarding the latter, the ability to detect and prevent capital flight or cash hoarding could reduce pre-enactment avoidance. Also relevant are various particulars of how the consumption tax would operate. For example, if consumer durables were treated using a prepayment approach, under which purchases would not be deductible as investment and sales proceeds would be exempt, there may be a substantial incentive for individuals to purchase consumer durables before enactment. The treatment of debt, tax-exempt institutions and foreigners (who may enter into transactions ex ante with taxable individuals and entities), consumption abroad, and other structural features could also have a substantial impact on the extent of avoidance. It should be emphasized that avoidance activity is doubly costly: it both is distortionary and reduces the amount of capital to which the transition capital levy would apply. (Note that if substantial avoidance is cheap and easy, such as through financial manipulations, the levy may largely be circumvented at only modest aggregate efficiency cost; nevertheless, the likely distortion per unit of revenue would be substantial in such a case.)

Further, note that, if the time period is sufficiently long, the anticipation effects will be highly detrimental even without any special maneuvering. After all, the straightforward incentive is to greatly increase current consumption at the expense of investment, a behavioral response that cannot readily be outlawed after the fact. Well in advance of any expected enactment, long-term investment projects would be eschewed (with the effect increasing as the time to enactment approaches), and closer to the effective date short-term projects would be discouraged as well.

4.2.3. Distribution

As indicated in subsection 2.3, a capital levy tends to have favorable distributive effects (without which it would have no appeal because one could instead change the grant component of the income tax, raising the same revenue and avoiding the problems of anticipation and repetition). That appeal, however, is limited by the imperfect relationship between capital holdings at any moment in time and underlying earnings ability (suggesting the possible superiority of a retrospective earnings tax over a capital levy). The single greatest problem is due to the life-cycle effect, a consequence of which is that a capital levy redistributes from middle-lifetime-income older individuals to younger individuals with no (or negative) savings but high expected lifetime income.[26]

As a first approximation, a consumption tax transition capital levy fits this mold because, as subsection 4.1.3 explains, the levy is best understood as caused by the introduction of a consumption tax of the type in scheme 2 rather than by repeal of the income tax, and this levy indeed applies to old capital. Nevertheless, the actual incidence will be influenced by numerous complications pertaining to the nature of the consumption tax that is ultimately enacted and the operation of a preexisting income tax, as discussed briefly in subsection 4.1.1 and further in some of the references cited therein. The incidence will also depend on the extent of relief that is provided and, some would argue, on the implicit compensation provided by the higher net-of-tax return to capital under a consumption tax, the subjects of subsections 4.3 and 4.5.

4.3. *What Counts as Full Relief?*

This subsection inquires into the appropriate nature of transition relief taking as given that the objective is to avoid a capital levy. This question has been analyzed, for example, in Bradford (1996a, 1996b), Kaplow (1995), and especially Bradford (1998).

Initially, consider the transition from a pure, accrual income tax (i.e., one that immediately recognizes all gains and losses) to a consumption tax—or from a no-tax regime to a consumption tax. If one wished to avoid any capital levy, it would be necessary in some fashion to avoid applying the new consumption tax to the full market value of pre-enactment assets. This might be accomplished by allowing individuals an immediate deduction for the full amount, which would entail refunds for many. (This formulation imagines, for simplicity, a flat-rate tax with refundability of losses.) Alternatively, deductions might be allowed over time, as long as the not-yet-deducted sum gave rise to a supplemental, ongoing deduction equal to the product of that amount and the interest rate, which would preserve the value of the write-offs.[27] (In either case, it is important to coordinate the treatment of pre-enactment debt, an important dimension that will not be discussed separately here.[28])

Suppose instead that the starting point for the transition to a consumption tax is an income tax more like the existing one, in which basis is often less than market value for a variety of reasons.[29] Then the question arises whether "full relief" entails protection of the entire market value at the effective date of the consumption tax or merely the basis of preexisting assets. It might appear that the answer is the latter, for protecting basis seems both necessary and sufficient to avoid "double taxation." However, this view is incomplete.

To analyze this problem, it is helpful to return to the two-step decomposition introduced in subsection 4.1.3, in which we consider (A) a transition from the income tax to a (scheme 3) wage tax, followed by (B) a transition from the wage tax to a consumption tax. Regarding step (A), examine first the case in which basis is below market value on account of unrealized capital gains. Under a wage tax, the capital gains will never be taxed. Hence, the question arises whether, in ending the income tax regime, there should be a tax on unrealized gains. On one hand, this would be more in accord with the income tax "ideal." However, that definitional ideal does not per se have normative force, and even if it previously did, it is not clear why this would remain so when the income tax is being repealed. If a positive view is taken of capital levies, this gain should be taxed, but similar analysis applies to the extent of basis as well. If instead one takes a full anticipation view, the prospect that unrealized capital gains would never be taxed due to transition to a wage tax would reduce the effective tax rate on investment ex ante, which would be desirable if the tax on capital income is overall taken to be distortionary, a likely motivation for substituting a wage tax.[30] (There would also be costs due to increased lock-in in the interim.)

Second, examine the case in which the below-market-value basis is due to expensing or accelerated depreciation under the original income tax. To that extent, consumption tax treatment is already provided. Accordingly, with respect to this gap between basis and market value, we have a situation akin to a transition from a consumption tax to a wage tax. As suggested previously, this should be viewed as a pure accounting change. Avoiding any levy (in this case, a negative one, that is, a windfall) would require ultimate taxation of the difference between market value and basis.

Third, consider retirement savings that, under the pre-existing income tax, were never subject to tax. In this case, basis is zero and consumption tax treatment has been provided with regard to the entire amount. Accordingly, to effectuate a transition to a wage tax that exacts no positive or negative levy would necessitate taxation.

Regarding step (B), the transition from a wage tax to a consumption tax, we have, as with the reverse move just mentioned, a pure accounting change. As previously suggested, if one does not wish to make such an event the moment to impose a capital levy, the market value of pre-enactment capital should not be subject to the consumption tax. Note that, considering this move in isolation, the concept of basis does not arise since basis has no role under a pure wage tax system.

If we combine the results from steps (A) and (B), thereby returning to the transition from an actual income tax to a consumption tax, we see that there is a reason to protect only basis, not full market value, in some cases, notably to the extent basis falls short of market value due to consumption-tax-like treatment of prior earnings.[31] In light of the analysis in subsection 4.1.3, it should not be that surprising that the reason for protecting less than full market value in some instances has to do with repeal of the income tax (in particular, hypothetically replacing it with a wage tax) rather than with introduction of a consumption tax (or using it to replace a wage tax).

Having stated what would constitute full relief, it is easier to appreciate the extent of the consumption tax transition capital levy if no relief is to be provided. For retirement accounts, expensed assets, and some others (see note 31 on consumer durables), since no basis protection is required to provide full relief, the failure to provide any relief would not constitute a capital levy. More broadly, because the current income tax is already like a consumption tax in many respects, transition to a scheme 2 consumption tax would entail a more limited capital levy than might first appear to be the case.[32]

4.4. Rate Changes under Consumption Taxation

Return yet again to Bradford's (1996a, 1996b, 1998) important lesson that the capital levy that arises when making a transition from an income tax to a (scheme 2 type) consumption tax is due to the introduction of the consumption tax rather than repeal of the income tax. This point carries the implication, which he also emphasized, that rate changes under such a consumption tax also cause capital levies. After all, introduction of a 25% consumption tax is equivalent to raising the rate from 0% to 25%. If that entails a substantial capital levy, then raising the rate from 25% to 30% would likewise constitute a capital levy, although a much smaller one. Similarly, reducing the rate from 25% to 20% would entail a negative levy, that is, a windfall to existing capital.[33]

Although many had examined how one could accomplish the initial transition to consumption tax with no capital levy (scheme 1), little attention had been devoted to how one might avoid (positive and negative) capital levies due to rate changes once a consumption tax was in place—assuming indeed that such was desirable. The most comprehensive treatment of the subject is in Bradford (1998). See also Boadway and Bruce (1984) and Weisbach (2003).

The basic approach (actually, one of two variants that Bradford offers) marries two ideas.[34] First, under an income tax, provision of economic depreciation renders income taxation, including rate changes, neutral with regard to asset values (the Johansson-Samuelson theorem). Second, the difference between an income tax and a consumption tax in steady state is due to the taxation of the time value of money (the return to waiting) under the former. Therefore, if one provides an ongoing, supplemental deduction equal to basis times the interest rate, this taxation would be eliminated. Accordingly, Bradford explains, the aforementioned alternative transition scheme of providing individuals basis that is deducted over time, with a supplemental and ongoing deduction for interest on the basis account, can be deployed so that consumption tax rate changes produce no capital levy (positive or negative).

Specifically, all assets—including those acquired under the consumption tax regime—would be subject to economic depreciation, combined with an additional annual deduction for interest on undepreciated basis, rather than providing for expensing, which is normally envisioned for a cash-flow consumption tax. If tax rates remain constant, these schemes are equivalent since the deductions provided under each have the same present value. If rates change, however, the augmented depreciation scheme avoids any capital levy. The reasoning parallels that of providing protection equal to market value when a consumption tax is implemented. When the consumption tax rate, say, increases, preexisting capital might otherwise be subject to a partial capital levy proportional to its market value. However, under the proposed scheme, there would exist a tax basis equal to market value at all times, giving rise to future deductions at the now-higher consumption tax rate. Since the present value of those remaining deductions (including the supplemental deductions for interest on basis) would equal the market value of the asset at the time of the rate increase, full protection would be provided. Analogously, if rates fell, the future deductions would be at the now-lower tax rate, thereby avoiding a negative capital levy.

Bradford demonstrated that this approach works in theory but also understood that it would be imperfect in practice. Providing true economic depreciation requires accurate prediction or contemporaneous measurement of changes in value. This is difficult when values fluctuate and especially challenging with regard to intangible assets. Indeed, as Bradford (2004) notes, many view such problems as the Achilles heel of the income tax. Because avoiding the need for such measurements is thus one of the principal reasons to move to a consumption tax, retaining such a system post-transition may seem unappealing.[35] It should be emphasized, however, that there would be a lower error cost if the accuracy of depreciation or other adjustments for changes in market value only mattered to the extent of rate changes. For example, a rate change of, say, 3% would only have one-tenth the impact of introduction of a 30% consumption tax (and, to the extent that pertinent distortions are proportional to the square of the tax rate, only one-hundredth of the efficiency consequence). The capital levy would be limited not only by the size of the rate change but also by the magnitude of the measurement error (specifically, it would be equal to the product of the two). In other words, ordinary rate changes reflecting fluctuations in revenue needs may usually be of modest significance to begin with, and their impact could further (if not fully) be mitigated, if such a scheme were worth the administrative cost.

4.5. Is Pre-Enactment Capital Compensated through Higher Returns?

Suppose that an income tax is replaced by a consumption tax that contains a transition capital levy (scheme 2). Suppose further that, as a result of removing the tax burden on capital income, the net-of-tax return on capital increases.[36] This latter effect produces a benefit that is greater for those who save more. Accordingly, some suggest that even a type 2 scheme provides significant implicit compensation for its capital levy, rendering it unnecessary to consider type 1 consumption tax schemes that contain no levy.[37] One could go further and argue that such no-levy schemes would instead provide a windfall to holders of capital because the benefit from the higher net-of-tax return would remain.

To assess this argument, it is best to begin by returning to the question addressed in section 2 of whether and why a capital levy may be beneficial or undesirable. Regarding the problem of repetition, if indeed full compensation resulted there would be no reason to fear recurrence of the combined policy. However, as discussed in subsection 4.2.1, the concern is not that individuals would anticipate repetition of the transition from an income tax to a consumption tax. Instead, the fear is that, since the capital levy can be separated from the pure, steady-state tax reform, the fact that a levy is imposed may raise the prospect that subsequent levies (in different forms) would be enacted. Nevertheless, if indeed the increased return approximated full compensation, the precedent set by the transition would be different, so repetition may be much less of a problem.

It is familiar, however, that the nature of "compensation" is highly uneven, due primarily to life-cycle effects (but also to differences in preferences and other factors).[38] Notably, young individuals with no savings receive the maximal benefit from higher future returns but bear none of the levy. Older individuals with large life-cycle savings are subject to the maximal levy yet receive the least compensation (that is, for given preferences and lifetime income). The breakeven point would be at some age in between. There is a substantial intergenerational redistribution.[39] But, importantly, the extent of what is given up by older individuals depends on the amount of their accumulated capital, so the compensation does not seem to be of a nature that would substantially erase the repetition concern.

For similar reasons, the anticipation problem is alleviated even less. Because the capital levy applies to the amount of capital one holds at the time of transition, the incentive to increase consumption and reduce investment remains. The basic problem is that the extent of the capital levy depends on past savings whereas the benefit depends on future savings. Of course, the two are related, in that individuals would not fully dissave before an anticipated transition and then fully restore their savings to the life-cycle optimum immediately thereafter (unless this could be accomplished through certain forms of financial avoidance activity). Although this point moderates the impact of an anticipated capital levy, it would do so even if there were no increase in the net-of-tax return. In sum, the implicit compensation does not substantially eliminate the adverse anticipation incentives due to the prospect of a capital levy.

Finally, consider distribution, which is the factor that seems closest in spirit to the loosely specified notions of equity that are often invoked in debates about the consumption tax versus the income tax and the problem of transition and compensation. As discussed in subsections 2.3 and 4.2.3, if the levy were distributionally unattractive, it probably should be avoided, since concerns about anticipation and repetition could only make matters worse. However, it was suggested that the distributive effects are likely to be attractive. To the extent that is the case, it seems odd that on equity grounds one would desire compensation, since perfect compensation would precisely destroy the beneficial distributive effects.

Here again, the life-cycle mismatch (and others) is pertinent. It was explained that a capital levy, such as that entailed by moving to a scheme 2 consumption tax, was only loosely correlated with underlying (lifetime) earning ability, and accordingly may well be distributively dominated by other regimes. Interestingly, the deviation between desired distributive effects and the capital levy mirrors the gap between the incidence of the levy and the purported compensation. The levy was only moderately desirable distributively primarily because it taxed the old too much and the young too little. The presence of compensation that is greatest for the young and least for the old does not improve the situation.

There is also an important conceptual question concerning the sense in which the enhanced net-of-tax return should be viewed as compensation for a capital levy. To see the problem, consider again, as suggested in Kaplow (1995), the two-step decomposition of the transition from an income tax to a consumption tax, with step (A) being the (hypothetical) move from an income tax to a wage tax and step (B) that from a wage tax to a consumption tax. Note that it is step (A) that is responsible for the increase in the net-of-tax return. If one were in fact simply moving to a wage tax, one could ask whether this benefit should be considered a windfall of sorts. To do so assumes that there is some sort of natural entitlement to the net-of-tax return under an income tax and that any deviation is distributively inappropriate. It is hard to identify why this should be so. Indeed, if a motivation for the reform is to eliminate intertemporal distortion, one might conclude the opposite. In a simple world, the move would constitute a Pareto improvement.[40]

The capital levy is solely attributable to step (B)—assuming that one moves from a scheme 3 wage tax to a scheme 2 consumption tax—and that step produces no compensation. This point further suggests the lack of nexus between the capital levy and the compensation. This conclusion is also illustrated by comparing two otherwise-identical individuals, one who saves a moment before enactment and the other a moment after; the capital levy hits only the first but the compensation is received by both.

The same ideas can also be illustrated with a different example.[41] Suppose that in the status quo there is a differential tax on chocolate. One day, it is repealed on account of its inefficiency (in distorting consumption between chocolate and vanilla). Would it be appropriate to accompany this transition with a one-time tax on chocolate lovers, and in particular, a tax that was an increasing function of age (perhaps it would be a function of lifetime chocolate consumption to date)? Such a suggestion would seem perverse for two reasons: the benefits of the reform are falling with age (fewer years over which to enjoy additional chocolate), and, perhaps more to the point, it is hard to see why elimination of the distortionary tax calls for any redistribution between chocolate- and vanilla-lovers in the first place (even without regard to the opposite lifetime incidence of the benefits of the repeal and the costs of the redistributive levy).

5. Literature on Dynamic Models of Taxation

5.1. Transition Simulations

In order to assess the effects of transition from an income tax to a consumption or wage tax on savings, growth, efficiency, and the inter- and intragenerational distribution of income, researchers have built dynamic simulation models. Most well known is the work in Auerbach and Kotlikoff (1983, 1987) and Auerbach, Kotlikoff, and Skinner (1983). Subsequent analyses providing greater detail along various dimensions include Altig et al. (2001), Auerbach (1996, 2008), Sarkar and Zodrow (1993), and Zodrow (2002). See also the discussions in Bernheim (2002) and Shaviro (2000).

Pertinent results are amply illustrated by the simulations in the various work of Auerbach, Kotlikoff, and Skinner. In basic simulations, moving to a consumption tax raises steady-state welfare by 6% whereas moving to a wage tax reduces it by 4%. The explanation is that the former reform involves a scheme 2 consumption tax—with a capital levy—and the latter involves a scheme 3 wage tax—without a capital levy. Also, as suggested in subsection 4.3, moving from an income tax to that type of wage tax may also entail a windfall to the extent assets received consumption-tax-like treatment under the income tax. With a positive capital levy, taxes in the future can be forever lower, so consumption and welfare can be higher. With in essence a negative capital levy, future taxes must be higher, which reduces consumption and welfare.

In this work and the commentary thereon—though not necessarily in the minds of all who may view the bottom-line results—it is well understood that these steady-state effects are substantially due to the differences in capital levies. (For example, Auerbach, Kotlikoff, and Skinner [1983, p. 81] state in their introduction that "It is this element of lump-sum taxation, and not the exemption from taxation of capital income *per se* that is crucial to the achievement of an efficient tax reform.") Furthermore, it is known that the steady-state effects are opposite for those in generations subject to the transition. Older generations subject to the consumption tax transition capital levy lose (though future generations gain), and the same groups gain under the wage tax transition capital give-away (though future generations lose). When the authors introduce the device of a lump-sum (intergenerational) redistribution authority to offset the intergenerational redistribution, much of the difference between the two types of transition disappears.[42]

These simulations provide quantification of the (positive or negative) capital levy under various scenarios. They are not, however, designed to illuminate issues pertaining to repetition or anticipation: most such simulations implicitly assume that there are no effects of either type. Some do consider anticipation and find, as one would expect, that the effect is adverse for transition to a (scheme 2) consumption tax but favorable for moving to a (scheme 3) wage tax, to an extent offsetting and possibly reversing the main results. One should also note the aforementioned simulation results of Howitt and Sinn (1989), who show that a substantial phase-in of a consumption tax can cause sufficient distortion due to anticipation effects during the transition to outweigh the otherwise positive effects of the capital levy.[43] Overall, given the conceptual focus of the present chapter, the primary relevance of this work is to illustrate concretely and provide some quantification for certain aspects of transition capital levies.

5.2. *Optimal Capital Taxation in the Long Run*

A substantial body of literature examines the optimality of capital taxation in infinite-horizon models. Representative contributions include Chamley (1986) and Judd (1985), with Auerbach and Hines (2002) and Bernheim (2002) providing surveys. It seems largely unappreciated, however, that these literatures can partly be understood as involving transitions from income to consumption taxation, and in particular transitions in which a sort of capital levy plays a central role.

In these models, time begins with a preexisting stock of capital. The government is permitted to tax the return to capital at up to 100%, and it also may tax labor income, which produces distortion. The optimum under standard assumptions has the character that capital income is taxed at 100% in initial periods, but ultimately 0% thereafter. (The duration of the 100% tax depends on the government's long-run revenue requirements, among other things, and there may be an intervening period in which an intermediate rate is employed.)

These models ignore repetition and anticipation; that is, they assume that commitment is possible and that the tax may be imposed starting at time zero. Regarding the latter, the preexisting capital stock is taken as given, which is to say, implicitly, that behavior during preceding periods during which income was earned and some of it was saved rather than consumed is taken to be unaffected by the prospect of the capital tax. Moreover, individuals are identical in these models, so distribution is moot.[44]

In this world, it would be optimal to employ a uniform lump-sum levy, which might raise all necessary revenue without distortion. This possibility is ruled out. In this regard, see the comments in subsection 2.3 on Ramsey-based models and also the references in notes 9 and 16 (the latter of which relate directly to the literature on capital taxation). As noted there, a capital levy may be seen as a substitute for lump-sum taxation—a perfect substitute, to the extent of the capital stock, if one can ignore repetition, anticipation, and distribution. The only difference here is that these models add the further restriction that the capital tax in any period may not exceed 100% of capital income.

At this point, the source of this part of the literature's results is apparent. Employing a 100% capital tax for a period of time is the best approximation the model will allow to a capital levy or a lump-sum tax. If revenue needs are small, one period (of perhaps less-than-100% taxation) will suffice. If revenue needs are larger, the 100% tax should be imposed longer. In this latter case, distortion arises after time zero; hence, it is best to use a 100% rate and end the tax as quickly as possible, so effects are maximally concentrated on old capital. Were it not for the 100% cap, it is obvious that attainable welfare would be even higher because the capital tax could then be imposed entirely in the initial period, making it precisely equivalent to a pure capital levy.[45] In sum, although the literature focuses on optimal capital taxation, it is useful to view some of its results as in the genre of capital levies. Accordingly, much of the analysis in this chapter bears on the significance of some of the results obtained in such models.

In addition, the form of the capital levy has a property in common with the transition to a consumption tax—or to a wage tax like that in scheme 4, in which a capital levy is included. The transition period corresponds to the first or initial periods, in which capital is taxed. The steady-state involves a pure wage (labor income) tax or consumption tax.

6. Conclusion

This chapter focuses on the question whether the transition to a consumption tax is an opportune occasion for the imposition of a one-time capital levy. To answer this question, it is necessary to delve more deeply into the three factors that bear on the desirability of a capital levy—repetition, anticipation, and distribution—and then to consider quite explicitly how these factors apply in the context of a consumption tax transition capital levy. Consideration of each factor presented issues that previously have received limited, if any, attention. Although no conclusion can be reached without a thorough inquiry into the political economy of the situation, which is not attempted here, the present analysis provides substantial reason for caution. The anticipation problem seems particularly acute, it is hardly obvious that repetition is not a serious concern, and even if on those grounds a capital levy were desirable, it may well be that alternative policies would be distributively superior.

This chapter also explores a number of subsidiary matters, including the relationship between the adoption of a consumption or wage tax and capital levies, what sort of transition relief would avoid imposition of any capital levy (if that were the objective), capital levies associated with tax rate changes and how they could be avoided, and whether the increased net-of-tax return to capital as a consequence of income tax repeal should properly be viewed as compensation for a consumption tax transition capital levy. In addition, the analysis was applied to existing literatures that offer dynamic models of taxation, both those that simulate transitions to a consumption or wage tax and those that determine optimal capital taxation in the long run. In each case, capital levies were seen to be central, a reasonably familiar theme in the former body of work but one largely unappreciated in the latter.

NOTES

I am grateful to James Hines, Kyle Logue, Joel Slemrod, and other conference participants for comments; Mary Bear, Clifford Chen, Shelley de Alth, and Stephanie Gabor for research assistance; and to the John M. Olin Center for Law, Economics, and Business at Harvard University for financial support. This chapter was first produced as a paper for "Key Issues in Public Finance: A Conference in Honor of David Bradford." My thinking about transitions has benefited greatly from discussions with David over the course of more than two decades in connection with each of our prior writings on the subject. The current chapter derives from a briefer treatment of capital levies and transitions in Kaplow (2008).

1. On transitions generally (and for more complete references to the wider literature), see, for example, Kaplow (1986, 1987, 2003) and Shaviro (2000).
2. For previous discussions of the transition to a consumption tax, many of which consider a broader range of issues, see, for example, the works of David Bradford (1996a, 1996b, 1998, 2004), Kaplow (1986, 1995, 2003), Sarkar and Zodrow (1993), Shaviro (2000), and Zodrow (2002). See also the literature discussed in section 5.
3. Kydland and Prescott (1977) also mention areas where the government has been less successful in restraining itself, including the imposition of price controls and windfall taxes on oil companies when prices spike, the prospect of which discourages exploration and production, and coming to the aid (through infrastructure projects) of those who build on flood plains, which action they might have found unprofitable but for the expectation of subsequent assistance.
4. In the United States, there exist constitutional provisions against ex post facto laws and takings of property without compensation. These and other proscriptions, however, have not in modern times been interpreted to significantly constrain the government's taxing powers.
5. See Friedman (1971).
6. Eichengreen does mention that in some instances, although capital levies were rejected, modest capital income taxes were imposed, but the latter can be viewed as modest capital levies, although of a less efficient form (see subsection 5.2). Additionally, he mentions instances of hyperinflation which, to the extent unanticipated, is similar to a capital levy on public debt (including money). Kennedy (1913) reports another fascinating instance, William Pitt's unsuccessful "Triple Assessment" in England in 1798, which was based on the previous year's expenditures in particular categories to limit avoidance, although it still was evaded.
7. Also, as noted, if enactment is not immediately (or, better yet from this perspective, retroactively) effective, but rather delayed, such as through a prolonged phase-in, there is additional time during which inefficient avoidance may take place.

8. It would be interesting to investigate whether the openly discussed capital levies in the 1920s had an impact on the market for public debt (the contemplated target).
9. Another example is Fischer (1980), who identifies the absence of a lump-sum tax instrument as the reason for the appeal of a capital levy but offers no explanation for why his model implicitly rules out this feature of a linear income tax. Criticism of the Ramsey framework along these lines originates in Atkinson and Stiglitz's (1976) seminal paper on optimal income and commodity taxation and is further discussed in Stiglitz (1987) and Kaplow (2008).
10. The life-cycle complication is especially important (and pertinent to the application in subsection 4.2.3 to the transition to a consumption tax). See also subsection 4.5. For example, a plain capital levy would redistribute from sixty-year-old school teachers who had saved a good deal to twenty-year-old future Bill Gates's. Another important factor bearing on the incidence of a capital levy concerns its base, for example, whether it includes social security or pension wealth. A caveat is that, in a fully dynastic world in which all individuals were linked to those in prior and succeeding generations, the life-cycle effects would substantially offset across different generations.
11. Rogers (1986) makes a different point regarding capital levies and distribution, namely that, to the extent a capital levy has undesirable distributive features, such levies may be discouraged, which would help alleviate the time inconsistency problem.
12. See, for example, Roberts (1984).
13. On account of risk aversion, mitigation would be optimal ex post, just as full insurance coverage for losses caused by nature or the market is optimal ex post. Another key assumption (relaxed in other parts of the analysis) is that the policy changes under consideration are optimal; however, because this postulate is primarily relevant to the sorts of transition effects not considered in this chapter, it will not be elaborated further here.
14. Effects in the former category include changes in the relative treatment of assets due to myriad imperfections in capital accounting (tax depreciation that does not match economic depreciation, expensing of some assets), the realization requirement, and differential tax rates for interest, dividends, and capital gains; changes due to the elimination of explicit tax preferences that may accompany such a reform; and changes with regard to imputed income (e.g., if housing is subject to the prepayment method under a consumption tax, so that the imputed rent from housing becomes effectively subject to tax). For prior treatments of these and other issues, see the literature cited in note 2. Observe that, as suggested by the two reforms involving Pigouvian taxes, the possible desirability of mitigating the effects of the accounting change aspect of transition to a consumption tax does not imply the desirability of mitigating otherwise-desirable incentive effects. In this regard, note that, as discussed in subsection 4.5, the prospect of present investment being subject to more neutral treatment in the future will

induce more neutral—that is, less distorted—investment incentives prior to enactment.

15. If the tax has graduated rates, there is no divergence if wages are uniform over time and individuals fully smooth consumption; otherwise, differences arise. Additionally, the text abstracts from uncertainty, which in idealized settings also does not affect the comparison. Finally, a consumption tax, being ex post, taxes inframarginal investment returns whereas a wage tax does not. These possible differences and others, however, are largely orthogonal to the present question concerning a capital levy.
16. Although it is familiar that one cannot compare second-best policies simply by counting the number of distortions, under the assumption of weak separability of leisure, the optimal tax (or subsidy) on capital is zero in basic models with an income tax that distorts labor supply in the process of redistributing income. See Atkinson and Stiglitz (1976) and the generalization in Kaplow (2006). For further discussion and qualifications, see, for example, Stiglitz (1987) and Kaplow (2008).
17. As Feldstein (1978) emphasizes, the extent of distortion is not indicated by the change in savings but instead by the effect of differential taxation on consumption across periods. Note, for example, that even if savings were unaffected, it would still be true that future savings falls relative to present consumption as the tax on capital income increases. The key distinction is that savings (adjusted for the net-of-tax interest rate) indicates expenditures on future consumption, not the quantity of future consumption itself.
18. For further analysis of how some of these factors affect possible transitions to a consumption tax, see, for example, Gentry and Hubbard (1997), Sarkar and Zodrow (1993), Seidman (1997), and Zodrow (2002).
19. In addition to previously mentioned simplifications, debt is ignored. See note 28.
20. Regarding administration, note for example that scheme 2, a consumption tax with a capital levy, can be implemented by imposing a sales tax or VAT and not providing any offset for preexisting assets.
21. Even here, the linkage in part depends on the manner in which the preexisting income tax operates. For example, if the Auerbach-Jorgenson (1980) system of depreciation were employed, under which there is immediate expensing in an amount equal to the present discounted value of the depreciation deductions that otherwise would be allowed, individuals would have no basis in such assets at the time of transition and hence no basis would be eliminated by moving to a consumption tax that provided no relief for pre-enactment basis.
22. As Bradford (1998) emphasizes, the Johansson-Samuelson theorem indicates that, under an accrual income tax, changing rates pose no special problems; thus repeal of such an income tax (i.e., changing the rate from the existing positive level to zero) has no effect on asset values. Accordingly, the capital levy, if any, should be associated with transition *to* a consumption tax.

23. On the other hand, if a transition were made to a consumption tax without a capital levy (scheme 1) and for administrative reasons there were idiosyncratic imperfections that resulted in gains to holders of some types of assets and losses to others, the problem would be more attenuated both in magnitude and in kind. Even assuming individuals anticipated that future reforms might also produce various mismatches, if they were largely random there would be little incentive effect. (Isolated anticipation effects would, however, arise to the extent that particular deviations were expected.)
24. Auerbach and Hines (1987) find that a perfect foresight model is, in most cases, much closer than a myopic model in explaining investor behavior in anticipation of U.S. tax reforms. Furthermore, the tax changes they study probably had briefer lead times and less phasing in than would likely be the case for a tax reform of the scope of replacing the income tax with a consumption tax.
25. By the same logic, anticipation problems would be reduced if the reform could be made effective retroactively, reaching back to consumption substantially prior to enactment. This outcome does not seem politically likely.
26. For a more detailed analysis of the incidence of a transition to a consumption tax, see Gentry and Hubbard (1997).
27. The former entails a greater short-run revenue loss, although there is no difference in the effect on the present value of revenue. Likewise, without regard to any capital levy, moving to a consumption tax rather than to a wage tax delays the collection of revenue on earnings that are saved. In either case, it is natural to contemplate adjustments to national debt to accommodate the change in the timing of government revenue.
28. One can interpret the discussion in the text as applicable to net assets, which would be appropriate for a cash-flow personal consumption tax (see, for example, Kaplow, 1995). (Amounts owed could be viewed as negative assets, one could provide negative basis, and so forth.) However, some consumption tax schemes have a real base—i.e., one that excludes financial transactions—in which the proper treatment of debt (a type of financial asset) may differ. The significance of this point can be appreciated through examples offered in Bradford (1996a, 1996b, 1998, 2004) in which a business purchases inventory, financed fully by borrowing, just prior to enactment of a consumption tax. Under some variations, the treatment of the business's inventory and borrowing would be offsetting, in which case different transition methods would affect whether there was a capital levy on the lender. Bradford also explores the related point: whether certain forms of consumption taxation (notably, a sales tax or VAT) will be accommodated by a one-time easing of monetary policy so that price levels increase by the amount of the tax; the degree of adjustment will affect the incidence of the transition between borrowers and lenders (if prices rise, repayment of principal stated in nominal terms will be with dollars of lower real value).
29. The analysis for basis in excess of market value is similar. Of course, due to the nature of actual depreciation schedules and the strategic realization of losses, this case is less important.

30. It might be noticed that the argument in the text suggests that retroactive relief for capital taxation would be efficient if indeed such relief would be anticipated. This point is generic to many transition settings. Thus, in the first example in section 3 involving a Pigouvian tax, it would be efficient for the tax to apply to external harm generated prior to enactment, again on the assumption that such a transition regime would be anticipated (see Kaplow,1986, 1987, 2003).
31. Another interesting case involves consumer durables, if a prepayment method is to be adopted under a consumption tax. No basis protection would be required because the proceeds from sales of such assets will be tax exempt.
32. Debt, if also not subject to transition provisions, further complicates the story. See also note 28.
33. Changing rates under a consumption tax—or under a wage or income tax—also results in a capital levy (negative for rate decreases) with regard to human capital, which is generally ignored here.
34. Bradford's other approach is to allow immediate expensing but also to provide a supplemental credit (which would be negative for a rate decrease) at the time the consumption tax rate changes, in an amount equal to the product of the market value of assets and the change in the tax rate.
35. Relatedly, because it is so difficult to provide true economic depreciation under an income tax, the Johansson-Samuelson theorem does not hold in practice, and accordingly rate changes under an income tax can also result in significant (positive or negative) capital levies. See, for example, Kaplow (1987).
36. At one extreme, such as in a small, open economy, the before-tax rate of return would be fixed so the net-of-tax return would rise by the full amount of the preexisting tax. At the other extreme, individuals' supply of capital is perfectly elastic at the pre-reform net-of-tax rate, so the market rate of return would fall by the amount of the tax, resulting in no change in the net-of-tax return. The discussion in the text is based on the premise that the result would be somewhere in between. See, for example, Bradford (1996a, 1996b).
37. See, for example, Graetz (1979). Another, related factor bearing on the extent of implicit compensation is that transitions may influence relative asset prices, differentially affecting old capital.
38. To the extent that implicit compensation arises through changes in asset prices or other simultaneous tax reforms (for example, repeal of the corporate income tax) that are favorable to old capital, the relation of compensation to direct loss would be closer.
39. It should also be noted that there are other means of influencing the intergenerational distribution—such as debt policy and social security—that are not a function of the extent of capital one chooses to accumulate.
40. Specifically, the argument of Atkinson and Stiglitz (1976) shows that the move is welfare increasing (with weak separability and identical preferences) and the generalization in Kaplow (2006) demonstrates how one can implement the move so as to generate a Pareto improvement (by means of a distribution-neutral reform).

41. Yet another perspective on the problem is provided by considering the fact that an increase in the net-of-tax return constitutes a change in relative prices (between consumption in different periods) and thus presents a price index problem, wherein welfare comparisons are made more difficult. This angle is pursued in Kaplow (1986, pp. 611–612, n. 322).
42. There still can be efficiency effects, depending on other changes and how the intergenerational redistribution is implemented, by comparison to the capital levy. In this regard, Bernheim (2002, p. 1195) observes: "It is natural to wonder about the sign and magnitude of pure efficiency effects when one eliminates surprise capital levies and subsidies (the third effect) by considering fully anticipated tax reforms, but [Auerbach, Kotlikoff, and Skinner] do not undertake such experiments."
43. Regarding distribution, some of the more recent work devotes more attention to the matter by allowing income-based heterogeneity and attending to differential transition effects on different types of assets.
44. A similar phenomenon also arises in some other literature on optimal taxation, such as that showing differential commodity taxation to be optimal if it can help tax unobservable preexisting endowments. The source of the initial endowments (prior labor earnings and savings) is outside the model, or, implicitly, in periods prior to the surprise enactment of the tax regime found to be optimal.
45. Although this chapter only touches upon matters of political feasibility, it seems difficult to believe that a prolonged capital income tax at a 100% rate would not be seen as tantamount to a capital levy, making it hard to understand why the former would be politically feasible and the latter not. This point is reinforced by the fact that a capital levy of a magnitude equal to the effect of the multiperiod 100% tax would be Pareto superior.

REFERENCES

Altig, David, Alan J. Auerbach, Laurence J. Kotlikoff, Kent A. Smetters, and Jan Walliser. 2001. "Simulating Fundamental Tax Reform in the United States." *American Economic Review* 91: 574–595.

Andrews, William D. 1974. "A Consumption-Type or Cash Flow Personal Income Tax." *Harvard Law Review* 87: 1113–1188.

Atkinson, Anthony B., and Joseph E. Stiglitz. 1976. "The Design of Tax Structure: Direct versus Indirect Taxation." *Journal of Public Economics* 6: 55–75.

Auerbach, Alan J. 1996. "Tax Reform, Capital Allocation, Efficiency, and Growth." In Henry J. Aaron and William G. Gale (eds.), *Economic Effects of Fundamental Tax Reform* (pp. 29–81). Washington, DC: Brookings Institution Press.

Auerbach, Alan J. 2005, August 25. "A Consumption Tax." *Wall Street Journal*, p. A8.

Auerbach, Alan J. 2008. "The Choice between Income and Consumption Taxes: A Primer." In Alan J. Auerbach and Daniel N. Shaviro (eds.), *Institutional Foundations of Public Finance* (pp. 13–46). Cambridge, MA: Harvard University Press.

Auerbach, Alan J., and James R. Hines, Jr. 1987. "Anticipated Tax Changes and the Timing of Investment." In Martin Feldstein (ed.), *The Effects of Taxation on Capital Accumulation* (pp. 163–196). Chicago: University of Chicago Press.

Auerbach, Alan J., and James R. Hines, Jr. 2002. "Taxation and Economic Efficiency." In Alan J. Auerbach and Martin Feldstein (eds.), *Handbook of Public Economics* (vol. 3, pp. 1347–1421). Amsterdam: Elsevier.

Auerbach, Alan J., and Dale Jorgenson. 1980. "Inflation-Proof Depreciation of Assets." *Harvard Business Review* 58: 113–118.

Auerbach, Alan J., and Laurence J. Kotlikoff. 1983. "National Savings, Economic Welfare, and the Structure of Taxation." In Martin Feldstein (ed.), *Behavioral Simulation Methods in Tax Policy Analysis* (pp. 459–493). Chicago: University of Chicago Press.

Auerbach, Alan J., and Laurence J. Kotlikoff. 1987. *Dynamic Fiscal Policy*. Cambridge, UK: Cambridge University Press.

Auerbach, Alan J., Laurence J. Kotlikoff, and Jonathan Skinner. 1983. "The Efficiency Gains from Dynamic Tax Reform." *International Economic Review* 24: 81–100.

Bernheim, B. Douglas. 2002. "Taxation and Saving." In Alan J. Auerbach and Martin Feldstein (eds.), *Handbook of Public Economics* (vol. 3, pp. 1173–1249). Amsterdam: Elsevier.

Boadway, Robin, and Neil Bruce. 1984. "A General Proposition on the Design of a Neutral Business Tax." *Journal of Public Economics* 24: 231–239.

Bradford, David F. 1986. *Untangling the Income Tax*. Cambridge, MA: Harvard University Press.

Bradford, David F. 1996a. "Consumption Taxes: Some Fundamental Transition Issues." In Michael J. Boskin (ed.), *Frontiers of Tax Reform* (pp. 123–150). Stanford, CA: Hoover Institution Press.

Bradford, David F. 1996b. *Fundamental Issues in Consumption Taxation*. Washington, DC: AEI Press.

Bradford, David F. 1998. "Transition to and Tax-Rate Flexibility in a Cash-Flow-Type Tax." In James Poterba (ed.), *Tax Policy and the Economy* (vol. 12, pp. 151–172). Cambridge, MA: MIT Press.

Bradford, David F. 2004. *The X Tax in the World Economy: Going Global with a Simple, Progressive Tax*. Washington, DC: AEI Press.

Bradford, David F., and the U.S. Treasury Tax Policy Staff. 1984. *Blueprints for Basic Tax Reform* (2nd ed.). Arlington, VA: Tax Analysts.

Chamley, Christophe. 1986. "Optimal Taxation of Capital Income in General Equilibrium with Infinite Lives." *Econometrica* 54: 607–622.

Eichengreen, Barry. 1990. "The Capital Levy in Theory and Practice." In Rudiger Dornbusch and Mario Draghi (eds.), *Public Debt Management: Theory and History* (pp. 191–220). Cambridge: Cambridge University Press.

Feldstein, Martin S. 1978. "The Welfare Cost of Capital Income Taxation." *Journal of Political Economy* 86: S29–S51.

Fischer, Stanley. 1980. "Dynamic Inconsistency, Cooperation and the Benevolent Dissembling Government." *Journal of Economic Dynamics and Control* 2: 93–107.

Friedman, James W. 1971. "A Non-cooperative Equilibrium for Supergames." *Review of Economic Studies* 38: 1–12.

Gentry, William M., and R. Glenn Hubbard. 1997. "Distributional Implications of Introducing a Broad-Based Consumption Tax." In James M. Poterba (ed.), *Tax Policy and the Economy* (vol. 11, pp. 1–47). Cambridge, MA: MIT Press.

Graetz, Michael J. 1979. "Implementing a Progressive Consumption Tax." *Harvard Law Review* 92: 1575–1661.

Grossman, Herschel I., and John B. Van Huyck. 1988. "Sovereign Debt as a Contingent Claim: Excusable Default, Repudiation, and Reputation." *American Economic Review* 78: 1088–1097.

Howitt, Peter, and Hans-Werner Sinn. 1989. "Gradual Reforms of Capital Income Taxation." *American Economic Review* 79: 106–124.

Judd, Kenneth L. 1985. "Redistributive Taxation in a Simple Perfect Foresight Model." *Journal of Public Economics* 28: 59–83.

Kaplow, Louis. 1986. "An Economic Analysis of Legal Transitions." *Harvard Law Review* 99: 509–617.

Kaplow, Louis. 1987. "Optimal Transition Policy: Replacing Horizontal Equity with an Ex Ante Incentives Perspective." Ph.D. diss., Department of Economics, Harvard University, Cambridge, MA.

Kaplow, Louis. 1995. "Recovery of Pre-Enactment Basis under a Consumption Tax: The USA Tax System." *Tax Notes* 68: 1109–1118.

Kaplow, Louis. 2003. "Transition Policy: A Conceptual Framework." *Journal of Contemporary Legal Issues* 13: 161–209.

Kaplow, Louis. 2006. "On the Undesirability of Commodity Taxation Even When Income Taxation Is Not Optimal." *Journal of Public Economics* 90: 1235–1250.

Kaplow, Louis. 2008. *The Theory of Taxation and Public Economics*. Princeton, NJ: Princeton University Press.

Kennedy, William. 1913. *English Taxation, 1640–1799: An Essay on Policy and Opinion*. London: G. Bell & Sons Ltd.

Kotlikoff, Laurence J. 2005, March 7. "The Case for the FairTax." *Wall Street Journal*, p. A18.

Kydland, Finn E., and Edward C. Prescott. 1977. "Rules Rather than Discretion: The Inconsistency of Optimal Plans." *Journal of Political Economy* 85: 473–491.

Roberts, Kevin. 1984. "The Theoretical Limits to Redistribution." *Review of Economic Studies* 51: 177–195.

Rogers, Carol Ann. 1986. "The Effect of Distributive Goals on the Time Inconsistency of Optimal Taxes." *Journal of Monetary Economics* 17: 251–269.

Sarkar, Shounak, and George R. Zodrow. 1993. "Transitional Issues in Moving to a Direct Consumption Tax." *National Tax Journal* 46: 359–376.

Seidman, Laurence S. 1997. *The USA Tax: A Progressive Consumption Tax*. Cambridge, MA: MIT Press.

Shaviro, Daniel. 2000. *When Rules Change: An Economic and Political Analysis of Transition Relief and Retroactivity*. Chicago: University of Chicago Press.

Stiglitz, Joseph E. 1987. "Pareto Efficient and Optimal Taxation and the New New Welfare Economics." In Alan J. Auerbach and Martin Feldstein (eds.), *Handbook of Public Economics* (vol. 2, pp. 991–1042). Amsterdam: North-Holland.

Weisbach, David A. 2003. "Does the X-Tax Mark the Spot?" *S.M.U. Law Review* 56: 201–238.

Zodrow, George R. 2002. "Transitional Issues in the Implementation of a Flat Tax or a Retail Sales Tax." In George R. Zodrow and Peter Mieszkowski (eds.), *United States Tax Reform in the 21st Century* (pp. 245–283). Cambridge, UK: Cambridge University Press.

CHAPTER 4

Comment 1

JAMES R. HINES, JR.

The standard practice in analyzing policy reforms is to compare the long-run suitability of alternative methods of achieving the same objective. This practice has the double benefit of simplifying the life of the analyst and focusing attention on the most salient and consequential properties of reform alternatives. Everyone knows that simple long-run comparisons are incomplete; getting from here to there entails a transition, one that is very possibly difficult or painful. Still, the method of long-run comparison holds considerable appeal, as evidenced by its near universal adoption. One can defend this practice by noting that most proposed policy reforms will never be adopted, so the problem of transition will never arise. By this reasoning, the exercise of analyzing reforms is purely conceptual, or academic, so the issues raised by transition become mere academic details. Hence the need to account for the effects of transition is something trivial, akin to the academic obsession with making sure that reference citations use the proper form.

The case for consumption taxation typically is based on its long-run features, the virtues and efficiency benefits of exempting from taxable income the returns to saving. Until recently the problem of transiting from a system that taxes income to one that taxes consumption received little if any attention. Advocates of replacing income taxes with consumption taxes—even those, such as Fisher and Fisher (1942) and Kaldor (1955), who offered specific recommendations—simply considered the steady state properties of their proposed alternatives to existing unsatisfactory income taxes. While the advocates were genuine in their desires, there seemed little danger at the time that governments would actually replace income taxes with consumption taxes.

In the realm of tax policy there is always the danger that governments will do what they are told. While governments in the second half of the twentieth century did not eliminate income taxes, they did move their tax systems in noticeable ways away from income taxation and toward consumption taxation. This is most evident in the case of value-added taxes (VATs).

Until the mid-1960s VATs were virtually unknown, but by 2004, 134 countries were using VATs to raise significant fractions of their tax revenue. These countries moved to partial consumption taxation without knowing exactly what their transitions might entail, and whether the consequences of any capital levies implicit in the transitions would ultimately be good or bad.

The experiences of other countries, together with the intellectual firepower that many analysts, among them most notably David Bradford, have brought to the issue of consumption taxation, make the adoption of a consumption-based tax a real possibility for the United States. As a result, it is time to think seriously about the consequences of transition from income to consumption taxation, and for serious thinking there is no better place to turn than Louis Kaplow. Kaplow's insightful chapter focuses on the critical issue of the capital levy implicit in a transition to consumption taxation. While the logic of this chapter is impeccable, it is worth pursuing some of the points that it raises in order to tease out their implications.

1. Anticipation

The great fear evoked by any capital levy is that the market will anticipate a repetition. Since moving from an income tax to a consumption tax typically reduces the value of existing capital, such a reform embodies aspects of a capital levy, as the Kaplow chapter carefully documents. Hence a transition to consumption taxation may encourage market participants to think that the government will impose additional future capital levies, with all of the associated costs of reduced capital investment and other actions undertaken to avoid the burdens of such taxes.

The critical question, it seems, is just how explicit a capital levy has to be in order to create the kind of anticipation that threatens to undermine future investment and economic activity. Certainly a government that announces plans to tax, just once, 20 percent of the value of existing capital must resign itself to the possibility that the market will think that what happens once might well happen twice. But the capital levy implicit in a transition to consumption taxation is considerably subtler than that, not only because the capital levy is inexplicit, but also because the magnitude of the capital levy depends on supply and demand elasticities whose values are not known with certainty. Indeed, even if one were willing to compensate owners of existing capital for losses that accompany a transition to a consumption tax, it is not clear how to design policies that would accurately do so. Under these circumstances, uncompensated introduction of consumption taxation might evoke fears that consumption tax rates would be increased again in the future, thereby exacting indirect levies on future capital—but it is difficult to see the introduction of consumption taxation as a precedent for future explicit capital levies.

How do markets actually form expectations of future policies? It is essential to understand expectation formation in order to predict the impact of capital levies on expectations of future capital levies, but it would be fair to say that there is much we do not know about this process. Certainly any reasonable observer of current U.S. tax policy would assign some positive probability to further movement away from income taxation and toward consumption taxation. If U.S. tax policy were to evolve in that direction—if the United States adopted a VAT, for example—then perhaps the market would conclude that further changes in the direction of consumption taxation were unlikely. In such a scenario, the adoption of a VAT and the accompanying capital levies would actually reduce expectations of future capital levies, thereby encouraging investment. While it is perhaps unlikely that the market would see things this way, it is certainly possible, which simply illustrates the importance of the process of expectation formation.

Finally, it is worth clarifying the cost of anticipated capital taxes. If the worst-case scenario were to materialize—if a government imposed a capital levy as part of a transition to consumption taxation, and markets reacted by expecting new capital levies every year—then the government might as well carry through with the annual capital levies, since otherwise its policies would produce deadweight loss without even any accompanying tax revenue. We already have a name for annual capital levies: property taxes. The cost of creating expectations of future capital levies is that the government effectively constrains itself henceforth to use property taxes. For the reasons identified in Kaplow's chapter, property taxes are inefficient compared to available alternatives. But economies manage to survive property taxes, so even this worst-case outcome is not disastrous.

2. Capital Levies in Practice

What has been the experience of countries that have moved in the direction of consumption taxation, including the vast majority of the world that has adopted VATs in recent decades? For the most part, consumption-oriented tax reforms have not been accompanied by explicit transition relief. In the absence of careful empirical investigation we simply do not know exactly what problems have been associated with these transitions—for example, whether saving rates have been depressed in these countries in anticipation of future additional capital levies. Since virtually all of the world's saving, outside of the United States, takes place in countries that use VATs, if there has been a noticeable negative effect of these transitions on saving rates, then world saving overall would likely be significantly depressed.

The adoption of certain types of consumption taxes, including VATs, not only imposes capital levies, but raises the possibility that the government will subsequently increase the rate of consumption taxation, thereby imposing a new capital levy. Experience suggests that this is a reasonable concern: VAT rates in 63 of the 134 countries with VATs in 2004 were greater than the rates in the years that these VATs were introduced.[1] In most political processes it is easier to increase the rate of an existing tax than it is to introduce the tax in the first place.

Kaplow discusses the instructive experience of European countries after the First World War. Most European countries ended the war with enormous accumulated government debts, and many were tempted to impose capital levies to offset these debts. In some cases, such as those of Hungary and Austria, governments enacted capital levies from which they ultimately obtained very little revenue, due largely to difficulties of practical implementation and the wildly unstable macroeconomic conditions of the time. Hyperinflation makes it very difficult to tax capital based on assessed values, since the stock-flow distinction becomes acute at such times.

The government of Great Britain contemplated but rejected a capital levy during the same period. Hicks et al. (1942) attribute the British government's reluctance to practical implementation problems, including its estimate that, given interactions with prevailing heavy taxes on income, capital gains, and estates, the proposed capital levy would raise rather little additional revenue. Subsequently, the Colwyn Committee (Colwyn et al., 1927) urged a reconsideration of the desirability of using capital levies, arguing that capital levies could raise revenue effectively and reasonably efficiently, assuming that the government found ways to surmount various implementation problems. Furthermore, the Colwyn Committee expressed confidence that the problem of anticipation could be overcome with "a form of guarantee against repetition of the levy for one or more generations" (p. 406), a promise that might, as events transpired, have proved difficult to keep in the aftermath of the subsequent war.

3. Human Capital Levies

It is by now understood that transitions from income taxation to consumption taxation generally reduce the after-tax value of existing physical capital. Such transitions also affect the value of human capital, the return to which comes in the forms of leisure and consumption financed out of after-tax wages. With enough information it would be possible to capitalize the value of the future wages and leisure that any individual expects to receive over his or her lifetime, and assign this value to an asset that can be called human capital. Thus any major tax reform, including a transition from income to consumption taxation, will affect the value of an individual's human capital asset.

Since the transition to consumption taxation will generally reduce the value of human capital assets, in part by imposing higher taxes on the returns to labor and in part by increasing after-tax interest rates, should this type of capital levy be a source of concern? Individuals invest in their human capital with education, self-improvement, and certain types of employment, and presumably will be less inclined to make these investments if they anticipate future capital levies. The literature on transitions to consumption taxation focuses on physical capital and various forms of intangible business capital, but not on the human capital that represents most of the economy, and it is far from clear that human capital should not receive symmetric consideration.

4. Open Economies

The textbook analysis of consumption tax transitions concerns closed economies. In a closed economy the government has many instruments with which to compensate residents who are negatively impacted by the transition to consumption taxation. In today's world matters are not so simple, since it is likely that nonresidents will be affected along with residents by the price changes that accompany a transition. Nonresidents can be affected through changes in the prices not only of local assets that they own, but also of foreign assets whose valuation is a function of local after-tax returns.

The standard approach to the open economy aspects of the problem is simply to ignore transition effects on foreign holders of domestic assets, or worse, to attempt to tailor policies to exploit foreigners. Foreigners are generally at greater risk of adverse policy reforms than are local residents, since they have so little influence over local politics. Anticipation of future policy reforms discourages foreigners from investing in assets that could lose value in the wake of reforms, thereby damaging the local economy in the ways that Kaplow documents in other contexts. One solution is to reassure foreigners that they would be compensated in any future changes, but the problems remain both how to perform such compensations and how effectively to commit to doing so in a way that foreign investors find credible.

5. Symmetry

It is customary to conceive of the transition problem as entailing capital levies that are costly in the long run because they discourage investment. The opposite is also possible: some transitions provide capital subsidies. For example, the U.S. Tax Reform Act of 1986 reduced the statutory corporate tax rate from 46% to 34% and removed various investment subsidies, thereby increasing the market value of old capital, whose return became taxed at a lower rate, and which faced reduced competition from new investment. This uncompensated transition, if anticipated, is costly in a direction opposite of the usual one, since it encourages excessive investment *ex ante*. It follows, from the persuasive logic of Kaplow, that sensible policy reforms would avoid such subsidies by imposing new charges on capital that benefits in transition.

Just about every change in economic policy entails a transition that is costly to some investors and beneficial to others. Indeed, viewed in the right way, almost all economic policies are merely transitional, doomed to be replaced in more or less short order by new policies based on new ideas or new political constellations. What this means for analysts is that the issues related to transitions are of first-order importance, as both David Bradford and Louis Kaplow clearly recognize.

NOTE

1. In 48 cases, VAT rates in 2004 were the same as when the VATs were introduced, and in 23 cases the 2004 VAT rates were lower than rates at introduction.

REFERENCES

Colwyn, Lord et al. 1927. *Report of the Committee on National Debt and Taxation.* London: His Majesty's Stationery Office.

Fisher, Irving, and Herbert W. Fisher. 1942. *Constructive Income Taxation: A Proposal for Reform.* New York: Harper & Brothers.

Hicks, J. R., U. K. Hicks, and L. Rostas. 1942. *The Taxation of War Wealth* (2nd ed.). Oxford: Oxford University Press.

Kaldor, Nicholas. 1955. *An Expenditure Tax.* London: Allen & Unwin.

CHAPTER 4

Comment 2

KYLE D. LOGUE

1. Introduction

Consumption tax scholars often point out that, in the absence of some form of special transition relief, the shift to a consumption tax will include a one-time tax on all existing capital in society. A capital levy of that sort, whether or not packaged as part of a transition to a consumption tax, would strike most individual taxpayers, at least those with any wealth to speak of, as an unusually bad idea. To economists, however, the idea of a surprise one-time tax on all existing wealth is pure genius. According to the conventional economic wisdom, a capital levy can enhance overall social welfare so long as it is unanticipated and its adoption does not create the expectation that another capital levy might be enacted in the future. What is so great about a surprise one-time wealth tax? It provides the tax policy equivalent of a silver bullet: a large lump-sum tax that is somewhat distributively appealing, in the sense that the tax burden would tend to fall heaviest on the relatively well off.

Historically, countries have used one-time society-wide capital levies as a means of paying off national debts, often the extraordinary debts created by wartime expenditures. Paying off war debt is not what consumption tax proponents apparently have in mind. Rather, the idea is that, with the revenue generated by a one-time consumption tax transition capital levy, Congress could reduce the more permanent marginal tax rates in society, which would reduce behavioral distortions and thus deadweight losses.[1] Indeed, for some economists, the possibility of a consumption tax transition capital levy is one of the main reasons to adopt a consumption tax.

In "Capital Levies and Transition to a Consumption Tax," Louis Kaplow makes a number of important observations about capital levies in general and consumption tax transition capital levies in particular. As is typical of Kaplow's writing, this chapter is exceptionally clear and is characterized by a remarkably high ratio of ideas to words. In this brief comment, I will review a few of the main insights of the essay, explain how those insights fit into

Kaplow's more general framework for analyzing legal transitions, and take one of the ideas that Kaplow mentions in passing and suggest a direction for future research on capital levies.

2. Separability, Incentive Effects, and Distributional Concerns

To my mind, the three most significant conclusions that Kaplow reaches in his chapter are: (1) that the transition to a consumption tax need not include a capital levy (that the two are separable); (2) that capital levies, whether adopted in connection with the move to a consumption tax or not, can be social-welfare enhancing only if they do not distort pre- and posttransition behavior; and (3) one-time capital levies are not as distributively appealing as one might initially suppose, given heterogeneity among wealth holders, especially in terms of age and hence future earning prospects, at the time of the transition.

As Kaplow makes clear, it is possible to transition to a consumption tax in a way that does not include a capital levy, and this is true no matter what form of consumption tax is chosen. Thus, if the U.S. Congress opted for a cash flow consumption tax, under which contributions to qualified accounts would be deducted and withdrawals taxed (similar to the current tax treatment of retirement savings), the capital levy could be avoided by allowing all pre-transition basis to be carried over to the new accounts.[2] Or, if the choice was made to switch to a pure wage tax (which, under certain assumptions, is equivalent economically to a consumption tax), the simple adoption of a tax on all posttransition wages would avoid the capital levy. Although it seems likely that the latter form of transition relief would be simpler to administer than the former, either approach would avoid a capital levy. In sum, the link between the transition to a consumption tax and a capital levy is not necessary. Which means the relevant question is whether a consumption tax capital levy is a good idea.

As with capital levies generally, the answer turns on the questions of incentive and distributional consequences. The sole efficiency benefit of liking a capital levy with the transition to a consumption tax would be that, for some reason, taxpayers would not see the levy coming and thus not alter their pretransition behavior in anticipation and, once the levy is imposed, would not distort their posttransition behavior in the expectation of future such levies. Neither of these outcomes seems likely, for reasons that Kaplow points out. In our democratic system, with our particular budgetary process that is covered in detail by commentators in academia and the media, it is almost inconceivable that taxpayers would be surprised by the outcome. Of course, the capital levy could be made nominally retroactive to apply to some date before the idea had even become a serious policy consideration, but such retroactivity would be highly controversial and, politically, close to impossible.

Moreover, unless lawmakers could tell some plausible story as to why such a levy would be only a one-time (or an extremely rare) occurrence, expectations of future levies would be increased by the imposition of a consumption tax capital levy, leading to further behavioral distortions. This is the familiar "time inconsistency" problem, and there is no easy solution to it.[3] Merely promising not to do it again would not be a sufficiently credible pre-commitment. Perhaps it might be thought that, because the transition to a consumption tax itself is likely to be a one-time event, the capital levy attached to that transition is likely to be a one-timer as well. But one could just as easily imagine a different, slippery slope sort of conclusion being drawn: Now that Congress has discovered the capital levy, what is to stop them from using it again?

Kaplow concludes that these problems of taxpayer expectations and the effect on those expectations on taxpayer incentives call into question the welfare-enhancing potential of a consumption tax capital levy.[4] I agree. Assuming we could somehow overcome these problems, however, the next question involves the distributional consequences of the levy. Obviously, the answer depends on one's view of the appropriate degree of redistribution through the tax system from the better off to the worse off in society. If some redistribution, or progressivity, in the tax system is deemed desirable, presumably it is a plus that a capital levy is a tax on those with wealth. Kaplow rightly points out, however, that the universe of capital owners at any given time is not homogenous. For example, there could be significant differences in age. Hence a flat rate tax on all capital could have regressive, or at least sloppy, redistributive effects as well—for example, young capital owners subject to the levy would disproportionately benefit from the reduced marginal rates on future income. This observation is sound and should be taken into account when assessing the merits of a capital levy.

Still, as taxes go, a capital levy has got to be a *relatively* progressive option, at least when compared with other classic lump-sum taxes, such as a head tax. Kaplow suggests another alternative, which might be even better: a one-time tax on the previous year's wages, which might allow more precise redistribution (with fewer regressive cross-subsidies).[5] Of course, even a nominally retroactive wage tax would entail some imprecision, since any given year's wage is an imperfect measure of economic well-being. Also, my intuition is that anticipation and repetition problems, as well as political opposition, would be even greater for a one-time nominally retroactive wage tax than for a consumption tax transition capital levy.

The upshot of Kaplow's analysis seems to be that, if we decide to make the transition to a consumption tax, we should seriously consider *not* imposing a capital levy, because of the uncertain incentive and distributional effects of such a levy. This conclusion calls into question the ideas that a capital levy is an inherent part of the transition to a consumption tax and that such a levy is necessarily welfare enhancing. Both are important points, and both are worth emphasizing, especially given that some scholars still regard the capital levy as one of the main reasons to switch to a consumption tax.

3. The Problem of Discouraging Efficient Anticipation: The Case for Allowing (Some) Windfall Gains

Kaplow also calls into question another justification for the consumption tax transition capital levy. This justification suggests that the taxpayers whose pretransition wealth was subject to the capital levy would receive at least partial compensation, because the value of their pretransition wealth would rise due to the switch from an income tax to a consumption tax. This boost in asset values at the time of transition would stem from the elimination of the tax on the return to savings inherent in an income tax. Indeed, it is the removal of the tax on savings that most commentators site as the primary reason to make the switch. And if pretransition assets go up in value because of this rule change, why not tax away some of that increased value—that "windfall gain"—to help fund lower marginal rates going forward, or so the justification goes.

Kaplow's analysis offers a rebuttal, and it has to do with anticipation and repetition concerns, although not exactly in the way described above. According to the now famous Kaplow transition framework, it is social-welfare enhancing to encourage some sorts of pretransition anticipatory investments, namely, those pretransition investments that anticipate a specific type of legal change: that which improves incentives.[6] For example, if polluting manufacturers make investments to reduce pollution *because* they anticipate the enactment of a new efficiency-enhancing, cost-internalizing Pigouvian tax, such anticipatory investments are themselves efficient and should be encouraged. That is, if polluters can guess right about new improvements in the law and act on them in advance, more power to them. Applying this idea to the consumption tax transition, if it is truly an improvement in overall tax policy to eliminate the tax on savings (because of the effect on savings incentives), then the sooner taxpayers begin investing in anticipation of the switch to a consumption tax, the better. Let them have their windfall gains as a sort of reward for good guessing about where the law is headed.

This is where the capital levy, unfortunately, comes in. If we impose a special tax on pretransition investments just as we switch to a consumption tax, one of two outcomes could occur: Either taxpayers would see the levy coming and would not engage in an efficient anticipatory increase in savings; or, perhaps worse, they would not see it coming and would make the desirable anticipatory investments only to have the gains taxed away by the levy. The ultimate result of the latter outcome would likely be that those taxpayers burned by the levy (and, arguably, every other taxpayer who saw the first group get burned) would become reluctant in the future to make any efficiency-enhancing investments in anticipation of desirable legal reforms. How large this effect would be is, of course, unknown.[7]

The point of this analysis, of course, is not that all pretransition anticipatory behavior is efficient. The whole point of *surprising* people with a one-time capital levy (or a one-time nominally retroactive wage tax) is to avoid some pretransition anticipatory incentive effects. One example of such undesirable anticipatory effects would be the distortion of labor choices. If taxpayers anticipate the introduction of a one-time capital levy, the prospect of such a tax will have much the same effect on labor choices as does the existing income tax, or as would a consumption tax for that matter. There would be an inefficient incentive to substitute leisure for labor.[8] That is the distortion we would like to avoid if possible. In effect, then, we should want to encourage anticipation of the positive legal change of switching to a consumption tax (if, indeed, it is a positive legal change) while simultaneously keeping the capital levy a surprise. Whether these two effects can be achieved simultaneously, as part of the same legislation, is unclear.

4. Breaking the Link between the Consumption Tax Transition and Capital Levies

Perhaps the best way to achieve these potentially conflicting goals would be to separate the capital levy from the consumption tax transition. That is, if we are going to use the surprise capital levy, perhaps we should think of a way of structuring it other than appending it to the transition to a consumption tax. On this view, the case for switching to a consumption tax would then have to stand on its own merits—that is, on the claim that the consumption tax overall is superior to an income tax without regard to the possibility of a capital levy. Likewise, the question of how best, if at all, to implement a capital levy would be kept entirely separate. On the former question a massive literature has already been generated. On the latter question, much less has been written. In the remainder of this essay, I will give the barest sketch of an idea for a system of periodic (though very rare) and largely unpredictable capital levies.

Recall that the original idea behind the capital levy was to provide a one-time, or rare, source of tax dollars to fund extraordinary national expenses. The quintessential example of such an expense is war debt. As it turns out, no one seems to hold the view today that the capital levy must be limited to reducing war debt. And so far as I know, no one insists that the levy must literally be "one time only." Rather, the point is that the levy must be largely unpredictable (total unpredictability is impossible) and structured in such a way that, when it occurs, the expectation of future capital levies is not significantly increased. These seem to be the necessary conditions for a time-consistent policy of capital levies.

So here is my idea, which I call "the insurance model of contingent capital levies" and is based on a paper by Barry Eichengreen (1990; this work is also cited and briefly discussed in Kaplow's chapter): The government promises *ex ante* never to impose a levy on capital, except in certain predetermined states of the world in which, by definition, tax dollars are extraordinarily valuable, such as during or after wars or, better yet, after catastrophic natural or manmade disasters. Whatever contingency is chosen to be the trigger, it must be widely understood, relatively unambiguous, and easily verifiable—all so that the government can be held to its precommitment only to impose the levy under specified conditions. In addition, the probability and magnitude of the trigger event must be entirely, or at least largely, outside of the government's control. All these conditions are necessary for the policy to be time consistent.

The analogy to insurance, and the notion of equalizing the marginal utility of income across states of the world, should be obvious. Unfortunately, the analogy to moral hazard is also evident. That is, if the government can control the likelihood or severity of the trigger event, there will be a tendency not to take steps to minimize those expenditures. This effect, of course, will be counterbalanced by the political pressure in the other direction. However, the potential political consequences for politicians' failing to plan adequately for natural or manmade disasters is not always as large or as predictable as one might expect. On the other hand, perhaps putting in place a program of disaster-contingent capital levies would also create a coalition of political actors with a financial interest in seeing that the government makes all reasonable disaster-cost-minimizing efforts. In any event, so long as the relevant trigger is not predictable, then the incentive problems normally associated with a capital levy (the anticipation and repetition problems) would be minimized.

Obviously, the difficulty with such a proposal would be in designing the trigger and the capital levy itself. As always, the devil is in the details. Would we limit the trigger to natural and manmade disasters above a certain threshold? If so, how would we define those categories, and where would we set the threshold? Would we want to include war expenditures as a trigger? If so, all the same questions arise: What is a war? Which types of wars count? How large would the levy be? Working out the details of such a program is obviously beyond the scope of this comment. The point is that, during these times, the ability to provide funding is especially critical, and it might be worthwhile to have in place a mechanism for raising revenue at those times in a way that is reasonably efficient and somewhat distributively appealing. A disaster-contingent capital levy might be such an idea. What is more, there is something normatively attractive about the idea that, when our country is struck by uncontrollable extraordinary disasters, we will ask those taxpayers with wealth to chip in and help out.

Or maybe not. Again, this is an idea that needs to be developed. The aim here has been merely to highlight the concept for future study and to emphasize that, if unanticipated capital levies might be said to have desirable efficiency and perhaps distributional properties, then more analysis should be directed at the best use of that policy tool on its own terms and not so much as an appendage to a consumption tax transition. I believe this to be one of Kaplow's main messages as well.

NOTES

This paper was prepared for "Key Issues in Public Finance: A Conference in Honor of David Bradford." David's writings, as well as numerous conversations with him over the years, have had a profound effect on my views of tax policy and on my understanding of what it means to be a good scholar.

1. See, for example, Auerbach, Kotlikoff, and Sinner (1983).
2. See also Kaplow (1995).
3. Kydland and Prescott (1977).
4. Kaplow is not the only person to make these points. Daniel Shaviro (2000) made a similar argument in his book on legal transitions.
5. See also Roberts (1984) and Levmore (1993).
6. Kaplow (1986). On this view, there is no social welfare gain from actions taken in anticipation of legal change designed to alter the distribution of wealth or simply to raise revenue to spend on public goods or legal change whose purpose is merely to alter the rules of accounting. See also Shaviro (2000), who develops this distinction in great detail.
7. The preceding is an efficiency argument for not taxing pretransition wealth. There is also a related fairness argument. According to David Bradford, one of the main reasons for switching from an income tax to a consumption tax is that doing so would eliminate the income tax's unfair discrimination in favor of "early consumers" over "late consumers." Furthermore, Bradford (1996) argued that protecting pretransition wealth accumulated under the income tax (that is, avoiding the capital levy on such pretransition investments) would minimize this particular unfairness over the life of the tax system, mercifully limiting the unfairness to "the duration of the income tax regime." The same sort of fairness concern seems to underlie Kaplow's example of the tax on chocolate: Imagine for years there was an inefficient tax on chocolate, one that distorted consumers' choices between chocolate and vanilla. If we decided to repeal the distorting chocolate tax, it would seem odd (even unfair) to simultaneously impose a one-time tax on all chocolate lovers.
8. Applying the Kaplow transition framework, this would be an example of a legal change with a distributional or pure fundraising purpose, and for which anticipatory behavioral changes should be discouraged.

REFERENCES

Auerbach, Alan J., and Laurence J. Kotlikoff. 1987. *Dynamic Fiscal Policy*. Cambridge: Cambridge University Press.

Auerbach, Alan J., Laurence J. Kotlikoff, and Jonathan Skinner. 1983. "The Efficiency Gains from Dynamic Tax Reform," *International Economic Review* 24: 81–100.

Bradford, David F. 1996. "Consumption Taxes: Some Fundamental Transition Issues." In Michael J. Boskin (ed.), *Frontiers of Tax Reform* (pp. 123–150). Stanford, CA: Hoover Institution Press.

Eichengreen, Barry. 1990. "The Capital Levy in Theory and Practice." In Rudiger Dornbusch and Mario Draghi (eds.), *Public Debt Management: Theory and History* (pp. 191–220). Cambridge: Cambridge University Press.

Kaplow, Louis. 1986. "An Economic Analysis of Legal Transitions." *Harvard Law Review* 99: 509–617.

Kaplow, Louis. 1995. "Recovery of Pre-Enactment Basis under a Consumption Tax: The USA Tax System." *Tax Notes* 68: 1109–1118.

Kydland, Finn E., and Edward C. Prescott. 1977. "Rules Rather than Discretion: The Inconsistency of Optimal Plans." *Journal of Political Economy* 85: 473–491.

Levmore, Saul. 1993. "The Case for Retroactive Taxation." *Journal of Legal Studies* 22: 265–307.

Roberts, Kevin. 1984. "The Theoretical Limits to Redistribution." *Review of Economic Studies* 51: 177–195.

Shaviro, Daniel. 2000. *When Rules Change: An Economic and Political Analysis of Transition Relief and Retroactivity.* Chicago: University of Chicago Press.

PART II

Fiscal Federalism, Corporate Finance, and Fiscal Language

CHAPTER 5

On the Theory and Practice of Fiscal Decentralization

WALLACE E. OATES

The traditional theory of public finance has made a strong case for fiscal decentralization. This case is based on an improved allocation of resources in the public sector, and is composed of four basic elements. First, regional or local governments are in a position to adapt outputs of public services to the preferences and particular circumstances of their constituencies, as compared to a central solution which presumes that one size fits all. Second, in a setting of mobile households, individuals can seek out jurisdictions that provide outputs well suited to their tastes, thereby increasing the potential gains from the decentralized provision of public services (Tiebout, 1956). Third, in contrast to the monopolist position of the central government, decentralized levels of government face competition from their neighbors; such competition constrains budgetary growth and provides pressures for the efficient provision of public services. And fourth, decentralization may encourage experimentation and innovation as individual jurisdictions are free to adopt new approaches to public policy; in this way, decentralization can provide a valuable "laboratory" for fiscal experiments.

However, this basic economic rationale for decentralization of the public sector is not quite so simple and compelling as it appears. Some of the more recent literature provides, first, a thoughtful and provocative critique of the traditional view of fiscal decentralization, and, second, some new approaches that reveal its dark side, especially in practice. There is emerging, in short, a broader perspective on fiscal decentralization that raises some serious questions about its capacity to provide an unambiguously positive contribution to an improved performance of the public sector.

My purpose in this chapter is twofold. First, I want to review the basic theory of fiscal decentralization. There are some loose ends to the traditional argument that open up some intriguing issues. Second, I want to turn to some of the new literature on fiscal discipline in multilevel government. This literature has focused attention on several basic and destructive forces that can undermine the economic performance of a relatively decentralized public sector. I find it helpful to begin by revisiting a decentralization theorem that I formulated long ago. As a point of departure, I want to explain briefly why I introduced the proposition and the rationale for its particular form and proof.

1. On the Decentralization Theorem and Its Motivation

In *Fiscal Federalism* (Oates, 1972), I proposed a straightforward decentralization theorem that formalized the basic efficiency argument for the decentralized provision of certain kinds of public goods. The theorem lays out a set of sufficient conditions for the decentralized provision of these goods to be Pareto-superior to a centralized determination of public outputs. It goes as follows:

> *The Decentralization Theorem:* For a public good—the consumption of which is defined over geographical subsets of the total population, and for which the costs of providing each level of output of the good in each jurisdiction are the same for the central or for the respective local government—it will always be more efficient (or at at least as efficient) for local governments to provide the Pareto-efficient levels of output for their respective jurisdictions than for the central government to provide *any* specified and uniform level of output across all jurisdictions. (p. 35)

The theorem seems almost trivially obvious, but I thought it useful at the time to have a more precise statement of the general idea for two basic reasons. First, it provides an explicit set of conditions under which decentralized provision is to be preferred (on efficiency grounds) to centralized control. As it turns out, some of the ingredients of the theorem are more problematic than I appreciated at the time. A reconsideration of them has opened up a whole range of alternative approaches and new interpretations. Second, as explored in the appendix to the chapter (1972, pp. 54–63), one approach to proving the theorem provides a straightforward algorithm (taken from Barzel, 1969) for determining the magnitude of the welfare gains from decentralization. This has the added virtue of identifying the key parameters that determine the size of the welfare gains from decentralized finance. David Bradford and I actually employed this approach in an exercise in which we measured the welfare gains from the decentralized determination of school budgets in New Jersey (Bradford and Oates, 1974).

Let me begin by going back to the conditions I imposed in the theorem. There are three issues that I want to address here. The first, and perhaps the most straightforward, is the matter of interjurisdictional spillover effects (or externalities). Second, there are the closely interrelated issues of the mobility of individuals across jurisdictions and the precise nature of the public good. The third matter, one which (for good reason) has gotten much attention, is the assumption in the theorem that the central government is constrained to provide a uniform level of output across all jurisdictions. I will take up each of these issues in turn.

First, the theorem assumes that the benefits from the consumption of the public good are limited to those individuals within the jurisdiction where it is provided. There are no interjurisdictional spillover effects associated with the good. Note that it is still a public good in the sense that it is jointly consumed (i.e., consumed in the same quantity) by all residents of the jurisdiction, but it has no impact on the well-being of those outside its borders. We are all familiar with the allocative distortions that typically occur when externalities are present, and this assumption simply rules out any such external effects.

There is an interesting and related matter that arises when this condition is violated. Suppose we are considering an assignment problem for a particular public good. The issue is whether or not to make the responsibility for its provision a central, or "local," government responsibility. If there are interjurisdictional spillover benefits present, this argues for assigning the function of providing the public good to the central government. But there is a cost here. If the central government provides a uniform output across all jurisdictions, then the welfare gains from diversifying outputs in accord with local preferences and conditions are lost. There is thus a basic trade-off in making this determination between the gains from accounting for the spillovers through centralized provision versus the losses from tailoring outputs to local circumstances. (In chapter 2 of the book, I provided an informal diagrammatic treatment and discussion of this trade-off.)

It is interesting that a trade-off of a similar spirit emerges from some of the more recent literature that is developing a so-called second-generation theory of fiscal federalism.[1] Drawing on a framework in which there is asymmetric information and incomplete contracts, Seabright (1996), for example, finds that centralization can increase welfare by improving "coordination" (by accounting for spillover effects), but this comes with a loss of "accountability" (local control over local outcomes). As Besley and Coate (2003) put it, "All of this notwithstanding, the key insight remains that heterogeneity and spillovers are correctly at the heart of the debate about the gains from centralization" (p. 2628).[2] At any rate, my theorem disposes of the problem by simply assuming that there are no external effects across jurisdictional lines.[3]

A second key issue in the theorem has to do with the precise nature of the public good. Often when treating public goods in general or those that are provided by a central government, the assumption is made that they are pure public goods in the Samuelsonian sense that an additional person can consume the output of the good without reducing the consumption of anyone else; in standard parlance, consumption is said to be "non-rival." National defense is the ubiquitous example. Most of the literature in local public finance, however, has adopted a different conception of public goods. So-called local public goods (as envisioned, for example, in the Tiebout model) are not pure public goods: they are subject to costs of congestion. Often the assumption is made that they are "fully congestible" (i.e., doubling the size of the group requires a doubling of inputs in order to maintain an unchanged level of consumption).

It is noteworthy that the Decentralization Theorem says nothing about this matter. It need not, because the theorem is sufficiently general to encompass a whole range of types of public goods, including both pure public goods and local public goods; they can be rival or non-rival in consumption. All that the theorem requires is that whatever the nature of these public goods, the cost of providing a given level of output in a particular jurisdiction is the same, be the provider the central or local government. This does, of course, rule out any economies of scale from central government provision.

However, this issue does raise some fundamental matters about how we conceptualize (or model) the decentralization problem. Of particular importance is what we assume about the mobility of economic units across jurisdictional boundaries (my second issue). The theorem finesses this matter by assuming a complete absence of mobility. One of the conditions specified in the theorem is that "the consumption [of the public good] is defined over geographical subsets of the total population." This implies that individuals are not able to move across jurisdictional lines; were this not so, the geographical subsets of the population would change as people altered their location. This condition is a bit stronger than it need be. What is required here is that there be no mobility *in response to changes in fiscal parameters* (i.e., changes in jurisdictional outputs of public goods or levels of taxes). In short, this is explicitly a non-Tiebout kind of world.[4]

In this respect, the Decentralization Theorem is quite restrictive. Several strands of the literature address the mobility issue explicitly and reach quite different sorts of results. Where mobility with respect to fiscal (and perhaps other) parameters exists, the precise character of the public good becomes crucial. In the Tiebout model, for example, there is costless mobility; individuals seek out a jurisdiction that provides exactly the level of output of the public good that they wish to consume. In so doing, they reveal their preferences for local public outputs and generate a Pareto-efficient outcome in the public sector. But the properties of the public good are critical here. For the Tiebout model to work, the public good must be fully subject to congestion (i.e., for each level of output, if we double the size of the population, we must double the quantity of inputs to maintain output at an unchanged level), and individuals must pay a tax (equivalent to a price) equal to the marginal cost of extending the output of the public good to encompass an additional consumer. Moreover, individual location decisions must not be constrained by anything other than fiscal variables (not, for example, by location of employment). For these reasons, the Tiebout model is typically taken to apply to metropolitan local finance, a setting in which individuals work in a particular urban setting that provides a wide choice of city and suburban jurisdictions in which to reside.[5]

If the set of local tax prices facing mobile individuals does not faithfully reflect marginal costs, then problems arise because location decisions can involve external costs on other persons in both the originating jurisdiction and destination (Buchanan and Wagner, 1970). In an influential paper, Flatters, Henderson, and Meiszkowski (FHM; 1974) departed from the Tiebout assumption by taking the public good to be a pure public good within the jurisdiction in which it is provided and by requiring that individuals must work in the same jurisdiction in which they reside. (On account of this latter condition, I prefer to call the model of Flatters et al. a "regional model" in contrast to Tiebout's "local model.") In this particular regional model, an individual's entry into a jurisdiction reduces the cost of providing the public good to other residents by the amount of the entrant's tax payment.

However, by increasing the stock of labor in the jurisdiction, the entrant drives down the marginal product of labor, and, hence, the wage. Because these effects involve external elements, a locational equilibrium in the model is not, in general, Pareto-efficient. A specific form of subsidy payments is needed to internalize the external costs and benefits associated with individual location decisions.

My basic point here is that the assumptions we make about mobility and about the nature of the public good interact in important ways in determining the kind of outcomes we obtain. We must think carefully about the settings in which we apply these models. The Tiebout model, for example, may provide a reasonably good description of behavior in a metropolitan setting (Fischel, 2001). In contrast, the FHM model has been helpful in understanding some of the issues where different regions have widely varying endowments of natural resources that affect both the productivity of private agents and the availability of tax bases.[6]

My third issue concerns the nature of central government provision of local public goods. It may help to be a bit more precise on this. In equation (5.1), let **G** be a vector of outputs of public goods where an element, g_i, is the level of public output in the ith jurisdiction:

$$G = G(g_1, g_2, \ldots, g_n) \tag{5.1}$$

The Decentralization Theorem equates centralized provision with a uniform level of public outputs (say g_0) across all jurisdictions; the theorem thus requires that $g_i = g_j = g_0$ for all i,j.[7] This obviously served my purposes quite well in the theorem by providing a benchmark against which to compare (favorably) a varied, decentralized pattern of outputs of public goods. But this condition has been contested in the literature. Why should we expect the central government to provide equal levels of public outputs in all jurisdictions? Why can't the central government simply provide the efficient level of output in each jurisdiction?

The rationale (or defense) for this constraint has taken two forms. The first is that there is an information issue. Local governments are closer to their constituencies; they have a knowledge of local preferences that the center cannot easily come by. It is hard for a central government to know the diverse preferences in the myriad of jurisdictions that constitute the country as a whole. In short, there is an asymmetry of information: local governments know local preferences; the central government does not. The second line of defense for this assumption suggests that there are political constraints on the center that prevent it from varying local outputs. That is, a national sense of equal treatment makes it difficult for a central government to provide more generous levels of public outputs in some jurisdictions than in others.

But these arguments are not fully convincing. We see in the real world a variety of pork-barrel projects under which central agents deliver special public programs to their own constituencies. But even at a more formal level, there is really nothing, in principle, to prevent the central government from obtaining the needed information on local cost functions and preferences (albeit costly to gather such information) and then to provide the Pareto-efficient level of output in each jurisdiction. In fact, central government responsibility for local public goods does not, in practice, rule out such sensitivity to local conditions. Under some administrative structures, the center may confer on their local agents both the responsibility and the authority to be responsive to local circumstances in their determination of local programs. Breton and Salmon (2007) describe the French system of administration under which *prefects* (appointed by the center) have the capacity and incentive to adapt national policies to local conditions. Thus, an outcome that is decentralized in spirit can, in principle, emerge from a structure of government with little in the way of real local autonomy.[8]

Some of the more recent literature has taken an entirely different tack on this whole issue. Lockwood (2002) and Besley and Coate (2003), for example, envision the determination of local outputs under a centralized system as taking place through the decisions of a central legislature, whose members are elected representatives of the individual jurisdictions. In such a setting, the elements of the vector **G** in equation (5.1) are set by the central legislative process, which can involve various kinds of logrolling and electoral maneuvers. This can give the problem a quite different character. If, for instance, the vector **G** is determined centrally by a minimum winning coalition in the legislature, allocative distortions occur that work to the disadvantage of those jurisdictions outside the coalition. Nevertheless, if spillovers in the provision of local public goods are sufficiently pervasive, a centralized outcome may still dominate a decentralized one.

The more general point here is that the Decentralization Theorem invokes a very strong condition or constraint on the central provision of public goods that makes it fairly easy to establish a presumption in favor of the decentralized provision of these goods (assuming an absence of significant spillover effects or large economies of scale). The problem of centralized versus decentralized provision can become much more complex when centralized outcomes are characterized in a more thoughtful way.

2. On Measuring the Welfare Gains from Fiscal Decentralization

The Decentralization Theorem also suggests a straightforward way to generate a cardinal measure of the welfare gains from the decentralized provision of public goods. Using an approach suggested by Barzel (1969), one can provide a proof of the theorem by simply maximizing the sum of consumer surpluses from provision of the good (Oates, 1972, pp. 59–63). This approach can be employed to measure the welfare gains from decentralization by simply calculating the difference between the level of aggregate consumer surplus under decentralized and centralized provision of the good.

Such an exercise, in addition to providing some sense of the size of the potential welfare gains from fiscal decentralization, has the further virtue of identifying the key parameters upon which these gains depend. Returning to the theorem, suppose that the costs of providing a unit of the good per person are the same across all jurisdictions. The only source of welfare gains in this case comes from diversifying outputs across jurisdictions in accordance with the differing demands for the local public good. It is straightforward to show for this case (Oates, 1997) that the magnitude of the welfare gains depends on the variation in demand across jurisdictions and on the price elasticity of demand for the good. The greater the differences in the efficient levels of output across the jurisdictions themselves, the more there is to gain from allowing each jurisdiction to provide its own efficient output level. Perhaps less obvious is the fact that the price elasticity of demand is a key parameter here. In particular, the more price inelastic the demand for the public good, the greater the gains from decentralization.[9]

Bradford and I (1974) employed this method in an exercise in which we estimated the potential welfare losses from moving from a system of decentralized school finance to one which imposed equal spending per pupil across all jurisdictions. Using a body of data on school finance from New Jersey, we first estimated a demand curve for per-pupil expenditure. We then took the observed spending per-pupil in each school district to be that which the local population desired (i.e., the efficient level). As our benchmark for centralized provision, we simply aggregated the school budgets across all jurisdictions and divided by the total number of pupils to get our figure for per-pupil expenditure for the case of centralized school finance. Since there was wide variation in expenditure per pupil within our sample ($295 to $547), and since our estimate of the price elasticity was low (−0.36), it is not surprising that we found the welfare losses from the centralization of school spending to be quite large. Our calculations suggested that the average deadweight loss associated with moving a dollar of expenditure from a high-spending district to a low-spending district was on the order of 50 cents.

This estimate assumes, of course, that there are no external effects associated with local school spending, an assumption one might well question. More generally, this approach has an admitted tendency toward large estimates of the welfare losses from fiscal centralization. First, it uses as a benchmark the assumption of uniform provision across jurisdictions under a centralized regime; it thus provides no scope whatsoever for the central authority to adapt outputs to local circumstances. Second, it assumes fully efficient local decision making by presuming that the observed outputs under decentralization are at Pareto-efficient levels. It is worth noting, in this context, that these kinds of measures are also likely to produce large estimates of welfare losses from centralization because the existing estimates of the price elasticity of demand for local public goods typically suggest highly price-inelastic demands. There is now a large body of econometric estimates of demand functions for a wide range of local public services, and they typically find price elasticities on the order of −0.3 to −0.5.[10]

Even if there is no variation in demands across jurisdictions, fiscal decentralization can produce welfare gains where costs vary, since with given demands, differing costs will result in differences in efficient levels of output.[11] Such variation in the costs of providing local public services can come from either of two sources. First, there may be actual differences in the production functions among jurisdictions. The costs, for example, of providing clean, clear roads are likely to be lower in areas where there is relatively mild weather than where winter (and summer) storms make road-clearing operations a more formidable task. Second, there is an altogether different and interesting source of variation in the cost per person of providing local services: the congestion properties of the public service. Suppose, for example, that the local public good is a pure public good within the jurisdiction in which it is provided. Then it will be less expensive *per person* to provide a given output in a relatively populous jurisdiction. And, hence, the efficient level of output, other things being equal, will be higher in such a jurisdiction.

It is easy to see for the case of varying costs that the gains from fiscal decentralization depend on the magnitude of the variation in costs across jurisdictions and, once again, on the price elasticity of demand (Oates, 1997). But for this case, the welfare gains are greater whereas the demand functions are more price elastic—just the opposite of the case where differences in efficient levels of output have their source in variation in demand.[12] Thus, the impact of the price responsiveness of demand on the magnitude of the welfare gains from decentralization depends on whether the divergences in efficient levels of local outputs have their source in differences in demands across jurisdictions or differences in costs.

An especially dramatic case of welfare losses from centralization with their source in cost differentials emerged a few years ago in the debate over the Environmental Protection Agency's (EPA) new arsenic rule for safe drinking water.[13] The removal of contaminants from drinking water involves processes with enormous economies of scale (in terms of population). It is typically much less expensive *per person* to provide safe drinking water in heavily populated areas than in those with fewer people. In this case, the EPA introduced a new and much tougher standard for arsenic concentrations in drinking water. The estimated benefits were quite modest. The problem was that the average cost *per household* to attain the standard varied from under $1 per household per annum in large water systems (e.g., New York City) to over $300 per household in the smallest systems. In benefit-cost terms, the new rule may have been defensible for large water districts, but (based on then-available estimates) the rule promised large welfare losses for smaller districts (Oates 2002). The setting of environmental standards in the United States often involves a single standard for all jurisdictions (a one-size-fits-all approach); following this precedent, the EPA's new standard was imposed on all water districts. However, as this case makes clear, a more decentralized approach to the setting of standards for many dimensions of environmental quality would make more economic sense.

The traditional economic case for fiscal (and regulatory) decentralization is thus founded on the potential welfare gains from diversifying local public outputs in accordance with local circumstances (encompassing both differences in preferences and costs). And the existing (if small) empirical literature suggests that these gains can be quite large. An optimal fiscal structure from this perspective is one in which a central government provides outputs of those public goods that are truly national in scope and decentralized levels of governments determine the appropriate levels of outputs of those public services whose consumption is limited to residents of their respective jurisdictions. In practice, however, there is much more to the story. To achieve efficient outcomes requires a set of public decision-making institutions that provides the needed incentives for effective budgetary choices. Much of the more recent literature suggests that this is much easier said than done. So to this I turn next.

3. On Fiscal Institutions and Decentralization

The earlier literature in fiscal federalism recognized the potential for distorted outcomes under certain spatial patterns of benefits from local public services and particular forms of taxation. McLure (1967, 1969) demonstrated this in his seminal work on tax exporting, in which he provided estimates of the extent to which various taxes levied in one state (or jurisdiction) were actually borne by residents elsewhere. McLure went on to develop the welfare implications of tax-exporting, pointing out that if local decision makers could expect outsiders to finance some portion of their local budget, there would exist incentives for excessive local expenditure. But it is in the more recent literature that the "dark side" of fiscal decentralization has been spelled out more fully.[14] This has been prompted, it seems to me, by two developments. First, we have seen several major fiscal and economic collapses (such as those in Argentina and Brazil), as well as more low-grade but persistent fiscal malfunctioning, that have important roots in the vertical structure of the public sector and, more particularly, in the behavior of decentralized fiscal authorities. This has prompted a careful examination of just what has gone wrong. Second, there have been important advances in the theory of fiscal structure and its operation that draw upon the new theory of the firm (e.g., Cremer, Estache, and Seabright, 1996). The recognition that asymmetric information, incomplete contracts, and the associated agency costs manifest themselves in public- as well as private-sector institutions has opened up a whole new perspective on fiscal decentralization.

A major issue in this literature is the raiding of the fiscal commons. This is not just a matter of corruption.[15] Such destructive behavior derives directly from the incentives that the political and fiscal system create for both public officials and the electorate. The very structure of intergovernmental finance in certain countries makes such behavior almost inevitable.

The source of these raids is the presence of "soft budget constraints" (a term from the seminal work of Kornai, 1979, 1980). Kornai originally introduced the term to describe the setting of state-owned enterprises in socialist countries, where managers could depend on the central government to bail them out of financial difficulties. This created an environment in which these managers could preside over chronic financial losses with little to fear from higher authorities. The scope of the term has, more recently, been broadened to encompass a range of economic entities whose financial losses will be underwritten by some form of "supporting organization" (Kornai, Maskin, and Roland, 2003). For my purposes here, the term can be understood to refer to officials in lower levels of government who operate with the *expectation* that their fiscal deficits will be covered by a higher level (often the central) government. This is a world in which provincial (state) governors or local mayors can expect fiscal bailouts from higher-level authorities; they need not, in short, keep their fiscal houses in order.

The key issue here is the source of such expectations. Since such bailouts can obviously undermine responsible fiscal decision making, how is it that a fiscal system can come to embody such a perverse set of expectations? The literature typically explains this phenomenon in terms of some kind of sequential, game-theoretic framework (e.g., Wildasin, 1997; Qian and Roland, 1998; Goodspeed, 2002). In the first stage of the game, the central government commits itself to a sensible, no-bailout position; it states explicitly that it will not come to the fiscal rescue of lower levels of government running deficits in their budgets. In the second stage of the game, decentralized officials must decide whether or not this claim is credible. As the literature makes clear, there are plenty of reasons why these officials may not find the center's claim to be persuasive. First, the central government presumably cares about the welfare of the citizenry (either for altruistic reasons or in order to be reelected). Second, the failure of a provincial or local government can have serious consequences not only for the well-being of its residents, but for others as well. As Wildasin (1997) has argued, such fiscal malfunctions can have important spillover effects on other jurisdictions. Moreover, in the complexity of hierarchical politics, governors or mayors may be in a position to shift the blame for their fiscal crises onto central public officials. Thus, the very political survival of central incumbents may well depend on their coming to the aid of lower-level fiscal authorities.

The credibility of the no-bailout claim is further complicated by the potentially important insurance role of the central government. As Lockwood (1999) and others have argued, there will be times when decentralized governments come under fiscal distress that has purely external origins. The central government can, under such circumstances, provide valuable assistance that will soften the impact of these external shocks. But, as with insurance in the private sector, there can be a real moral hazard problem here. Especially in a contentious political setting, it may not always be easy to distinguish clearly fiscal deficits that have their source in external shocks from those that result from poor fiscal management.

Thus, for a complex of reasons, decentralized governments may decide that the center's claim to a no-bailout position is not credible. In consequence, they may proceed in the second stage of the game to intentionally expand the budget beyond levels for which they have funding in the expectation that central officials will come to their rescue with grants or loans. [If, alternatively, decentralized governments find the center's commitment to a no-bailout strategy to be persuasive and so behave responsibly in fiscal terms, the game ends at this juncture.] Confronted by these provincial or local deficits, the central authority must then decide whether or not to come to the rescue with additional financial resources. And, as we have discussed, there may often be compelling reasons (both economic and political ones) for a bailout.

This "game" raises the crucial issue of the structural source of these perverse expectations. What are the elements in a fiscal and political system that create an environment that undermines fiscal discipline? There is a not a simple answer to this question. In a fascinating and enlightening set of case studies, Rodden, Eskeland, and Litvack (2003) suggest that soft budget constraints typically have a multiplicity of sources that encompass existing fiscal institutions, the structure of the political system, the absence (or weakness) of certain key markets, and the specific history of intergovernmental fiscal relations in the country. In short, each nation has its own story to tell. But there are some important lessons here. For example, as Rodden at al. point out, soft budget constraints frequently arise in settings where fiscal responsibility is ill defined. In some countries, there exist serious ambiguities about which level of government is responsible for providing certain services (such as health care or pensions) or at least the funding of them. Where spending and revenue authority and responsibility are not clearly defined, there may be good reason for governors or mayors to expect fiscal assistance from higher levels. In short, Rodden et al. find that "unclear or shared responsibilities have a cost in terms of accountability and incentives" (p. 16).

Soft budget constraints are also more likely where decentralized levels of government have weak tax systems and rely heavily on higher levels of government for fiscal transfers. Rodden et al. describe such a setting as involving "transfer dependency." In order to make the tough fiscal decisions and weigh the benefits against the costs of new or expanded programs, public officials need to be in a position of raising the monies from their constituencies through their own state and local tax systems. A heavy reliance on transfers creates incentives for turning to an expansion of these transfers rather than increasing taxes in one's own jurisdiction.

Another major element of soft budget constraints is often debt finance. One way to fund a potential deficit (if assistance is not directly forthcoming from above) is through the issue of bonds. There are numerous instances, for example, in which powerful provincial governors (in countries like Argentina) have had access to the public banking system (or other state-owned enterprises) to absorb their bond issues. In such a setting, public officials can simply sell the requisite bonds to regional or national banks to cover prospective deficits. Soft budget constraints thus often manifest themselves both in terms of transfer dependency and a poorly functioning banking system that is subject to manipulation by public officials for funding deficits.[16]

The absence of a strong and effective set of private markets constitutes a further impediment to a system of hard budget constraints. Well developed and efficient capital markets, for example, can provide needed fiscal discipline by imposing higher borrowing costs and limiting access to credit for provincial or local governments that perform poorly. Similarly, an effective set of land markets in the presence of mobile factors of production can support sound fiscal decision making through the capitalization of superior or poor fiscal performance (encompassing the quality of local outputs and levels of local taxation) into local property values. Thus, a strong system of private markets can itself be an important contributor toward a hardening of budget constraints.

In addition, there is the critical matter of history and precedents. The U.S. experience is instructive in this regard. Reviewing its history of relatively hard budget constraints, Inman (2003) argues that, since the founding of the Republic and the War of 1812, the United States' essentially clean record of any strategic bailouts owes much to one important historical episode. In the 1840s, a wave of defaults occurred encompassing eight states and the Republic of Florida as a result of poorly conceived public investments in transportation and banking projects. The federal government explicitly rejected efforts by these states to obtain fiscal assistance. Because Congress said no, it put an end to any real prospects for strategic fiscal bailouts. The point here is that a refusal to provide such assistance can build upon itself and create a setting where expectations of bailouts no longer have much foundation. History, in short, matters.

At any rate, building a system of hard budget constraints is clearly a formidable (but by no means impossible) task that involves dimensions not only of the fiscal system, narrowly defined, but also of political and market structure.[17] This is truly a problem in political economy, and I want next to explore briefly three aspects of this issue. The first is the topic of intergovernmental grants, a fundamental source of soft budget constraints. The second is the issue of political structure and fiscal responsibility. And the third is the complex interrelationship among markets, politics, and fiscal performance.

As we have discussed, Rodden at al. (2003) have identified "transfer dependency" as one of the predominant sources of soft budget constraints. This issue actually has a long history in the literature on fiscal federalism where it has been called the problem of "vertical fiscal imbalance." There is, I think, fairly general agreement that for a sound fiscal system, the various levels of government need their own sources of tax revenues. Proposals for additional spending need to be evaluated in a setting in which benefits are weighed against their costs, and having to rely on own revenues (rather than transfers) provides incentives for a more careful balancing of these two sides of the ledger. A condition of vertical fiscal imbalance (or transfer dependency) is said to exist where own-revenue systems are weak and lower-level governments rely heavily on transfers from above.

The issue here is the extent and nature of a sensible system of intergovernmental grants. It is important to recognize at the outset that nearly all systems of multilevel government finance incorporate significant grant programs and that there is an explicit, and quite compelling, rationale for their role. Public-finance economists have traditionally seen such grants as serving two basic purposes. First, in the Pigouvian tradition, they provide a needed incentive for lower-level governments to expand public outputs that have important spillover effects into other jurisdictions. The appropriate fiscal instrument here is a matching grant that serves to internalize the spillover benefits. Second, there exist major programs of fiscal equalization in most federal countries (although not at the federal level in the U.S.) that serve to transfer resources to relatively poor regions. These are typically justified on redistributive grounds or, more recently, in terms of providing a more level playing field for interjurisdictional competition. In addition to these two functions, it is often pointed out that the central government may have a kind of comparative advantage in raising tax revenues. Nationwide taxes (with uniform provisions and rates), so the argument goes, have fewer distortionary effects on flows of mobile resources than do state and local taxes with differing rates, definitions of tax base, and so forth. Moreover, a national tax structure permits a higher degree of progressivity, which promotes distributive objectives. There may also be some (modest) economies of scale in tax administration. So the argument here is that we can have a better overall tax system if we rely more heavily on the central government and use transfers to provide some portion of state and local funds.

This raises the tough question of whether or not an extensive system of such intergovernmental transfers is consistent with a fiscal structure with hard budget constraints that encourages efficient fiscal decision making. This is not an easy question to answer. Let me consider first the case against intergovernmental transfers. We have already seen the concern raised by Rodden et al. and others that such transfers can easily become an instrument that governments abuse in the pursuit of fiscal bailouts. In addition, there is some troubling evidence that intergovernmental grants often do not function as the normative theory would have them do, even in the context of a system of relatively hard budget constraints. Studies in the United States suggest that where such transfers presumably have a role in internalizing interjurisdictional spillover effects, they have not done so very effectively. Moreover, the design of many of these programs runs counter to this objective (Oates, 2004). For example, for many years, the federal matching grants for interstate highway construction involved a cost-sharing formula under which the federal government's share was 90 percent of construction costs. Such a federal matching share surely far overstates the fraction of benefits accruing to other states. Moreover, most federal matching-grant programs (in the U.S. at least) have caps at fairly modest levels of expenditure. Once the cap is reached, federal cost-sharing ceases, and there is no incentive at the margin for any expansion of the program. More generally, Inman (1988), in a study of U.S. federal grant programs to state and local governments, found that the basic economic objectives of efficiency and equity do not take us very far in explaining the actual structure and functioning of the federal grant system. He had much more success in explaining (econometrically) the pattern of grant allocations using a model of political influence.[18]

As we have noted, another basic role for intergovernmental transfers is fiscal equalization. In many federal countries like Canada, Australia, and

Germany there are major programs to transfer resources from more wealthy jurisdictions to those with relatively small tax bases (and, perhaps, high fiscal need). But these programs too can have perverse and unintended consequences. In an intriguing recent study, Padovano (2007) looks at the process of income convergence among regions, where he contrasts the experience of the United States, a country with essentially no fiscal equalization by the federal government, with that of Italy, where there have been large fiscal transfers from the wealthy North to the South. Padovano finds that in the United States the process of income convergence has proceeded expeditiously as economic theory would predict, with a movement of industry and employment to relatively low-wage areas and a consequent narrowing of interregional income differentials over time. This process of income convergence has not happened in Italy. Padovano argues that this is largely the result of the transfer system which has muted the incentives for the factor movements that generate convergence.[19]

While a more systematic and comprehensive review of the experience with intergovernmental transfers goes beyond the scope of this chapter, there is surely enough evidence here to suggest that these grant systems have often not been designed properly, frequently have not functioned very well, and in some cases have had perverse, if unintended, consequences. The case against grants, based on their actual use, is not easily dismissed.

At the same time, I am reluctant to throw out intergovernmental transfers as simply a bad idea in practice. They have an important *raison d'être,* and there are ways to address their ills. Moreover, they are firmly entrenched; we probably are destined to live with them whether we want to or not. The challenge is how to make them work better. In that light, the two key issues are proper design and proper use. In terms of design, transfers must provide a set of incentives consistent with their objectives. Most notably, they must not encourage poor fiscal practices; for example, Rodden et al. (2003) point out that the mandated German formula for fiscal equalization makes it clear to the smaller and poorer states that poor fiscal performance will be rewarded with increased transfers (p. 443). This is obviously a recipe for undermining fiscal discipline. In practice, moreover, a grant system needs to be transparent and predictable. There needs to be a well understood set of rules such that the system cannot be gamed to one's own advantage. This may well involve limiting the discretion of the central government in the distribution of funds so as to preclude political manipulation of grant distributions. This is obviously a topic for an extended treatment in its own right. The design and operation of an effective system of intergovernmental grants ranks, in my view, right at the top of the research agenda in fiscal federalism.

A second issue on which I want to comment briefly is the intimate relationship between fiscal behavior and politics. The fiscal system is embedded in a larger political system, and the way in which fiscal decentralization works clearly depends on political, as well as fiscal, institutions. This has been the subject of both important theoretical and empirical work. I mentioned earlier the papers by Lockwood (2002) and Besley and Coate (2003), in which central legislatures composed of locally elected representatives determine the vector of local public outputs described in equation (5.1). Depending on how the legislature behaves (e.g., a minimum-winning coalition or a cooperative outcome), the pattern of local outputs will exhibit different sorts of distortions. Seabright (1996) has taken a somewhat different tack in a model in which an incumbent central government determines the vector of local outputs in such a way as to maximize the probability of its reelection. The crucial variable for each local jurisdiction in this approach is the probability that the jurisdiction is decisive (or pivotal) in determining the election of the central government. Localities for which this probability is relatively high obviously tend to get more favorable treatment in terms of relatively high levels of local public outputs. These are simply a few examples of a larger body of ongoing theoretical work in which we find that local fiscal outcomes depend in crucial ways on how the political system works.

The critical role of political structure also comes through clearly in recent empirical work. In the illuminating collection of country studies to which I have made frequent reference, Rodden et al. (2003) find that certain properties or characteristics of the political system have profound implications for the presence or absence of hard budget constraints for decentralized levels of government. Most notably, they find that in countries where the central legislature is itself a loose coalition of regional interests, budget constraints tend to be relatively soft with sometimes devastating results (as in the cases of Argentina and Brazil). In such a setting, some fiscal outcomes have been the result of extensive logrolling behavior among regional interests that result in fiscal bailouts for decentralized authorities. This work leads to the rather paradoxical and ironical finding that for fiscal decentralization to function effectively, there is a real need for a strong central government with a sufficient presence to be able to resist opportunistic moves by provincial and local interests. A weak center, in short, is often an integral part of a fiscal system with soft budget constraints and poor performance.

My third, and final, topic is the broad umbrella that covers the whole constellation of fiscal structure, the political system, and market institutions. The general point here is that, in the end, fiscal performance emerges from this larger system. Weingast and his co-authors have stressed the fundamental interdependence of the private and public sectors in their work and have been able to tie various elements together in terms of what they call "market-preserving federalism."[20] On the one hand, an effective system of markets requires a supportive political and fiscal environment. One of the basic threats to efficient markets is the encroachment of powerful political interests. "Preserving markets requires that the state be effective yet limited" (Qian and Weingast, 1997, pp. 83–84). On the other hand, efficient markets contribute to hard budget constraints and improved fiscal performance. From the Weingast et al. perspective, this crucial interdependence is best addressed in terms of a decentralized public sector in which regulatory and fiscal powers are diffused among state and local entities. Competition among these decentralized authorities restricts their capacity to intrude on the efficient operation of markets. Efficient markets, in turn, constrain the fiscal activities of public-sector agents. As we noted earlier, in a setting with mobile factors and relatively efficient land and credit markets, poor fiscal performance will penalize a jurisdiction through restricting local government access to credit markets, raising the interest rates on local public debt, and through the capitalization of the poor quality of local outputs and high taxes into local property values. There is thus a kind of mutual reinforcement between markets and fiscal decentralization that enhances the performance of both the private and public sectors of the economy and that gives them a self-enforcing character. Weingast (1995) suggests that we can find historical examples of such systems in eighteenth-century England and in the United States in the nineteenth century.

The essence of such systems is a combination of fiscal and market institutions that provides a set of incentives to individual agents for efficient behavior. A relatively decentralized public sector, characterized by competition among jurisdictions in a setting of a common market without barriers to trade, can provide a powerful inducement for public decision makers to behave in ways that promote the welfare of their constituencies and sustain the efficient performance of private markets.

There is, however, no detailed, universal blueprint for the optimal system. As we have seen, the construction of a viable and efficient structure involves a delicate balancing act. A self-sustaining system must, on the one hand, be sufficiently decentralized to promote competition among jurisdictions and to limit the capacity of the center to undermine the efficient operation of markets. At the same time, however, the central government must be strong enough to credibly resist moves by decentralized agents to raid the commons. The right balance is likely to vary somewhat from nation to nation depending on the particular history and character of the country.[21] The political economy of fiscal decentralization is thus a very complicated and challenging issue. As Wildasin (2004) indicates, it offers us a rich research agenda with a potentially enormous payoff.

NOTES

I am grateful for helpful comments on an earlier draft of this paper to Emma Galli, Charles McLure, Fabio Padovano, Harvey Rosen, John Wallis, and David Wildasin.

1. For a survey of this new literature, see Oates (2005).
2. The more recent literature provides a number of new perspectives on this assignment issue (e.g., Lockwood, 2002). In some instances, they provide a somewhat different slant on the trade-off between centralization and decentralization. Janeba and Wilson (2005), for example, construct a model in which tax competition among local governments is the source of inefficiency in local provision, while inefficiencies at the central level have their source in decisions by a minimum winning coalition in a central legislature. In another approach, Brueckner (2004) poses the trade-off in terms of the inefficiencies stemming from local taxation versus the gains from Tiebout-sorting under local provision.
3. Another (and traditional) way of addressing this problem is through a set of (Pigouvian) taxes and subsidies that serve to internalize the external effects. A system of properly designed matching grants, for example, can provide the appropriate incentives to expand outputs of public services to encompass the benefits to those outside the jurisdiction.
4. An interpretation of the theorem that allows mobility with respect to other nonfiscal variables does complicate matters a bit, for it makes the population of a given jurisdiction (and hence the pattern of efficient outputs of public goods) specific to a particular locational equilibrium.
5. For a review and assessment of the Tiebout model, its evolution, and its contribution, see Oates (2006).
6. This issue has received extensive attention in Canada, where the treatment of oil revenues in the oil-rich provinces has been a contentious matter at both national and regional levels. This has provided some of the motivation for a major program of fiscal equalization among the provinces. For a formal analysis of the problem, see Boadway and Flatters (1982).

7. For purposes of measuring the welfare gains from fiscal decentralization, I took g_0 to be arithmetic mean of the demands of all the individuals in the country (Oates, 1972, pp. 59–63).
8. There is a kind of semantic issue here. In my earlier book (1972), I characterized an *economic* definition of federal government as one in which *outcomes* at decentralized levels "are determined largely by the demands for these [public] services of the residents . . . of the respective jurisdiction" (p. 17). I contrasted this with *political* definitions of federalism that focus more on political autonomy, often expressed in the form of a constitution. The point here is that one can associate decentralization either with the nature of the outcomes or with the process by which these outcomes are determined. In this sense, I suppose one could characterize the prefect system (from an economic perspective) as possessing important federal elements.
9. It is interesting to note that this is precisely the opposite result from the case of deadweight losses in taxation. For the tax case, we all learn that the welfare losses from an excise tax on a specific good (at least in a partial-equilibrium framework) become larger as demand curves become more price elastic, because a given tax causes a larger response (distortion) in terms of the change in quantity purchased. In contrast, the welfare losses from fiscal centralization are greater, the more price inelastic is the demand curve, because given changes in quantities on the horizontal axis moving away from an efficient level generate greater losses in consumer surplus where demand curves are relatively steep.
10. For surveys of this econometric literature, see Rubinfeld (1987) and Oates (1996).
11. The Decentralization Theorem assumes that cost functions for local public services are identical across all jurisdictions. It thus focuses solely on differences in demand as the source of welfare gains from fiscal decentralization.
12. This is like the case of distorting taxes in that the source of the variation manifests itself on the price, rather than the quantity, axis.
13. More generally, the removal of contaminants from drinking water involves processes that exhibit huge differences in cost per person across water districts of different population sizes. See U.S. Congressional Budget Office (1997) and Dinan, Cropper, and Portney (1999) for studies that explore the case for decentralized standard-setting for safe drinking water.
14. Prud'homme (1995) and Tanzi (1996) raised a range of specific concerns regarding the dangers inherent in fiscal decentralization.
15. There has emerged a large literature on corruption in the public sector, much of it empirical in character. One of the important questions posed in this literature is whether corruption is likely to be a more serious problem at the central or at decentralized levels of government. My reading suggests the jury is still out on the answer.
16. As Wildasin (2004) discusses, there is typically an intimate relationship between intergovernmental transfers and public debt. An increase in transfers from the center may often be financed by an increase in the center's deficit so that central

borrowing may effectively substitute for borrowing at decentralized levels of government.

17. Another mechanism for the hardening of budget constraints is a system of explicit rules on fiscal behavior that introduces measures such as a balanced-budget restriction on the current account. The limitations on deficit spending and levels of public debt embodied in the Stability and Growth Pact as part of the European Monetary Union (EMU) appear to have had some impact on restraining public spending in various EMU countries (Franco et al., 2003). There is also a large literature on fiscal rules in the U.S. states that suggests that *appropriately designed* measures can have some effect in constraining budgetary behavior.
18. See also Gamkhar (2002).
19. Likewise, McKinnon (1997) and McKinnon and Nechyba (1997) have suggested that fiscal equalization has, in several countries, impeded the standard process of "equalization through competition."
20. See, for example, Weingast (1995), Qian and Weingast (1997), McKinnon (1997), and Weingast (2005).
21. In their illuminating study of fiscal decentralization in Canada, Bird and Tassonyi (2003) argue that an objective examination of fiscal structure suggests that Canadian provinces should have relatively soft budget constraints. Yet provincial fiscal behavior has not been characterized by opportunistic raiding of the commons. They suggest that this is largely the result of a political system that limits provincial influence in the central legislature and of strong markets. In addition, they note that national temperament may itself be important. They contend that "generally prudent fiscal behavior has become an institutionalized norm in Canada, in part because fiscal profligacy . . . has not proven an effective long-run electoral strategy" (p. 113).

REFERENCES

Barzel, Yoram. 1969. "Two Propositions on the Optimum Level of Producing Collective Goods." *Public Choice* 6 (Spring): 31–37.

Besley, Timothy, and Stephen Coate. 2003. "Centralized versus Decentralized Provision of Local Public Goods: A Political Economy Approach." *Journal of Public Economics* 87: 2611–2637.

Bird, Richard M., and Almos Tassonyi. 2003. "Constraining Subnational Behavior in Canada: Different Approaches, Similar Results?" In Jonathan A. Rodden, Gunnar S. Eskelund, and Jennie Litvack (eds.), *Fiscal Decentralization and the Challenge of Hard Budget Constraints* (pp. 85–132). Cambridge, MA: MIT Press.

Boadway, Robin, and Frank Flatters. 1982. "Efficiency and Equalization Payments in a Federal System of Government: A Synthesis and Extension of Recent Results." *Canadian Journal of Economics* 14 (November): 613–633.

Bradford, David F., and Wallace E. Oates. 1974. "Suburban Exploitation of Central Cities and Governmental Structure." In H. Hochman and G. Peterson (eds.),

Redistribution through Public Choice (pp. 43–90). New York: Columbia University Press.

Breton, Albert, and Pierre Salmon. 2007. "Francc: Forces Shaping Centralization and Decentralization in Environmental Policymaking." In Albert Breton et al. (eds.), *Environmental Governance and Decentralization*. Cheltenham, UK: Edward Elgan (pp. 457–494).

Brueckner, Jan K. 2004. "Fiscal Decentralization with Distortionary Taxation: Tiebout vs. Tax Competition." *International Tax and Public Finance* 11: 133–153.

Buchanan, James, and Richard Wagner. 1970. "An Efficiency Basis for Federal Fiscal Equalization." In Julius Margolis (ed.), *The Analysis of Public Output* (pp. 139–158) New York: Columbia University Press.

Cremer, Jacques, Antonio Estache, and Paul Seabright. 1996. "Decentralizing Public Services: What Can We Learn from the Theory of the Firm?" *Revue d'Economie Politique* 106 (Jan.–Feb.): 37–60.

Dinan, Terry M., Maureen L. Cropper, and Paul R. Portney. 1999. "Environmental Federalism: Welfare Losses from Uniform National Drinking Water Standards." In *Environmental and Public Economics* (pp. 13–31). Cheltenham, UK: Edward Elgar.

Fischel, William A. 2001. The Homevoter Hypothesis. Cambridge, MA: Harvard University Press.

Flatters, Frank, J. Vernon Henderson, and Peter Mieszkowski. 1974. "Public Goods, Efficiency, and Regional Fiscal Equalization." *Journal of Public Economics* 3: 99–112.

Franco, Daniele, Fabrizio Balassone, and Maura Francese. 2003. "Fiscal Policy in Europe: The Role of Fiscal Rules." *National Tax Association Proceedings, Ninety-Fifth Annual Conference, 2002* (pp. 7–17). Washington, DC: National Tax Association.

Gamkhar, Shama. 2002. *Federal Intergovernmental Grants and the States: Managing Devolution*. Cheltenham, UK: Edward Elgar.

Goodspeed, Timothy J. 2002. "Bailouts in a Federation." *International Tax and Public Finance* 9: 409–421.

Inman, Robert P. 1988. "Federal Assistance and Local Services in the United States: The Evolution of a New Federalist Fiscal Order." In Harvey Rosen (ed.), *Fiscal Federalism: Quantitative Studies* (pp. 33–74). Chicago: University of Chicago Press.

Inman, Robert P. 2003. "Transfers and Bailouts: Enforcing Local Fiscal Discipline with Lessons from U.S. Federalism." In J. Rodden et al. (eds.), *Fiscal Decentralization and the Challenge of Hard Budget Constraints* (pp. 35–83). Cambridge, MA: MIT Press.

Janeba, Eckhard, and John D. Wilson. 2005. "Decentralization and International Tax Competition." *Journal of Public Economics* 89: 1211–1229.

Kornai, Janos. 1979. "Resource-Constrained Versus Demand-Constrained Systems." *Econometrica* 47 (4): 801–819.

Kornai, Janos. 1979. 1980. *Economics of Shortage*. Amsterdam: North-Holland.

Kornai, Janos, Eric Maskin, and Gerard Roland. 2003. "Understanding the Soft Budget Constraint." *Journal of Economic Literature* 41 (December): 1095–1136.

Lockwood, Ben. 1999. "Inter-Regional Insurance." *Journal of Public Economics* 72 (April): 1–37.

Lockwood, Ben. 2002. "Distributive Politics and the Costs of Centralization." *Review of Economic Studies* 69: 313–337.

McKinnon, Ronald I. 1997. "Market-Preserving Federalism in the American Monetary Union." In M. Blejer and T. Ter-Minassian (eds.), *Macroeconomic Dimensions of Public Finance: Essays in Honor of Vito Tanzi* (pp. 73–93). London: Routledge.

McKinnon, Ronald I., and Thomas Nechyba. 1997. "Competition in Federal Systems: The Role Of Political and Financial Constraints." In John Ferejohn and Barry R. Weingast (eds.), *The New Federalism: Can the States be Trusted?* (pp. 3–61) Stanford: Hoover Institution Press.

McLure, Charles. 1967. "The Interstate Exporting of State and Local Taxes: Estimates for 1962." *National Tax Journal* 20 (March): 49–77.

McLure, Charles. 1969. "The Inter-Regional Incidence of General Regional Taxes." *Public Finance* 24: 457–483.

Oates, Wallace E. 1972. *Fiscal Federalism.* New York: Harcourt Brace Jovanovich.

Oates, Wallace E. 1996. "Estimating the Demand for Public Goods: The Collective Choice and Contingent Valuation Approaches." In D. Bjornstad and J. Kahn (eds.), *The Contingent Valuation of Environmental Resources* (pp. 211–230). Aldershot, UK: Edward Elgar.

Oates, Wallace E. 1997. "On the Welfare Gains from Fiscal Decentralization." *Journal of Public Finance and Public Choice* 2/3: 83–92.

Oates, Wallace E. 2002. "The Arsenic Rule: A Case for Decentralized Standard Setting? *Resources* 147 (Spring): 16–18.

Oates, Wallace E. 2004. "Fiscal Structure in the Federal System." In J. Richard Aronson and Eli Schwartz (eds.), *Management Policies in Local Government Finance* (5th ed., pp. 39–60). Washington, DC: International City/County Management Association.

Oates, Wallace E. 2005. "Toward a Second-Generation Theory of Fiscal Federalism." *International Tax and Public Finance* 12 (August): 349–374.

Oates, Wallace E. 2006. "The Many Faces of the Tiebout Model." In William A. Fischel (ed.), *The Tiebout Model at Fifty* (pp. 21–45). Cambridge, MA: Lincoln Institute of Land Policy.

Padovano, Fabio. 2007. *The Politics and Economics of Regional Transfers: Decentralization, Interregional Redistribution, and Income Convergence.* Cheltenham, UK: Edward Elgar.

Qian, Yingyi, and Gerard Roland. 1998. "Federalism and the Soft Budget Constraint." *American Economic Review* 88 (December): 1143–1162.

Qian, Yingyi, and Barry R. Weingast. 1997. "Federalism as a Commitment to Preserving Market Incentives." *Journal of Economic Perspectives* 11 (Fall): 83–92.

Prud'homme, Remy. 1995. "The Dangers of Decentralization." *World Bank Research Observer* 10: 201–220.

Rodden, Jonathan A., Gunnar S. Eskeland, and Jennie Litvack. 2003. *Fiscal Decentralization and the Challenge of Hard Budget Constraints.* Cambridge, MA: MIT Press.

Rubinfeld, Daniel L. 1987. "The Economics of the Local Public Sector." In Alan Auerbach and Martin Feldstein (eds.), *Handbook of Public Economics* (*Vol. 2*, pp. 571–645). Amsterdam: North Holland.

Seabright, Paul. 1996. "Accountability and Decentralization in Government: An Incomplete Contracts Model." *European Economic Review* 40: 61–89.

Tanzi, Vito. 1996. "Fiscal Federalism and Decentralization: A Review of Some Efficiency and Macroeconomic Aspects." In *Annual World Bank Conference on Development Economics, 1995*. Washington, DC: World Bank.

Tiebout, Charles M. 1956. "A Pure Theory of Local Expenditures." *Journal of Political Economy* 64 (October): 416–424.

U.S. Congressional Budget Office. 1997. *Federalism and Environmental Protection: Case Studies for Drinking Water and Ground-Level Ozone*. Washington, DC: U.S. Government Printing Office.

Weingast, Barry R. 1995. "The Economic Role of Political Institutions: Market-Preserving Federalism and Economic Development." *Journal of Law, Economics and Organization* 11 (April): 1–31.

Weingast, Barry R. 2005. "The Performance and Stability of Federalism: An Institutional Perspective" In Claude Menard and Mary Shirley. (eds.), *Handbook of the New Institutional Economics*. Dordrecht, The Netherlands: Springer-Verlag (pp. 149–198).

Wildasin, David E. 1997. "Externalities and Bailouts: Hard and Soft Budget Constraints in Intergovernmental Fiscal Relations." Unpublished paper.

Wildasin, David E. 2004. "The Institutions of Federalism: Toward and Analytical Framework." *National Tax Journal* 57 (June): 247–272.

CHAPTER **5**

Comment 1

CHARLES E. MCLURE, JR.

Wallace Oates has provided an extremely useful summary and update of many aspects of the theory and practice of fiscal decentralization. I will discuss three issues that Oates does not cover: tax exporting, tax assignment, and the impact of public employee unions. The first two topics, although crucial to the analysis of fiscal decentralization, are somewhat esoteric, and are often misunderstood, even by specialists in public finance. The last has important implications for Oates's analysis that should not be ignored.

1. Tax Exporting

As Oates notes, tax exporting is justifiably viewed as generally undesirable. Unless the exported tax reflects benefits of public services—an oft-neglected qualification—tax exporting is unfair, it distorts the tax prices residents of subnational jurisdictions pay for public services, and it may lead to excessive provision of such services. Tax exporting is, however, probably less common than many believe, and its primary source may not be generally recognized.

Deductibility. The deduction for state and local income (or sales) and property taxes in calculating federal income tax liability implies that nonresidents, in effect, pay a substantial fraction of these taxes. Forty years ago I estimated that deductibility was, by far, the most important source of tax exporting in the United States (see McLure, 1967), and I suspect that it still is. That deductibility, which is easily fixed, may encourage overexpansion of state and local government is, of course, an indictment of deductibility, not of decentralization.[1]

Property tax. Whether property taxes are exported raises a key methodological choice, that between the old and new views of the incidence of the tax. Is the primary distributional effect of the tax to reduce the return to capital (new view), some of which may be owned by nonresidents, or are property taxes borne primarily by local consumers, renters, labor, and owners of factors that cannot move, such as land and natural resources (old view)? (For more on these issues, see Mieszkowski, 1972; Aaron, 1975; McLure, 1977; and Zodrow, 2008.)

While the new view is useful in appraising the incidence across income classes of the national "system" of property taxes, only the old view is relevant for the question of overexpansion of the public sector caused by tax exporting. Moreover, similar analysis is generally appropriate for appraising the incidence and exporting of production taxes, sales taxes on business inputs, and corporation income taxes levied by state and local governments.

Production taxes. A state production tax (e.g., a severance tax on oil, gas, or coal) cannot be exported to out-of-state purchasers just because the taxed product is exported; it depends on whether the taxing state dominates the relevant market. (It may also depend on the presence of long-term contracts with pass-through provisions.) This simple economic verity was often overlooked during the energy crisis of the 1970s and probably will be again.

Sales taxes and excises. Sales taxes and excises levied by state and local governments on sales to consumers are not likely to be paid in significant amounts by nonresidents, except for tourists, business travelers, commuters, and cross-border shoppers. Exporting to the first three groups may not be problematic, because these groups consume public services provided by the taxing jurisdictions, although perhaps less than residents. Cross-border shopping between states probably causes problematic tax exporting only where major metropolitan areas straddle state lines. By comparison, exporting of local sales taxes to cross-border shoppers can be quite problematic, especially where big box retailers and auto malls draw customers from other localities (and tax revenue is not assigned to localities where automobiles are registered). This—along with the inherent difficulty of applying local sales taxes to remote sales—suggests that local governments should not levy sales taxes where there are viable alternatives such as local individual income taxes.

The retail sales taxes levied by U.S. states and localities and by Canadian provinces apply to substantial amounts of sales to business. Since market dominance is rare in today's globalized world, this production-related component of the sales tax is unlikely to be exported to nonresident purchasers of the goods and services produced with the taxed business inputs.

Corporate income taxes. The corporate income taxes levied by the U.S. states and Canadian provinces all rely on formulas to divide the nationwide income of the taxpayer among the taxing jurisdictions. Formula apportionment converts these levies to taxes on whatever factors are used to apportion income, commonly payroll, property, and sales in the U.S. and payroll and sales in Canada (see McLure, 1980). The portions of the tax attributable to in-state labor and to sales are unlikely to be exported, for reasons just outlined. Like the property tax, some of the part attributable to property may be exported. With the U.S. shift toward placing greater (or sole) weight on the sales factor that has occurred over the last quarter century, state corporate income taxes have probably become somewhat less likely to be exported.

2. Tax Assignment

The tax assignment problem is usefully described as "Who (which level of government) should tax what, and how?" Unfortunately, too much literature asks only "Who should tax what?" and fails to ask "and how?" "How" can be answered at a general level or, as explained in McLure (2000), in detail for specific taxes. If "How" is not answered satisfactorily—or inherently cannot be, as in the case of local sales taxes—"Who should tax what" may need to be reconsidered. On the other hand, if, in practice, "Who should tax what" is answered badly, exemplified by state corporation income taxes, "How" may become very important.

State taxes, surcharges, tax sharing, and revenue sharing. States can legislate and administer their own taxes, rely on surcharges on the federal tax base, receive a share of federal revenue from a particular tax that is returned to its state of origin, or share in a pool of federal revenues. State taxes and surcharges give individual states the power to set tax rates—by far the most important attribute of tax assignment, as it determines how much spending can be financed. By comparison, under tax sharing and revenue sharing, individual state governments cannot determine tax rates, which are chosen by the federal government (or by all states acting collectively). Thus both tax sharing and revenue sharing are best seen as a form of federal grant, and both may nurture attitudes that lead to a soft budget constraint.

State taxes and surcharges differ in the degree of state autonomy over the tax base and administration. A surcharge levied on a uniform tax base, like tax sharing, avoids gaps and overlaps in taxation, but entails loss of state fiscal sovereignty. Harmonization of state tax bases and administration, which can be more or less complete, provides the benefits of uniformity to a lesser degree, while retaining greater state sovereignty. Centralized administration avoids unnecessary costs of compliance and administration, but runs the risk in some countries that the central government will not disburse state revenues, belying the impression that these are truly state funds.

"Market-preserving federalism" provides incentives for state governments to adopt policies that are consistent with free markets and thus encourages good economic performance (see Weingast, 1995). State taxes, surcharges, and tax sharing may all be consistent with market-preserving federalism, as a state's revenue depends on its economic performance. By comparison, under revenue sharing the amount of revenues a particular state receives depends on the performance of all states, not just its own—or it may depend negatively on it.

3. Public Sector Unions

A discussion of the implications of public sector unions is notably absent from Oates's otherwise excellent paper. He could have reasonably overlooked the widespread unionization of these employees in 1972, when it was still a relatively new phenomenon, but unionization now raises issues that can no longer be ignored.

The effects of public sector unions resemble those of private sector unions in some respects, but there are also important differences (see Freeman, 1986; Gunderson, 2005). Based on conventional analysis of the effects of collective bargaining, one might expect unionization of the public sector to result in excessive wages or overly generous fringe benefits and under-provision of public services. If the demand for public services is price inelastic, expenditures on salaries of public sector employees would be higher and we would pay more to get less.[2]

In the private sector, union demands may be tempered by competition in the product market—a force that is strengthened by globalization; excessive demands may cause the employer to go bankrupt, shut down plants, or relocate. By comparison, demands of public sector unions are unlikely to cause governments to go bankrupt or shut down most activities, much less relocate. There is no foreign competition, although there may be competition from the private sector for the supply of some services, for example, by contracting out. Public officials may have less incentive to resist union demands than their private sector counterparts, although tax competition—and the threat that taxpayers will leave if they are not getting what they pay for—may help hold spending down.

Unionization may also affect productivity, but evidence on this score is inconclusive. Gunderson (2005) notes:

> Clearly more empirical work is merited to determine the productivity of public sector inputs and how that productivity is affected by different forms of employee voice including unionization. It is particularly important to link that determination to alternative forms of market structure for the delivery of public sector services, given the growing tendency towards privatization, deregulation, outsourcing, competition in public service delivery, and the provision of public services through private sector delivery agencies. (p. 404)

Freeman and Medoff (1979) argue that unions do more than bargain collectively; they also provide "voice" for their members. While some aspects of voice may be negative for society, as well as for employers (e.g., fostering excessively adversarial relations and inhibiting beneficial turnover), some may be positive (e.g., enhancing morale and loyalty). Gunderson (2005) emphasizes that voice may have two faces, what we might call voice in the workplace and voice in the political arena, and indicates why political voice can be expected to be more important in the public sector than in the private sector.

The political activities of public sector unions—so-called public interest advertising and lobbying (for tax increases and deductibility, as well for particular spending programs), campaign contributions to governors and legislators, etc.—shift the demand curve for unionized labor, making it virtually certain that expenditures on public sector salaries are greater than in the absence of unionization.[3] Gunderson (2005, p. 395) notes, "There are also reasons to believe that union voice in the public sector is likely to take on a more muscle-type bargaining face than the positive communication face. That is, the union voice function in the public sector takes on a cloak that is closer to the monopoly face of unions in the private sector."[4] In some countries (e.g., Argentina) this has aggravated the problem of soft budget constraints.

Unionization of public sector employees potentially has implications for many aspects of the theory and practice of fiscal decentralization. It may affect the allocation of resources between the private and public sectors and within the latter. It may adversely affect public sector (and thus private sector) productivity. It may create or aggravate soft budget constraints. Tax competition may place a damper on the negative effects of unionization, or those negative effects may occur despite the highly touted disciplinary effects of Tiebout competition, undermining the economic performance of a state.

Finally, this analysis emphasizes the importance of the distinction between public *production* of services and public *provision* of services (with production occurring in the private sector). The problem described here is much greater for public production than for public provision of services and creates a presumption in favor of the latter.

NOTES

1. Of course, deductibility is also questionable on equity grounds, as it is available only to those who itemize and depends on the taxpayer's marginal tax rate. The risk that ending deductibility would create confiscatory taxation is easily addressed by allowing a deduction for federal income tax in calculating liability for state and local income taxes—a result analogous to what occurs automatically for sales taxes.
2. See Freeman (1986, pp. 51–52) for reasons that public sector demand for union labor may not be inelastic. He also notes, however, that the early empirical literature on the relation between unionization and compensation may understate the effect of unionization and that, as in the private sector, unions may have a greater impact on fringe benefits than on wages. Gunderson (2005) surveys evidence on these effects.
3. Freeman (1986, p. 44) hypothesizes that, "public sector unions seek to shift demand for labor rather then simply to raise wages, so that their effects are as much on employment and total budget as on wages." While I was Deputy Assistant Secretary of the Treasury, representatives of state and local governments, especially those from high-tax states, and unions of government employees strongly opposed the Treasury Department proposal to eliminate the federal income tax deduction of state and local taxes (see McLure, 1986).
4. The two faces of unions (collective bargaining and voice) cannot conveniently be pigeon-holed. Arguing that the primary explanation for the growth of public sector unions has been the legislation and executive orders that have made such unions legal, Freeman (1986, pp. 45–49) surmises that the "[g]eneral lack of management opposition to public sector unionism" is "possibly due to the political power of unions."

REFERENCES

Aaron, Henry J. 1975. *Who Pays the Property Tax?* Washington: Brookings Institution.

Freeman, Richard B. 1986. "Unionism Comes to the Public Sector." *Journal of Economic Literature*, 24(1): 41–86.

Freeman, Richard B., and James Medoff. 1979. "The Two Faces of Unionism." *Public Interest* 7(April): 69–93.

Gunderson, Morley. 2005. "Two Faces of Union Voice in the Public Sector." *Journal of Labor Research* 26(3): 393–413.

McLure, Charles E., Jr. 1967. "The Interstate Exporting of State and Local Taxes: Estimates for 1962." *National Tax Journal* 20(1): 49–77.

McLure, Charles E., Jr. 1977. "The 'New View' of the Property Tax: A Caveat." *National Tax Journal* 30 (March): 69–75.

McLure, Charles E., Jr. 1980. "The State Corporate Income Tax: Lambs in Wolves' Clothing." In Henry J. Aaron and Michael J. Boskin (ed.), *The Economics of Taxation* (pp. 327–346). Washington: The Brookings Institution.

McLure, Charles E., Jr. 1986. "Tax Competition: Is What's Good for the Private Goose also Good for the Public Gander?" *National Tax Journal* 39(3): 341–348.

McLure, Charles E., Jr. 2000. "Tax Assignment and Subnational Fiscal Autonomy." *Bulletin for International Fiscal Documentation* 54(12): 626–635.

Mieszkowski, Peter. 1972. "The Property Tax: An Excise Tax or a Profits Tax?" *Journal of Public Economics* 1 (April): 73–96.

Weingast, Barry R. 1995. "The Economic Role of Political Institutions: Market-Preserving Federalism and Economic Development." *Journal of Law, Economics and Organization* 11 (April): 1–31.

Zodrow, George R. 2008. "Property Taxation." *New Palgrave Dictionary of Economics* (2nd ed.). New York: Palgrave/Macmillan.

CHAPTER 5

Comment 2

The Old Time Fiscal Federalism Religion—Is It Good Enough for Me (and Thee)?

HARVEY S. ROSEN

1. Introduction

In his chapter "On the Theory and Practice of Fiscal Decentralization," Wallace Oates provides an authoritative survey of developments in the theory of fiscal federalism since the early 1970s. The chapter focuses on recent challenges that have arisen to some theories that were commonly accepted several decades ago, particularly with respect to the desirability of decentralizing fiscal responsibilities in a federal system of government. As well as being lucid and well-argued, this essay is also gracious: much of the received wisdom that has been critiqued in recent years is due to Oates himself, yet the chapter contains not the slightest hint of defensiveness either in tone or substance. Rather, Oates bends over backward to put the newer research in the best light possible. In this note I argue that he may have bent over a bit too far. In many ways, the older literature on fiscal federalism provides a better framework for thinking about the pros and cons of fiscal decentralization.

2. The Old Time Religion

The traditional theory of fiscal federalism argues that fiscal decentralization can improve the allocation of resources in the public sector. In his opening paragraph, Oates provides a cogent summary of the argument, which is worth quoting in full:

> Regional or local governments are in a position to adapt outputs of public services to the preferences and particular circumstances of their constituencies, as compared to a central solution that presumes one size fits all. [Moreover], in a setting of mobile households, individuals can seek out

> jurisdictions that provide outputs well suited to their tastes, thereby increasing the potential gains from the decentralized provision of public services . . . [Finally], decentralization may encourage experimentation and innovation as individual jurisdictions are free to adopt new approaches to public policy; in this way, decentralization can provide a valuable "laboratory" for fiscal experiments.

The argument is attractive, particularly to economists, who are used to the notion that, for most commodities, decentralized decision making can lead to efficient outcomes. The exceptions to this rule and the associated possibilities for market failure are, of course, well-known. Nevertheless, the presumption in mainstream economics is that decentralized markets are the best mechanism for allocating resources, and the argument that it can be extended to the public sector (where feasible) resonates strongly.

3. Challenges to the Orthodoxy

Nevertheless, as Oates notes, "this basic economic rationale for decentralization of the public sector is not quite so simple and compelling as it appears. . . . some new approaches [to fiscal decentralization] reveal its dark side, especially in practice." What are the causes for this ominous sounding warning? Oates brings up a variety of challenges to the traditional view; here I would like to focus on three. First is externalities. The behavior of one jurisdiction can affect the welfare of another jurisdiction in a way that is external to the market. Depending on how property rights are assigned, this may lead to a suboptimal allocation of resources. There is not much to say on this except that exactly the same phenomenon is present in the analysis of private goods, and the main result is the same: The resulting allocation of resources may be inefficient, and under certain circumstances, the government can implement a variety of policies that could improve the allocation. In the fiscal federalism context, the central government would play this role.

Second is the assumption that the central government tends to provide a uniform level of the public good across all jurisdictions. This is bound to be inefficient, because both preferences and costs of provision differ across jurisdictions. As Oates observes, this gives rise to a natural query: Why can't the government figure out the efficient level of the public good for each jurisdiction, and provide each jurisdiction with just the right amount? The traditional response is that the central government doesn't have the information to know the preferences and costs in every jurisdiction, and even if it did, political constraints prevent it from treating different jurisdictions differently. However, challengers to the orthodox view are more insistent that these problems can be overcome. As Oates states,

> But even at a more formal level, there is really nothing, in principle, to prevent the central government from obtaining the needed information on local cost functions and preferences (albeit costly to gather such information) and then to provide the Pareto-efficient level of output in each jurisdiction. In fact, central government responsibility for local public goods does not, in practice, rule out such sensitivity to local conditions. . . . [A]n outcome that is decentralized in spirit can, in principle, emerge from a structure of government with little in the way of real local autonomy. . . . The problem of centralized versus decentralized provision can become much more complex when centralized outcomes are characterized in a more thoughtful way. (section 1)

This issue of information and the costs of obtaining it leads to a third general concern that might weaken the traditional case: "The recognition that asymmetric information, incomplete contacts, and the associated agency costs manifest themselves in public- as well as private-sector institutions has opened up a whole new perspective on fiscal decentralization" (section 3). Although these information phenomena raise a host of issues, Oates focuses particularly on the problem of soft budget constraints at the subfederal level. In this case, the central government may have less information about the fiscal situation of the subfederal jurisdiction; consequently, subfederal jurisdictions may spend more than the efficient level, believing that the central government will bail them out in the event of a fiscal crisis. However, it should be pointed out that some strains in the new fiscal federalism literature allow for the possibility that the central government can obtain excellent information about the situation at the local level and act upon it (see the discussion above about the tastes for and costs of local public good provision), while others (such as the soft budget constraint literature) make the diametrically opposed assumption.

4. Evaluating the Challenges

Are the challenges compelling? The question is not whether the conclusions of the new literature logically follow from the assumptions. Rather, one must ask whether the new view provides a better guide to thinking about the division of responsibilities between the central and local governments than the orthodox view. Let's start with the notion that the central government can obtain all the information that the subfederal government has, and then can use it to make efficient decisions with respect to local public good provision (and presumably other choices, such as local tax structure and regulatory policy as well). The argument strikes me as being more than a bit reminiscent of an old idea in the history of economic thought: Oskar Lange's theory of market socialism.[1] Lange argued that a centrally planned economy can be as efficient, or even more efficient, than a decentralized market economy. The key is for government central planners to use the price system to mimic a market economy. The planners announce prices to the managers of government enterprises, who then maximize profits conditional on these prices. If the prices do not clear the market, this information goes back up to the planners, who announce a new set of prices. The process continues until equilibrium is obtained.

Neither policy makers nor academic economists talk much about this kind of idea anymore. They realize that, in practice, the informational requirements for central planning are too enormous, and the incentives to get the information and act on it appropriately are too weak, for such a scheme to work. In addition, the theory of market socialism does not account for the importance of innovation, and the necessity of providing an environment in which risk-taking can be rewarded. (I return to the topic of innovation in the provision of publicly provided goods and services later.) I think that the story is pretty much the same when it comes to a central government deciding how local governments should run their jurisdictions; both the information and incentives to do it correctly are missing.

Is there any evidence to back up this view? I think that even though Oates does not make the connection, some evidence on the competence of the central government in this context is provided by his discussion of federal grants policy. As is well-known, in the presence of positive externalities across jurisdictions, Pigouvian subsidies for the externality-producing activities can enhance efficiency. Surely a central government that could efficiently plan the entire structure of subfederal public finance could get the (relatively) simple task of implementing Pigouvian subsidies right. But to the contrary, Oates notes, "Studies in the United States suggest that where such transfers presumably have a role in internalizing interjurisdictional spillover effects, they have not done so very effectively" (section 3). He cites research documenting that U.S. federal grants to state and local governments have enhanced neither efficiency nor equity and mentions no evidence to the contrary. Of course, this does not prove that the subfederal governments are more efficient at organizing their public sectors than the federal government would be. But looking at the experience with externalities gives one no confidence that the presumption of the orthodox view—that both informational and incentive issues favor decentralization—is to be taken lightly.

The subject of externalities is closely linked to another issue that is prominent in critiques of the orthodox view of fiscal federalism. This is the notion that competition among jurisdictions does not lead to efficient amounts of spending at the subfederal level. Rather, it leads to a "race to the bottom," in which subfederal levels of government, for example, cut their fiscal activities below the efficient levels in order to attract businesses to locate there. It is extremely difficult to document in any definitive way whether states and localities are in fact racing their way to the bottom. But a few very simple calculations would perhaps provide a reality check. Between 1980 and 2004, the gross domestic product (GDP) increased by a factor of 4.20. During the same period, state and local government tax receipts increased by more, a factor of 4.55.[2] Presumably, one of the major externality-producing expenditure functions is education; between fiscal year 1979 and fiscal year 2002, these expenditures increased by a factor of 4.66.[3] I emphasize again that such calculations are no substitute for a careful empirical analysis, but the figures do suggest that if there is a race to the bottom going on, someone may have turned the sign pointing to the finish line in the wrong direction.

Finally, I would like to turn to two problematic issues for the new approach to decentralization on which Oates is basically silent. As he noted in the passage I quoted at the beginning, one of the key tenets of the orthodox view is that decentralization encourages experimentation and innovation in the design of public policy. As Supreme Court Justice Louis Brandeis famously observed, "It is one of the happy incidents of the Federal system that a single courageous state may, if its citizens choose, serve as a laboratory, and try moral, social and economic experiments without risk to the rest of the country."[4] Indeed, just as many economists now view innovation as one of the key benefits of a market system (and one of the main reasons why proposals such as market socialism are bound to fail), many students of public finance view state and local experimentation with social policy as one of the key benefits of fiscal decentralization. From all appearances, Brandeis's laboratories are busily at work. For example, as the nation grapples with the extremely difficult policy issues surrounding health care, all eyes will be on

Massachusetts, which recently enacted a set of policies designed to achieve universal health insurance coverage. It is noteworthy that Oates's discussion of the new federalism contains no citations to papers that attempt to show, either theoretically or empirically, that one could expect a centralized system of local public good provision to lead to more or better experimentation than a decentralized system. My own limited experience working for the federal government suggests that, aside from pork barrel "demonstration projects," it is practically impossible for the federal government to attempt meaningful policy experiments at the state and local level.

The other noteworthy silence relates to the use (or lack thereof) of the new approach to fiscal federalism as a framework for estimating empirically the gains to decentralization. As Oates writes, the proof of the traditional decentralization theorem "provides a straightforward algorithm . . . for determining the magnitude of the welfare gains from decentralization." Oates devotes the entire second section of his chapter to issues that arise in implementing this algorithm, focusing in particular on a paper that he published in 1974 with David Bradford, whose memory we honor with this volume. In typically modest fashion, Oates carefully lists all the problems with the assumptions that he and Bradford had to make in order to implement the algorithm. But the key point is that the orthodox theory does provide a usable framework for empirical analysis. Now, scholars who study methodological issues debate whether theory, in order to be deemed valuable, needs to be amenable for use as a structure for applied work of one kind of another. Without opining on this issue, I merely note that Oates cites no example where the new federalism literature has been used as a framework to do an actual calculation of the benefits (or costs) of decentralization in any context. Apparently, the models are too complicated and/or the informational requirements are too burdensome to be useful in this way.

5. Conclusion

As part of his critique of some of the assumptions that underlie the traditional approach to fiscal federalism, Oates states, "[W]e must think carefully about the settings in which we apply these models" (p. 7). It is certainly a fair comment, but it applies to the critiques of the traditional work as well. And viewed through this lens, the traditional method that he pioneered compares very well indeed to the new approaches to federalism.

NOTES

1. Oskar Lange, *On the Economic Theory of Socialism,* University of Minnesota Press, 1938.
2. Calculations based on *Economic Report of the President 2006,* Washington, DC: United States Government Printing Office (pp. 280, 382).
3. Calculations based on *Economic Report of the President 2006,* p. 383.
4. *New State Ice Co. v. Liebman,* 285 U.S. 262 (1932).

CHAPTER 6

Dividends and Taxes

ROGER GORDON

MARTIN DIETZ

Our objective in this chapter is to provide an overview of the existing debate about the behavioral and efficiency effects of taxes on dividends. The tax treatment of dividends differs widely across countries and has changed dramatically since 2001 in the United States.

In order to be in a position to assess how dividend taxes affect behavior and efficiency, we first need to provide an explanation for why firms pay dividends, in spite of their unfavorable tax treatment. Certainly firms need to provide a payoff to their equity holders. But providing this return through dividends has in the past subjected their shareholders to higher tax liabilities than they would face if the funds, for example, were used instead to repurchase shares in the firm, reinvested in productive assets, or used to acquire other firms, in each case generating income for shareholders that is taxable as capital gains. Section 1 briefly describes this longstanding dividend puzzle.[1]

There are a variety of explanations proposed in the tax and finance literature for dividend payments. Here we describe and compare in a simplified setting the two most commonly used theories. The "new view," summarized in section 2, assumes that firms are not allowed to repurchase shares or to acquire shares in other firms, so that dividends are the only feasible way to pay out profits to shareholders. The signaling model, summarized in section 3, argues that managers choose to pay out profits in order to signal to investors that the firm has more than enough cash on hand, and so is doing well. Having a more costly signal, such as dividends, may be attractive since equilibrium signals will be smaller.

In section 4, we summarize the economic forecasts of the two theories for firm behavior, and compare these forecasts with patterns clearly seen in the data. While both theories forecast dividend payments, they vary in the consistency of their other implications with the data.

We then explore the implications of each theory for the efficiency and distributional effects of dividend taxes. Here, the new view forecasts no behavioral effects or efficiency costs of dividend taxes, at least when imposed on firms currently paying dividends.[2] The tax simply reduces share values. In the signaling model, dividend taxes also have no efficiency consequences when imposed on firms that both pay dividends and repurchase shares.[3] Firms do respond to the tax by changing the mixture of their payouts, doing so to leave the effective cost of a signal unchanged. In this theory, share prices remain unchanged, or can even increase for firms that gain from having available a more costly signal.

Neither theory, as it stands, is consistent with all of the evidence available to date about patterns of dividend payout behavior. Of the two theories, though, the signaling model is consistent with a broader range of the evidence. However, even this theory cannot explain why firms might simultaneously issue new shares and pay dividends, why so many firms neither issue dividends nor new shares, why dividend payout rates are so stable, why share prices seem to fall in response to increases in the dividend tax rate, or why patterns of share repurchase are so different from patterns of dividend payouts. If a theory for dividends cannot explain the full range of dividend behavior we see, it is premature to say anything with confidence about the efficiency and distributional effects of a tax on dividends.

1. Initial Model of the Dividend Puzzle

In order to make clear the nature of the dividend puzzle and in the process define notation for the subsequent discussion, consider the after-tax return received by an investor in corporate equity:[4]

$$R_t = (1-m)\frac{D_{t+1}}{V_t} + (1-z)\left(\frac{V_{t+1} - V_{t+1}^N}{V_t} - 1\right) \tag{6.1}$$

Here, R_t denotes the after-tax return per dollar invested in equity; m is the personal income tax rate on dividend income, D_{t+1}; z is the "effective" tax rate on accruing capital gains; V_t is the value of the individual's equity holdings at date t; while V_{t+1}^N is the amount of new issues of equity (or repurchases if negative) during the period. Throughout, we assume that $m>z$, since capital gains have commonly faced a lower statutory tax rate, and these taxes are deferred until realization and avoided entirely if the shares are held until death.[5]

Let ρ denote the net-of-tax rate of return that the investor can get elsewhere.[6] Since bonds are the obvious alternative outlet for savings, let $\rho = r(1-t)$, where r is the market interest rate and t is the statutory tax rate on interest income.[7] The value of the firm then adjusts each period so that equity earns a return equal to that available elsewhere, implying that $R_t = \rho$. Therefore,

$$\left(1+\frac{\rho}{1-z}\right)V_t = \left(\frac{1-m}{1-z}\right)D_{t+1} + V_{t+1} - V_{t+1}^N \tag{6.2}$$

Substituting for successive values of V_{t+1} and using the standard transversality condition, we find that

$$V_t = \sum_{i=1}^{\infty} d^i \left[\left(\frac{1-m}{1-z}\right)D_{t+i} - V_{t+i}^N\right] \tag{6.3}$$

where $d = 1/(1+\rho/(1-z))$. The presumed objective of the firm at each date is to maximize the current share value. It does so subject to the cash flow constraint

$$(1-\tau)\pi_t(L_t,\ K_t) + V_i^N = D_t + I_t, \tag{6.4}$$

where $K_{t+1} = K_t + I_t$.

Here π_t denotes the after-tax profits at date t, τ is the corporate tax rate, K_t denotes the firm's capital stock, L_t equals the labor supply (taken to be exogenous), while I_t denotes new investment at date t.[8] The available choices for the firm include D_t, I_t, and V_t^N. The one constraint is that dividends must be nonnegative.

The tax effects on capital accumulation are summarized in the shadow price of capital:

$$q_t = \sum_{i=1}^{\infty} d^i \frac{(1-\tau)(1-m)}{1-z}\pi_i'. \tag{6.5}$$

Here, q_t measures the market value of the after-tax present value of the return on a marginal investment, so corresponds to Tobin's q. In equilibrium, investors are willing to invest an extra dollar in the firm only if the after-tax returns they get, in present value, equal a dollar.

Consider then the effects on current share values of an increase in dividends by a dollar in some period $t + k$, financed by an increase in new share issues by a dollar in that period. Equation (6.3) then implies that share values change by

$$d^k\left(\frac{1-m}{1-z} - 1\right) \tag{6.6}$$

This expression is negative whenever $m > z$. As a result, a manager can increase firm value by simultaneously cutting dividends and cutting new share issues or increasing share repurchases.[9] In the process, income taxed at rate m is replaced by income taxed at rate z, so that the shareholder gains with no offsetting costs to the firm. The only equilibrium is one with no dividend payments. Of course, the dividend tax then collects no revenue, but also generates no excess burden since repurchases, taxes aside, are a perfect substitute for dividends for both the firm and its shareholders.

The trouble with this model is that dividends are clearly nonzero in the data, and most firms pay dividends.[10] This is the dividend puzzle.

Of course, any model solving the dividend puzzle must explain the use of dividends, in spite of these tax incentives. In addition, there are a number of other obvious stylized facts or strongly confirmed empirical results that should be consistent with the forecasts from a model. Among these are:

Stability of dividends: Dividend payments by a firm tend to be very stable over time, much more so than firm profits (see Lintner, 1956). Some firms, though, do not pay any dividends.

Occasional new share issues: New share issues occur occasionally both among firms that do not pay dividends and among firms that do pay dividends.

Share repurchases: Share repurchases are increasingly common, though repurchases by a given firm are highly volatile over time.[11]

Response to tax: Dividend payout rates increase when the tax rate on dividends falls.[12]

Mergers and acquisitions: Mergers and acquisitions are very common but do not seem to respond to the dividend tax rate.[13]

2. New View

Probably the most commonly cited explanation for dividend payments in the public finance literature is known as the "new view."[14] The key difference of the new view model from the model in section 1 is the additional constraint that $V_t^N \geq 0$, ruling out repurchase of shares or acquisition of shares in other firms. Repurchase of shares has been legally barred in the United Kingdom.[15] In the United States, if repurchases occur on a periodic basis and in proportion to each shareholder's initial holdings then the resulting capital gains will be treated as a dividend for tax purposes by the IRS. While this legal restriction alone is not really sufficient to justify the constraint that $V_t^N \geq 0$, at the time the new view was developed repurchases in the United States were sufficiently small that this assumption was broadly consistent with the data.[16]

How do results change when this constraint is added to the prior model? Equation (6.6) still measures the change in firm value if dividends and new share issues are increased simultaneously, and this expression remains negative. We therefore conclude that dividends and new share issues cannot both be positive simultaneously. At least one of these variables must equal zero.

This result creates three different potential regimes.

(1) If $D_t = V_t^N = 0$, then the firm simply retains and invests all earnings.
(2) If $V_t^N > 0$ but $D_t = 0$, then $q_t = 1$.
(3) If $V_t^N = 0$ but $D_t > 0$, then in equilibrium $q_t = (1-m)/(1-z)$ or equivalently,

$$1 = \sum_{i=1}^{\infty} d^i (1-\tau)\pi'_i. \tag{6.7}$$

Now the marginal investment is being financed through a dollar no longer paid as dividends, so costs the shareholders $(1-m)/(1-z)$, yet still provides a return of q_t.

In this model, what are the effects of an increase in the tax rate m on the investment rate and on economic efficiency? Until 2001, the tax rates on dividends and interest income were equal, so they changed together. We will now examine two policy changes: one in which both tax rates increase together, and one in which just the dividend tax rate changes.[17] In each case, the impact of a tax change on firm behavior and on economic efficiency varies depending on the regime a firm is in. We focus on steady-state situations to simplify the algebra.

As long as the firm is in regime (1), behavior and economic efficiency cannot be affected by a dividend tax. Firms would not normally remain in regime (1) in steady state, so we focus on the other two regimes.

For firms in regime (3), as seen from equation (6.7), the tax rate m does not affect the equilibrium capital stock. If only m changes, then the equilibrium capital stock is left unaffected. We then infer from the firm's cash flow constraint that dividends do not change either. The only effect is on firm values. Any effects on efficiency then arise solely from the general equilibrium effects caused by the wealth redistribution, analogous with the results reported in Auerbach and Kotlikoff (1983).

The tax rate t enters implicitly in equation (6.7), however, since $d^{-1} = 1 + r(1-t)/(1-z)$. If t and m increase together, then equation (6.7) implies that the equilibrium capital stock increases, since the alternative asset is now less attractive. Dividends then fall temporarily, to finance the additional investment.

In general, the efficiency implications of this increase in investment are unclear.[18] As emphasized in Bradford (1975), the efficiency implications of the extra investment per se depends on what else was foregone in order to finance the additional investment. If the financing comes from extra savings, then the additional investment creates an efficiency gain as long as $\pi' > \rho$. If the financing comes from a drop in investment in some other sector, then the answer depends on the difference in the equilibrium pre-tax returns in the two sectors. For example, if the funds would otherwise have been invested abroad, earning a pretax return of r, then there is an efficiency gain only if $\pi' > r$. In steady state, equation (6.7) implies that

$$\pi' = \frac{r(1-t)}{(1-z)(1-\tau)} \qquad (6.8)$$

implying that $\pi' > \rho$. However, $\pi' > r$ if and only if $\tau + z(1-\tau) > t$ (i.e., only if corporate income had been taxed more heavily than interest income).

What happens in regime (2)? In a steady state, in which the capital/labor ratio remains unchanged at the value satisfying equation (6.5), equation (6.5) implies that

$$\pi' = \frac{\rho}{(1-m)(1-\tau)}. \qquad (6.9)$$

If just the dividend tax rate increases, then the required rate of return on capital goes up and the equilibrium capital stock falls. If $t = m$ and both tax rates increase together, then investment is unchanged *if* the interest rate is unchanged. What happens to the domestic interest rate depends on whether the economy is open or closed. For a small open economy, r should remain unchanged, and then so should investment.

What happens to economic efficiency as a result? The same complications as before enter. If the economy is open, then investment is unchanged when m and t both increase, but savings fall, implying an efficiency loss since $\rho < r$.

How successful is this model in explaining the stylized facts? The model of course was designed to explain the existence of dividends, and to explain why not all firms pay dividends. The response of dividend payments to variations in the dividend tax is also consistent with the model if all past tax changes have involved simultaneous changes in both t and m, since an increase in t results in an increase in investment and a fall in dividends.[19]

The model is not consistent with the other facts, however:

Stability of dividends: For firms in regime (3) that pay dividends, dividends are a residual: $D_t = \pi_t - I_t$. Given how volatile profits are, and the bunched time pattern for new investment,[20] dividends should be highly volatile, inconsistent with their stable pattern.

Occasional new share issues: Firms in regime (1) issue new shares and pay no dividends, but the model cannot explain why firms might both issue new shares *and* pay dividends.

Share repurchases: Of course, the model assumes repurchases cannot occur.[21]

Mergers and acquisitions: If $q < 1$ in equilibrium, then it becomes cheaper for a firm to buy new capital through acquiring a firm that already owns this capital than to buy the new capital directly. The higher is m relative to z, the stronger this tax incentive. If mergers involve no real cost, then the equilibrium has $q = 1$, and so no dividend payments. If mergers are costly, they should still respond strongly to m, contrary to the evidence.

3. Signaling Model for Dividends

The second model focuses on the use of dividends to signal to investors the true value of the firm. There are several papers modeling the use of dividends as a signal of firm profits;[22] we build our discussion on the model by Miller and Rock (1985).

To capture a signaling explanation for dividends, we alter the basic model in several ways. Enough complications are added that we chose to simplify by restricting the model to two periods, so that the resulting initial value of the firm to shareholders equals

$$V_0 = E\sum_{i=1}^{2} d^i \frac{1-m}{1-z} D_i - d(EV_1^N - EV_1^R) + d^2 E(K_2 + (1-\tau)\pi(K_2) - D_2),$$

where the expectations, denoted by E, are taken as of time 0.

To generate the incentives for signaling requires a number of key changes to the initial model. First, outside investors cannot fully monitor the firm. In particular, assume that all that outside investors can observe is the industry and any dividend payments, share repurchases, or new share issues on the public exchanges undertaken by the firm.[23] Let their unconditional expected profits at date 1 be denoted by $\bar{\pi}_1$, so that the true profits π_1, satisfy $\pi_1 = \bar{\pi}_1 + \tilde{\epsilon}_1$. The manager observes $\tilde{\epsilon}_1$ while outside investors can only try to infer its value, based on the observable behavior of the firm. Assume in addition that $E(\tilde{\epsilon}_2|\tilde{\epsilon}_1) = \lambda\tilde{\epsilon}_1$, so that the manager also knows more than outside investors about profits in the second period.

Second, we assume that $\tilde{\epsilon}_i$ is uncorrelated with any movements in the market, so that investors impose no risk premium for bearing this risk. We also assume that the manager is risk neutral, so ignore an offsetting incentive for the manager to underinvest due to being more risk-averse at the margin than outside investors.

Third, we assume that the manager determines the size of the dividends D_1, investment, I_1, share repurchases, V^R, or new share issues, V^N.[24,25] In contrast with the new view model, we impose no constraint on share repurchases, forcing the model to come up with some other explanation for dividends.

Fourth, we assume that the manager cares about the current share price as well as the true value of the firm. In particular, assume that the manager initially owns $n + s$ shares out of a total of N shares. Of these, the manager plans to hold n shares until the firm liquidates, but to sell s shares in period 1 at the market-clearing price p, after the firm announces any dividends and any plans to buy or sell shares but before these measures take place. The manager's objective is then to maximize

$$sp + \frac{n}{N}\frac{1-m}{1-z}D_1 + \frac{n}{N^R}dV_2^{true}, \tag{6.10}$$

where N^R is the number of shares left after repurchases. Maximization is subject to the cash flow constraint $D_1 + I_1 + V^R = (1 - \tau)\ (\bar{\pi}_1 + \tilde{\epsilon}_1) + V^N$.

Fifth, we assume that the manager fixes *ex ante* the fraction of payouts that take the form of dividends versus share repurchases, and then chooses *ex post* (once profits are revealed) the total payouts.[26] In particular, for each dollar of overall payouts, we assume that β dollars are dividends and $(1 - \beta)$ dollars are used to repurchase shares.[27]

Finally, if the firm chooses to issue new shares, we assume that the firm must file a prospectus through an investment banker, listing a given number of shares for sale on the market at a given price. This prospectus should in itself reveal information to the market about the state of the firm. Optimistically, we assume that the prospectus per se reveals $\tilde{\epsilon}_1$.[28] That the firm's current profits are low enough to induce it to issue new shares is bad news from the perspective of the market, consistent with the empirical evidence in Ibbotson (1975) and Eckbo and Masulis (1995) that share prices fall on the announcement of a new share issue.

Issuing such a prospectus is costly, however. Assume that the costs are C, reducing the amount of retained earnings available for investment by this amount.

3.1. *Signaling by Firms with Sufficient Internal Funds*

Consider first the decisions of a firm that has sufficient internal funds so that it chooses not to pay these fixed costs, implying $V^N = 0$. The market price per share of the firm cum dividend in period 1, after the announcement that P dollars will be spent in total on dividends and share repurchases, equals

$$p = \frac{1}{N}\frac{1 - m}{1 - z}\beta P + \frac{1}{N^R} dE(V_2^{true}|P). \tag{6.11}$$

Since the only information known by the manager and not known by the market is $\tilde{\epsilon}_1$, there is an implicit function

$$EV_2(\tilde{\epsilon}_1, P) = E(V_2^{true}|P)$$

The manager's first-order condition for the optimal dividend payout rate, after some simplification, then equals:

$$(1 - \tau)\pi'_2 = \frac{\rho}{1 - z} - \frac{m - z}{1 - z}\beta d^{-1} + \left(1 - \frac{n}{s + n}\frac{N}{N^R}\right)\frac{\partial EV_2}{\partial \tilde{\epsilon}_1}\frac{\partial \tilde{\epsilon}_1}{\partial P}. \tag{6.12}$$

In equilibrium, the firm uses existing profits to finance either new investment or a combination of dividends and share repurchases until at the margin both options are equally attractive. The gross return to more new investment is measured by the left-hand side of equation (6.12). The net benefits from paying out the funds instead are measured by the three terms on the right-hand side. The first measures the return that can be earned on these funds elsewhere. The second measures the tax cost of the payouts that take the form of dividends, while the last measures the signaling benefit of payouts arising from the induced capital gain on shares.

If there were no informational effects of the payouts, then the last term equals zero, so that the remaining terms describe the payout rate that maximizes share values, for any given β. Consistent with the data, and consistent with the model (as shown below), shareholders will infer that firms that can afford larger payouts must have a larger $\tilde{\epsilon}_1$. The resulting increase in EV_2 and in p benefits the manager directly, by returning a higher price for any shares he or she sells in period 1. However, the higher p also means that the funds used to repurchase shares in period 1 result in fewer shares being repurchased, so that the manager receives a smaller share of the firm's value in period 2. As a result, the sign of the expression in parentheses is ambiguous in general, though for purposes of discussion we presume it is positive.

If the expression in parentheses is positive, then this last term raises the required rate of return, reducing the capital stock below the level that maximizes share values based on full information. The weight on this last term, and so the size of this effect, is smaller the lower is N^R. Therefore, firms with a larger $\tilde{\epsilon}_1$, who then pay out more funds leading to a lower N^R, also invest more.[29] For firms that pay out more funds, moreover EV_2 is higher not only because the inferred value of $\tilde{\epsilon}_2$ is higher but also because the inferred capital stock is higher.

3.2. Corporate Financial Behavior by Firms Issuing New Equity

For firms that choose to issue new shares, we assumed that the prospectus reveals $\tilde{\epsilon}_1$, so that the manager then chooses how many new shares to issue (and how much to invest) to maximize firm value. For these firms,

$$\pi'_2(1-\tau) = \frac{\rho}{1-z}. \tag{6.13}$$

These firms will use all available funds to finance investment, neither paying dividends nor repurchasing shares. Dividends have a clear tax cost, while with symmetric information there no longer is any signaling benefit from share repurchases.

3.3. Market Equilibrium

Given their fixed cost, the minimum size of new issues is at least equal to C. In addition, the return provided by the increased capital stock has to cover not only the cost of capital, but also the fixed costs. Thus, the amount of capital invested has to jump discretely for marginal firms. Marginal firms that are indifferent to issuing new shares or not but choose not to issue new shares must then have

$$\pi_2'(1-\tau) > \frac{\rho}{1-z}. \tag{6.13a}$$

This marginal firm trades off the fixed cost C of issuing shares with the benefits of raising the capital stock to the level satisfying equation (6.13).

Given their fixed cost, the minimum size of new issues is at least equal to C, so that firms that choose not to issue shares end up with a capital stock that is smaller by an amount at least equal to C. Given the tax disadvantage of dividends and given that they are the lowest quality type among the dividend paying firms, the Pareto-dominating signaling equilibrium would then have these marginal firms pay no dividends and repurchase no shares.

In general, there are multiple signaling equilibria among dividend payers. If there were pooling at some level of dividends, (e.g., zero dividends), then there must be a discrete jump in dividends for firms with $\tilde{\epsilon}_1$ slightly above the range of $\tilde{\epsilon}_1$'s that pool. Otherwise, firms with an $\tilde{\epsilon}_1$ just below the upper bound of $\tilde{\epsilon}_1$'s that pool will prefer to increase their payouts slightly, resulting in negligible costs but a discrete jump in firm value. If there are no gaps in the distribution of dividend payout rates, then there can be no pooling. In that case, all other firms with higher $\tilde{\epsilon}_1$ than this marginal firm would pay positive dividends determined by equation (6.12).

We also assume that the value of β prevailing in the market equilibrium is the value that maximizes *ex ante* share values, before managers observe $\tilde{\epsilon}_1$. With a lower β (a smaller fraction paid out as dividends), payouts are cheaper given the tax disadvantage of dividends. However, the equilibrium payout rate will be higher, leading to yet more underinvestment. The optimal β trades off these two offsetting effects, generating the optimal cost of a signal, subject to the constraint that dividends must be nonnegative.[30] If the optimal cost of a signal is above the cost of paying dividends, then there should be dividends but no share repurchases. For a somewhat lower optimal cost, we would see a mixture of dividends and share repurchases, while for a low enough optimal cost of a signal we would see only repurchases being used. The equilibrium β can then vary by industry.

How do the above results change if the manager also owns stock options? Those holding an option do not receive any dividends but do benefit from the capital gains that result from share repurchases. This reduces the benefits of payouts, for any given β. It also lowers the value of β that maximizes the *ex ante* utility of managers.

To what degree is this model consistent with the various stylized facts laid out in section 1? The model is consistent with some firms paying dividends and others not (those that issue new equity). Unless there is a pooling equilibrium at zero dividends for some range of firms, there would be no firms that neither pay dividends nor issue new shares.

This model implies more stable dividends than under the new view, since higher $\tilde{\epsilon}_1$ leads to more investment, even with an unchanged profitability of future investment. Firms that signal their quality move away from a first best investment rule, see equation (6.12), where higher quality firms invest more despite the fact that they have assumed that there are no differences in productivity.

Also, some firms in the model do issue new shares. However, according to the model, we should never see such firms also paying dividends.

The model is easily consistent with firms paying both dividends and repurchasing shares. The two payouts should move together, however, contrary to the data suggesting that repurchases are much more volatile. The size of repurchases relative to dividends should grow as managerial compensation shifts toward options and away from stock compensation. The model also is easily consistent with the dividend payout rate falling as the tax rate on dividends increases. Finally, the model has no direct implications for the rate of mergers and acquisitions.

What then does the model imply about the efficiency effects of a tax on dividends? Here, our results correspond to those in Bernheim (1991). According to the model, there is an optimal cost of a signal. If firms can achieve this cost with $0 < \beta < 1$, then they can continue to achieve this cost for a higher tax rate on dividends, by decreasing β appropriately, leading to a drop in the dividend payout rate, an offsetting increase in repurchases, and no other real effects. In particular, the net cost of the signal, the overall payout rate, tax payments, and share values are all unchanged. At the margin, the dividend tax has no real effects.

When the optimal cost of a signal is higher than the cost of paying dividends, however, then firms would not repurchase shares and signal solely with dividends. In this case, raising the tax rate on dividends moves the cost of a signal closer to the value that maximizes *ex ante* share values, and raises revenue as well! In response to the higher dividend tax rate, share values should rise and investment should increase.

The optimal tax rate on dividends should then be high enough that all dividend-paying firms also repurchase shares. Any higher tax rate has no real effects.

4. Discussion

How successful are each of these models in explaining the list of stylized facts described in section 1? Clearly both models were designed to forecast dividend payments, and both can explain why only some firms pay dividends.[31]

Table 6.1 summarizes how each of the models does in explaining the stylized facts laid out in section 1. One clear observation from the data is that a firm's dividend payout rate is very stable over time. The new view model, in which dividends change dollar for dollar with any fluctuations in profits,

Table 6.1. Forecasts versus Data

	New View	Signaling	Data
D stable	No	Somewhat	Yes
V^N and D	No	No	Possible
V^R and D	No	Probable	Possible
$\partial D/\partial m$	$= 0$	< 0	< 0
$\partial I/\partial m$	$= 0$ existing	$\geq$ existing	??
	< 0 new	> 0 new	
∂(efficiency) $/\partial m$	$= 0$	> 0	??
$\partial V/\partial m$	< 0	> 0	< 0?

yields forecasts sharply different from what is seen in the data. In the signaling model, dividends vary less than dollar for dollar with profits, since some of the extra profits in equilibrium are retained to finance extra investment, though it is still hard to reconcile the stable dividend payouts often seen in the data with a model that forecasts that each period's dividend helps signal new information about that period's profits.

The second stylized fact is that new share issues occur, sometimes in conjunction with dividend payments. Both models can generate new share issues; however, in both models, if a firm issues new shares it would not simultaneously pay dividends.

The data also show that many firms both pay dividends and repurchase shares. The new view model rules out share repurchases by assumption, though Auerbach and Hassett (2003) describe an extension in which some share repurchases can occur. In the signaling model, the optimal signal often consists of a combination of dividends and share repurchases, though whether or not this is true can vary by industry.

Another well-documented observation is that the dividend payout rate falls when the dividend tax rate increases. The signaling model is certainly consistent with this observation. The new view model forecasts no effects of a permanent increase just in the dividend tax rate. However, the new view would still forecast a fall in the dividend payout rate in response to an increase in the tax rate on other financial income and in response to a transitory increase in the dividend tax rate. Past changes in U.S. dividend tax rates have always been combined with changes in tax rates on other financial income and were inevitably viewed to be transitory changes.

As seen from the summary in Table 6.1, neither model is entirely consistent with the range of behavior clearly seen in the data. The signaling model comes closer, since it can readily explain the use of share repurchases as well as dividends, and generates somewhat more stable dividend payout rates. In principle it can explain why a group of firms might neither pay dividends nor issue new shares, if there were a pooling equilibrium for some firms at zero dividend payments and a separating equilibrium among firms that have positive dividend payments. However, the signaling model cannot explain simultaneous new share issues and dividend payments, or the volatility of share repurchases compared with the very stable observed dividend payout rates.

The two models also have very different forecasts for the effects of a dividend tax on corporate investment rates. According to the new view, a permanent increase in the dividend tax rate has no effect on investment in existing firms, though it discourages entry of new firms.[32] In the signaling model, however, the dividend payout rate falls and the extra retained earnings generate extra real investment among existing firms.[33] Note that the sign of this effect is directly contrary to the traditional view that an increase in the dividend tax rate should reduce investment. In contrast with the traditional model, new firm entry is encouraged according to the signaling model, since the cost of any future signals either remains unchanged or shifts closer to its optimal level. Past empirical studies of taxes and investment provide only limited evidence for *any* effects of taxes on investment, and these past results are certainly not adequate at this point to say anything about the effects of a change in the dividend tax rate per se on investment.

The two models differ in their forecasts for the effects of an increase in the dividend tax rate on firm values. According to the new view, the *only* effect of a permanent increase in the dividend tax rate is a reduction in firm values. In contrast, the signaling model forecasts that an increase in the dividend tax rate has no effect on the share value of firms that both pay dividends and repurchase shares, while it should increase the share values of firms that are not repurchasing shares but do pay (or anticipate paying) dividends. Providing evidence of the effects of a dividend tax increase on share values requires some care, since it means identifying the specific date at which the market learns about a possible increase in the tax rate. Auerbach and Hassett (2006) attempt to identify such dates for the 2003 cut in the dividend tax rate, and find that share values did increase in response, consistent with the new view model, but inconsistent with a signaling model.[34] Clouding this result is the fact that the change in the dividend tax was linked to many other tax changes.

The choice of model has important consequences for forecasts of the efficiency effects of changes in the dividend tax rate. In the new view model, a permanent change in the dividend tax rate has no real effects on behavior among existing firms, so there are no first-order efficiency consequences there, although it does discourage entry of new firms. The signaling model implies that increasing the dividend tax rate leaves entirely unaffected firms that are both paying dividends and repurchasing shares, but shifts the cost of a signal closer to its optimal value in firms that are paying dividends but not repurchasing shares (and in the process raising efficiency). The tax also encourages entry to the extent that entering firms expect to benefit from having a higher cost signal at some point in the future, further raising efficiency.

These sharply different forecasts from the two models for the efficiency effects of a dividend tax make it valuable for empirical work in public finance to focus on tests that help differentiate among these models. Certainly, the past literature includes evidence beyond the stylized facts listed in section 1, although these papers did not focus in particular on testing among these various models.

Bernheim and Wantz (1995), for example, document that share prices respond more strongly to announced changes in the dividend payout rate during years when the dividend tax rate is higher. This pattern is consistent with a signaling model, since the level of dividend payouts falls in response to a higher dividend tax rate, but the range of underlying share values being signaled remains unchanged. It is harder to see how to reconcile the new view model with this evidence.

The recent articles by Chetty and Saez (2005) and Brown et al. (forthcoming) both document that the cut in the U.S. dividend tax rate in 2003 induced a larger increase in the dividend payout rate in firms where managers owned more shares, and a smaller response where managers owned more options. While the new view model forecasts that the dividend payout rate should increase in response to a temporary fall in the dividend tax rate, it does not forecast a differential increase depending on the compensation scheme of the manager. These observations are readily consistent with a signaling model, where the manager decides on the payout rate, since that choice depends on the manager's incentives.

Finally, consider the evidence reported in Gordon and Bradford (1980) that the estimated market value of higher expected dividend payouts, as judged by the degree to which equilibrium expected share appreciation is lower to offset the higher expected dividends, is cyclical: dividends are valued more highly during boom periods and less during recessions. The estimated values are considerably higher than $(1 - m) / (1 - z)$ during booms and considerably lower than $(1 - m) / (1 - z)$ during recessions. This evidence is certainly inconsistent with the forecasts from the new view model, where the market value of a dollar of extra dividends should always be equivalent to $(1 - m) / (1 - z)$ in expected capital gains.

The signaling model may have some chance to explain the Gordon and Bradford estimates, since in this model dividends are stochastic. Following convention, the estimation procedure used in Gordon and Bradford assigned a risk premium to shares based on the covariance of the *ex post* capital gain on a share with that on the market, implicitly assuming that dividends are risk free. Yet if dividends are stochastic, the risk premium should instead be based on the covariance of the *ex post* overall return on a firm's equity with the overall return on the market portfolio (adjusting for taxes). By ignoring the possibility that dividends are stochastic, the resulting misspecification forces a reinterpretation of the coefficients. If the resulting bias to the coefficient on expected dividends were positive during boom periods and negative during recessions, then a signaling model could be consistent with the reported evidence.

These other sources of evidence on dividend behavior therefore seem largely consistent with the signaling model, while they cannot readily be reconciled with the new view model. The one exception is the apparent response of share prices to announced changes in the dividend tax rate, which is consistent with the new view but inconsistent with a signaling model.

On net, it appears that the signaling model is consistent with some of the evidence, but cannot readily explain why firms might simultaneously issue new shares and pay dividends, why so many firms neither pay dividends nor issue new shares, why dividend payout rates are so stable, why share prices seem to fall when dividend tax rates are increased, or why patterns of share repurchase are so different from patterns of dividend payouts. The new view model is consistent with some firms neither paying dividends nor issuing new shares and with a fall in share prices when the dividend tax rate is increased, but is otherwise yet more inconsistent with the past evidence. In particular, under the new view made, forecasted dividend payout rates are particularly unstable, repurchases should not exist, dividend payout rates should not respond so consistently to tax rates, share prices should not respond to dividend announcements nor should the size of this response depend on the size of the dividend tax or the state of the business cycle, and mergers and acquisitions should be strongly encouraged by the dividend tax.

Given the many differences between the forecasts from either model with patterns clearly seen in the data, it seems inappropriate to rely on either model as they currently stand to make forecasts regarding other aspects of behavior such as investment rates or, more generally, the efficiency and distributional effects of a dividend tax.

NOTES

We would very much like to thank Alan Auerbach, George Zodrow, William Andrews, and the other participants of the "Key Issues in Public Finance" conference for comments on an earlier draft. Dietz thanks the Fritz-Thyssen-Stiftung for financial support.

1. For an earlier statement of the dividend puzzle, see Black (1976).
2. Dividend taxes discourage entry of new firms, however.
3. Dividend taxes, though, can aid firms that pay dividends but do not repurchase shares, since these firms can gain from having available a more costly signal.
4. Our notation is largely conventional, and in particular is drawn from Poterba and Summers (1985).
5. To justify this description of capital gains taxes, we can assume that the individual will sell the shares at a random date, based on events unrelated to the *ex post* return on the shares (e.g., consumption needs). To the degree to which shareholders respond to tax incentives by realizing capital losses quickly and deferring the realization of capital gains, the effective capital gains tax rate is reduced further, and may not even by positive. See Constantinides (1983) or Stiglitz (1983).
6. For simplicity, we assume that all shareholders have the same opportunity cost, ρ.
7. Until recently, in the United States the tax rates on dividends and interest were equal, in which case $m = t$.
8. To simplify notation, we ignore depreciation. Allowing for depreciation introduces standard extra terms, with no change in the qualitative results.
9. Another alternative is to use the funds freed by a cut in dividends to buy shares in another firm. The formal derivation would be entirely unchanged.
10. Recently, the number of firms paying dividends has fallen while the total amounts paid out to investors has roughly stayed constant. See Fama and French (2001) and DeAngelo, DeAngelo, and Skinner (2004).
11. In the United States, the importance of share repurchases has been increasing since the mid-1980s. Nowadays, dividends and share repurchases are of roughly equal size in aggregate. See Grullon and Michaely (2002).
12. This empirical result has been documented many times. See, e.g., Poterba (2004), Chetty and Saez (2005), and Brown, Liang, and Weisbenner (forthcoming).
13. See, e.g., Auerbach and Reishus (1988).
14. This model was derived independently by King (1977), Auerbach (1979), and Bradford (1981).
15. Acquisition of shares in other firms remained possible, however.
16. Acquisitions, though, have always been an important use of firm funds.
17. In 2001, both m and t fell, but m fell by more.
18. Of course, any tax change affects behavior throughout the economy. We focus solely on the efficiency effects of the resulting changes in dividend and investment behavior.

19. If the increase in m is temporary, dividends would also drop even if t is left unchanged.
20. See Doms and Dunne (1998) for evidence on the time pattern of new investment for a firm.
21. Auerbach and Hassett (2003) develop a hybrid model that allows for a limited amount of repurchases.
22. See, e.g., Bhattacharya (1979), Miller and Rock (1985), Williams (1988), Bernheim (1991), and Bernheim and Redding (2001).
23. We do assume below that when new shares are issued, further information is revealed.
24. Note the change in notation from the prior model. In the signaling model, it is useful to distinguish explicitly between new share issues and share repurchases.
25. We further assume that the manager and the board of directors have the same information and the same incentives, so do not distinguish between them.
26. With this assumption, there is a one-dimensional signal *ex post* that is sufficient in itself to reveal information about a one-dimensional unobserved variable: profits. *Ex ante,* however, the firm chooses the optimal form of the signal.
27. This assumption raises the question of whether the IRS will classify the share repurchases as dividends for tax purposes. We assume here that the firm can manipulate the timing of share repurchases to avoid this.
28. Clearly a prospectus reveals some information. Our assumption that it reveals all relevant information is an extreme one. If the prospectus instead does not reveal anything directly about $\tilde{\epsilon}_1$, this information could still be inferred by the size of the new share issue, see Krasker (1986). Qualitative results therefore do not change. However, the resulting investment incentives change, since issuing more shares affects the equilibrium price paid in the latter case but not the former.
29. Firms with higher profits repurchase more shares, so that any further increase in share price brought on by yet more repurchases is particularly costly, since this price increase applies to more shares. Finding repurchases increasingly costly, firms with higher profits will also invest more.
30. See Bernheim (1991) for a more formal exploration of the optimal cost of such a signal.
31. In the signaling model, at least in a separating equilibrium, firms can either pay dividends or issue new shares but only one firm does neither.
32. In addition, firms are smaller at entry due to the tax. See, e.g., Sinn (1991) and Dietz (2005).
33. More specifically, in a signaling model investment should increase in firms that pay only dividends and not change in firms that both pay dividends and repurchase shares.
34. They also report that share values increased particularly among firms not currently paying dividends. They rationalize this result by pointing out that equation (6.3) implies that the present value of dividends is a higher fraction of firm value to the extent that the present value of new share issues (minus share repurchases) is larger.

REFERENCES

Auerbach, Alan J. 1979. "Wealth Maximization and the Cost of Capital." *Quarterly Journal of Economics* 93: 433–446.

Auerbach, Alan J., and Kevin A. Hassett. 2003. "On the Marginal Source of Investment Funds." *Journal of Public Economics* 87: 205–232.

Auerbach, Alan J., and Kevin A. Hassett. 2006. "The 2003 Dividend Tax Cuts and the Value of the Firm: An Event Study." In edited by Alan J. Auerbach, James R. Hines, and Joel Slemrod (eds.), *Taxing Corporate Income in the 21st Century*. Cambridge: Cambridge University Press.

Auerbach, Alan J., and Laurence J. Kotlikoff. 1983. "National Savings, Economic Welfare, and the Structure of Taxation." In Martin S. Feldstein (ed.), *Behavioral Simulation Methods in Tax Policy Analysis*. (pp. 459–498). Chicago: University of Chicago Press.

Auerbach, Alan, and David Reishus. 1988. "Taxes and the Merger Decision." In John Coffee, Louis Lowenstein, and Susan Rose-Ackerman (eds.), *Knights, Raiders and Targets* (pp. 300–313). Oxford: Oxford University Press.

Bernheim, B. Douglas. 1991. "Tax Policy and the Dividend Policy." *RAND Journal of Economics* 22: 455–476.

Bernheim, B. Douglas, and Lee S. Redding. 2001. "Optimal Money Burning: Theory and Application to Corporate Dividends." *Journal of Economics & Management Strategy* 10: 463–507.

Bernheim, B. Douglas, and Adam Wantz. 1995. "A Tax-Based Test of the Dividend Signaling Hypothesis." *American Economic Review* 85: 532–551.

Bhattacharya, Sudipto. 1979. "Imperfect Information, Dividend Policy, and 'the Bird in the Hand' Fallacy." *Bell Journal of Economics* 10: 259–270.

Black, Fischer. 1976. "The Dividend Puzzle." *Journal of Portfolio Management* 2: 5–8.

Bradford, David F. 1975. "Constraints on Government Investment Opportunities and the Choice of Discount Rate." *American Economic Review* 65: 887–899.

Bradford, David F. 1981. "The Incidence and Allocation Effects of a Tax on Corporate Distributions." *Journal of Public Economics* 15: 1–22.

Brown, Jeffrey R., Nellie Liang, and Scott Weisbenner. forthcoming. "Executive Financial Incentives and Payout Policy: Evidence from the 2003 Dividend Tax Cut." *Journal of Finance*.

Chetty, Raj, and Emmanuel Saez. 2005. "Dividend Taxes and Corporate Behavior: Evidence from the 2003 Dividend Tax Cut." *Quarterly Journal of Economics* 120: 791–833.

Constantinides, George. 1983. "Capital Market Equilibrium with Personal Tax." *Econometrica* 51: 611–636.

DeAngelo, Harry, Linda DeAngelo, and Douglas J. Skinner. 2004. "Are Dividends Disappearing? Dividend Concentration and the Consolidation of Earnings." *Journal of Financial Economics* 72: 425–456.

Dietz, Martin D. 2005. "Dividend and Capital Gains Taxation in a Cross-Section of Firms." Mimeo.

Doms, Mark, and Timothy Dunne. 1998. "Capital Adjustment Pattern in Manufacturing Plants." *Review of Economic Dynamics* 1: 409–429.

Eckbo, B. Espen, and Ronald W. Masulis. 1995. "Seasoned Equity Offerings: A Survey." In Robert A. Jarrow, Vojislav Maksimovic, and William B. Ziemba (eds.), *Handbooks in Operations Research and Management Science* (vol. 9, pp. 1017–1072). Amsterdam: North Holland.

Fama, Eugene F, and Kenneth R. French. 2001. "Disappearing Dividends: Changing Firm Characteristics or Lower Propensity to Pay?" *Journal of Financial Economics* 60: 3–43.

Gordon, Roger H., and David F. Bradford. 1980. "Taxation and the Stock Market Valuation of Capital Gains and Dividends: Theory and Empirical Results." *Journal of Public Economics* 14: 109–136.

Grullon, Gustavo, and Roni Michaely. 2002. "Dividends, Share Repurchases, and the Substitution Hypothesis." *Journal of Finance* 57: 1649–1684.

Ibbotson, Roger. 1975. "Price Performance of Common Stock New Issues." *Journal of Financial Economics* 2: 235–272.

King, Mervyn. 1977. *Public Policy and the Corporation.* London: Chapman and Hall.

Krasker, William S. 1986. "Stock Price Movements in Response to Stock Issues under Asymmetric Information." *Journal of Finance* 41: 93–105.

Lintner, John. 1956. "Distribution of Income of Corporations among Dividends, Retained Earnings, and Taxes." *American Economic Review, Papers and Proceedings* 46: 97–113.

Miller, Merton H., and Kevin Rock. 1985. "Dividend Policy under Asymmetric Information." *Journal of Finance* 40: 1031–1051.

Poterba, James. 2004. "Taxation and Corporate Payout Policy." *American Economic Review, Papers and Proceedings* 94: 171–175.

Poterba, James M., and Lawrence H. Summers. 1985. "The Economic Effects of Dividend Taxation." In Edward Altman and Marti Subrahmanyam (eds.), *Recent Advances in Corporate Finance* (pp. 227–284). Homewoood, IL: Richard D. Irwin.

Sinn, Hans Werner. 1991. "The Vanishing Harberger Triangle." *Journal of Public Economics* 45: 271–300.

Stiglitz, Joseph. 1983. "Some Aspects of the Taxation of Capital Gains." *Journal of Public Economics* 21: 257–294.

Williams, Joseph. 1988. "Efficient Signalling with Dividends, Investment, and Share Repurchases." *Journal of Finance* 43: 737–747.

CHAPTER 6

Comment 1

WILLIAM D. ANDREWS

1. Introduction

Gordon and Dietz begin their chapter by stating that in order to solve the "dividend puzzle" they must determine "why firms pay dividends, in spite of their unfavorable tax treatment." To do this, they introduce the "new view" model and the signaling model as "the two most commonly used theories" for explaining dividend payments. They compare each theory's predictions with various "stylized facts" about dividend behavior, and conclude that while neither model explains everything, "the signaling model is consistent with a broader range of the evidence."

Their comparison is misconceived because these two theories are functionally quite different from one another. The signaling model is indeed a behavioral theory about what corporate management and directors are trying to do when they set dividend policy. Taxation is only one factor in the equations. The model is sufficient to yield predictions of dividend behavior by which it can be tested.

The new view, by contrast, says nothing about why corporations pay dividends. It only says that the tax treatment of dividends is less generally unfavorable than the traditional view would have it. More specifically, it asserts that *if* all a corporation's distributions, present and future, *were* subject to tax at the same effective rate as present dividends, then there *would be* no bias against present dividends. The reason is that accumulation would then only defer the dividend tax and extend it to earnings on the deferred amount. This is important, but it does not produce any prediction of dividend behavior unless we have some idea of what that behavior would have been in the absence of tax, which the new view does not provide.

Ignoring this fundamental difference, Gordon and Dietz have erroneously attributed absurd behavioral predictions to the new view. I will here discuss only two: (1) that the new view forecasts dividends to be highly variable, when in fact they are remarkably stable; and (2) that the new view forecasts an absence of share repurchases, when in fact they are now quite common.

2. The Stability of Dividends

As Gordon and Dietz report, "[d]ividend payments by a firm tend to be very stable over time, much more so than firm profits." Individual dividend-paying corporations rarely reduce dividends from what they were the year before, and increases are guarded and modest. But, they say, under the new view "For firms... that pay dividends, dividends are a residual: $D_t = \pi_t - I_t$. Given how volatile profits are, and the bunched time pattern for new investment, dividends should be highly volatile, inconsistent with their stable pattern." This statement is simply wrong; the new view makes no such absurd prediction. Several reasons for these assertions are as follows.

First, the new view only deals with the distorting effect of taxes on dividend and investment behavior. If the directors have reasons to try to make dividends stable, that will require paying out a different portion of variable profits from year to year, and since all the distributions involved are taxable dividends the new view asserts that dividend taxes will neither impede nor subsidize such stabilization. So the only prediction supported by the new view is that dividends will be as stable or variable as the directors, for nontax reasons, want them to be.

Second, the assertion that dividends are a residual seems to mean that somehow profits and investment will be independently determined and then dividends will be ascertained by simple subtraction. But the equation $D_t = \pi_t - I_t$ does not prove or even express that idea very well. The equation is mathematically equivalent to $I_t = \pi_t - D_t$, which would suggest that investment is the residual. The equation looks like an oversimplified version of a standard cash flow constraint, which is usually interpreted as meaning that total uses of funds—dividends and investment—must equal total sources—in this case, profits—without specifying which item or items will be adjusted to maintain the equation.[1]

Third, even if the equation were accepted as determining dividends, it does not support a prediction of great variability, because variations in investment are not independent of variations in profit. To see why, consider what exactly must be included in investment. Gordon and Dietz refer to "the bunched time pattern for new investment," which suggests that they are thinking of the purchase of business capital assets. But if I_t were only capital equipment, then the equation is manifestly false since it fails to take account of changes in working capital, nonbusiness investments, and all the myriad of other things in which accumulated profits may be stored.

Moreover, if I_t meant the gross cost of capital equipment, then the equation cannot be true without a deduction for debt. It is common business practice to borrow a substantial portion of the cost of capital expenditures, repaying the loan over some part of the useful life of the acquired asset, in order to offset much of the "bunched time pattern" of such expenditures.

In short, to make the equation true, I_t must be defined comprehensively to mean total net increase in shareholder equity, which in the case under discussion is simply undistributed profit ($I_t = \pi_t - D_t$). If an item of income is accrued, the corresponding account receivable must be taken into account as part of investment. So variations in profit are not independent of fluctuations in investment. Instead variations in profit will automatically go hand-in-hand with corresponding variations in I_t, and dividends will be just as stable or variable as the directors choose to make them.

Now suppose there is an opportunity to make a large business capital investment, one not previously planned. Is that precluded by the formula limiting investment to undistributed profits? The answer is of course not if the corporation can borrow to pay the cost, since debt-financed investment is not included in net equity investment until the loan is paid. Borrowing for capital investment is regularly understood as spreading out the burden of lumpy expenditures over some part of the life of the acquired asset.

Over a longer period of time, if borrowing seems too high, the corporation might reduce investment expenditures or dividends (or both), or raise new equity capital by the issue of shares (or all three), in order to bring borrowing down. The formula only asserts that dividends, gross investment, and borrowing must be set so that the sum of the first two minus the third equals profits.

Fourth, setting the new view aside, one can easily imagine reasons why directors might assign a high priority to keeping dividends stable. Many investors want a steady dividend stream for reasons of personal convenience, and are distressed if a dividend is missed or cut. That distress may be reflected in stock prices. That being so, corporate directors try to avoid cutting dividends, and to set dividend levels they are confident can be maintained. Therefore, a dividend increase tends to demonstrate such confidence and implies that all the various sorts of nonpublic information to which directors and management have access are consistent with it. The negative implications of a dividend cut are also reinforced by the knowledge that directors would try hard to avoid it.

Now suppose a dividend-paying corporation suddenly has a favorable investment opportunity for which it needs additional funds. Assume its debt/equity ratio is high, and a new issue of stock is proposed to raise the funds. But then a tax-sensitive director points out the opportunity to save taxes by cutting the dividend instead.[2] What should be done?

Presumably *this* dividend cut would be explained to shareholders as good news, not bad. But should investors accept that explanation? There have been accounts from time to time of such an explanation not preventing a drop in share price. The tax-sensitive director may blame that on investor ignorance or intransigence, but acceptance of this explanation would appreciably complicate the interpretation of dividend behavior. So maybe the market drop produces a desirable result after all, by preserving the clear and simple understanding that a dividend cut signifies trouble.

Perhaps some similar explanation can be constructed for why corporate share repurchases by public corporations have not entirely replaced dividends. As affirmed by Gordon and Dietz, share repurchases have not acquired the stability of dividends. It would be interesting to know to what extent they have replaced special dividends, which used to be paid with a specific warning not to expect recurrence. It might even be found that repurchases serve a useful nontax purpose by communicating that message with less confusion than when the message took the form of a cautionary verbal statement accompanying a dividend increase.

This explanation has some things in common with the signaling model considered in Gordon and Dietz's chapter, but without the subtleties involved in figuring out when and why "burning money" is a signal of financial (and other?) well-being, or of distinguishing between a signal and a mere demonstration. More particularly, it certainly does not make the counterfactual assumption that the ratio of dividends to share redemptions is fixed prior to determining the total amount to be distributed.

In sum, if directors desire to have stable dividends, they may have to retain part of earnings in profitable years to supplement earnings in bad years. Or they may have to pay out in bad years, counting on future earnings to make up for the current shortfall. The new view asserts only that the dividend tax will not create any bias for or against such behavior.[3]

3. Share Repurchases

According to Gordon and Dietz, the principal distinguishing characteristic of the new view is that it assumes no share repurchases. This assumption is stated in mathematical terms[4] and later, without having interacted with anything else, treated as a prediction that there will in fact be no share repurchases. For this the new view gets very low marks because there are now substantial share repurchases by American corporations, publicly held as well as closely held.

This is absurd. The function of an assumption is not to make a prediction but to indicate what a model does and does not cover. The new view asserts that *if* all distributions by a corporation, present and future, *were* subject to the dividend tax (or an equivalent), *then* the increment to share value resulting from accumulation of earnings *would* be the amount accumulated minus the deferred dividend tax, which is just what a shareholder would have had after tax if the dividend were paid. As a result, the tax *would not be* biased for or against the payment of dividends. The constraint that $V_t^N \geq;0$ is simply the mathematical expression of the *"if"* clause. If the facts are not consistent with the constraint, then the model makes no prediction at all since it does not apply.

Does that mean the new view is now irrelevant with respect to American corporations?[5] I believe not, for at least the following two main reasons.

First, while the presence of distributions free of the dividend tax makes the pure and simple version of the new view descriptively inapplicable, continued payment of substantial taxable dividends makes the underlying principle applicable *pro tanto*. In simple English, delete *if* and substitute *to the extent that*, so the assertion is

> To the extent that future distributions by a corporation are expected to be taxable as dividends (or subject to some equivalent tax burden), the price at which shares can be expected to sell will be discounted from corporate asset value to reflect the burden of that deferred dividend tax. Accordingly, the bias against paying a dividend and simply accumulating earnings instead will be significantly less than what is asserted in the traditional view.

A mathematical expression of this idea seems to me to be contained in Gordon and Dietz's chapter, not as part of the new view but in equation 6.3 of section 1 (Initial Model of the Dividend Puzzle):

$$V_t = \sum_{i=1}^{\infty} d^i \left[\left(\frac{1-m}{1-z} \right) D_{t+i} - V_{t+i}^N \right], \tag{6.3}$$

Where D and V^N represent expected dividends and share issues (or repurchases if negative), respectively, for all future years. Expected future distributions cannot be measured simply or directly, but the general idea expressed in the equation seems indisputably correct. It also contradicts the traditional view of dividend taxation which asserts that earnings accumulated in any particular year will increase share value by their whole amount, without any reduction for the taxes whose payment has been deferred.

The essential lesson of the new view is that a prerequisite for distortion—opportunity for gain by taxpayers—is that distributions can be made, currently or in the future, that escape the burden of the dividend tax. Gordon and Dietz's equation (6.3) asserts the same thing. And the arguments and examples in their chapter confirm the same lesson, focusing as they do on the profit to be made from substituting share repurchases for payment of taxable dividends.

Equation (6.3) discounts the after-tax value of all future distributions at a single rate—the interest rate on bonds. It might work better to apply a lower discount rate to dividends than to other distributions, for reasons already suggested in section 2, and in any event to specify something higher than the bond rate as a reference.

Privately held corporations have often redeemed shares, since before there was an income tax. The redemption price has generally been set by somehow evaluating the whole business and dividing the result pro rata among the shareholders. Public corporations generally did not redeem any substantial number of shares until after 1980. Since then redemptions have risen to represent roughly half of total corporate distributions. Why?

The primary reason for share redemptions by closely held corporations has nothing to do with taxes; it is simply because otherwise investors would very likely be unable to find any other purchaser from whom to get fair value on liquidation of their investments. Of course the tax advantage of redemptions over dividends was quickly apparent, and since 1920 redemption proceeds have been taxed as dividends unless "not essentially equivalent to a dividend." That standard has been elaborated in the statute and in a plethora of judicial and administrative decisions, and other exceptions have been added, but the general standard of dividend equivalence remains central. In general, any pro rata redemption from all shareholders (including any redemption of less than all the shares of a sole shareholder) is taxable as a dividend, while a complete redemption of all the shares of an individual (and related parties as specified in the statute) is not; intermediate cases may or may not fit within some more specific rule than dividend equivalence. With careful planning, death of a shareholder is apt to present substantial opportunities for share redemptions not taxable as dividends.

The traditional view of dividend taxation fits closely-held corporations relatively well. Accumulated earnings enhance share value by something approaching their full amount because they are likely to be later distributed, in substantial part, through share redemptions not subject to the dividend tax.

Prior to 1980 share redemptions by public corporations were rare. This was partly because of uncertainties about the application of the tax and securities laws. But the principal reason was just that the point of a public market for shares was to give shareholders a satisfactory way to liquidate their investments, and shareholders clearly got capital gain treatment for market sales, so it was not obvious how corporate repurchases would produce any better result than that.

The unobvious answer is that if shares trade at a discount from asset value to reflect prospective dividend taxes, as predicted by the new view, the corporation will be able to repurchase them for less than a pro rata portion of corporate assets, thus increasing the value of unredeemed shares. But according to the traditional view of dividend taxation, which prevailed more or less unchallenged until the late 1970s, the market value of shares should reflect accumulated earnings in full, without any such discount for prospective dividend taxes.

Why did public corporations shift after 1980 to making half their distributions by share repurchase rather than dividends? Partly because doubts about the possible unfavorable application of the tax and securities laws were resolved. And partly, in some cases, because employee stock option holders would share in the benefit of a value increase produced by redeeming shares for less than a pro rata share of corporate assets, while they would not share in simple dividends. But, most of all, because corporate financial officers and advisors came to understand and believe that stock was trading at some sort of discount that could be captured for the benefit of continuing shareholders (and option holders) by a corporation repurchasing its own shares. It is not accidental that this broader understanding took hold soon after the new view made its appearance in the economics literature!

Finally, why do half of total corporate distributions continue to occur in the form of taxable dividends? My guess is that stable dividends earn a discount rate lower than for other distributions by enough to offset the extra tax burden.[6]

Second, for many, the principal purpose of the new view has always been to describe what can be, not what is, and for this purpose a strict version of the new view remains very relevant. Most of the distortions traditionally attributed to our system of double taxation of corporate income could be eliminated or immensely mitigated, without revenue loss, by extending the burden of dividend taxation to all corporate distributions, including share repurchases and buyouts. As to these it would be inappropriate to impose the whole burden on the seller by taxing the proceeds as a dividend, but it would be quite feasible either to tax continuing shareholders as if they had received the distribution and spent it to purchase the redeemed shares,[7] or to impose a tax of similar burden on the corporation itself.[8]

This conclusion does not depend upon having "a theory for dividends [that explains] the full range of dividend behavior we see" but only on recognizing the validity of equation (6.3) in Gordon and Dietz's basic model.

NOTES

1. See discussion following Gordon and Dietz's initial equation (6.1) in section 1 of their chapter.
2. See Gordon and Dietz's text immediately following equation (6.6).
3. Gordon and Dietz are not the first to describe the new view as asserting that dividends are a residual. In my view they have advanced the ball by making it explicit how that assertion depends on mistreating a cash flow constraint as a prediction.
4. $V_t^N \geq 0$. V_t^N is new share issues and a negative value for this term would represent share repurchases.
5. Better to be wrong than irrelevant!
6. One report from the trenches suggests a different reason: An outside corporate director was appalled by a management proposal to substitute share repurchases for dividends because it would divert a significant part of the return on the shareholders' investment into the hands of employee option holders before they had made any contribution to corporate capital or even any commitment to contribute to that capital themselves. He viewed the asserted tax advantage of share repurchases as a smokescreen.

7. Marvin Chirelstein, "Optional Redemptions and Optional Dividends: Taxing the Repurchase of Common Shares," 78 *Yale aw Journal* 739 (1969).
8. Reporter's Study of the Taxation of Corporate Distributions, especially Reporter's Proposal R2, in American Law Institute, *Federal Income Tax Project,* Subchapter C 327, 401 (1982).

CHAPTER 6

Comment 2

GEORGE R. ZODROW

The debate over the economic effects of the taxation of dividends at the individual level has been long and contentious, sparked in large part by a fundamental contribution by David Bradford (1981). Bradford's paper, along with those of King (1977) and Auerbach (1979), developed what is still commonly known as the "new view" of dividend taxation, a view with the striking implications that (1) dividend taxes have no effect on marginal incentives for new investment financed with retained earnings, and (2) personal-level dividend taxes are fully capitalized into stock prices, implying that Tobin's q, the ratio of the market price of new capital relative to its replacement cost, is less than one. By comparison, the traditional view holds that dividend taxes reduce investment by raising the cost of capital while distorting decisions regarding the level and composition of investment, the financing of investment, the choice of organizational form, and the choice between dividends and retentions. This view holds that dividends are paid to shareholders, despite their tax disadvantages (attributable to the fact that dividends are typically taxed more heavily than the capital gains that arise when earnings are retained), because they provide shareholders with valuable offsetting benefits. These benefits are typically assumed to be either (1) clear signals regarding uncertain current or future profits, or (2) a solution—in the form of limiting managerial tendencies to overinvestment or "empire building" by forcing payouts of past profits—to the agency cost problems that arise due to the separation of ownership and control between shareholders and firm managers. In addition, the traditional view holds that future dividend taxes are not capitalized into share values, and that the marginal source of equity finance is new share issues. A resolution of the long-standing debate between the new and traditional views of dividend taxation—or a definitive determination of the extent to which the views apply to which firms in the marketplace—is as critical as ever. This is especially true because recent reforms in the United States are moving the tax system toward business-individual income tax integration via the dividend exclusion approach, and the two views of dividend taxation have dramatically different implications for the desirability of this approach.

The comprehensive chapter by Gordon and Dietz is an important contribution to this literature, as it synthesizes the new view and one version of the traditional view in compact and elegant yet relatively simple models that clearly illustrate the underlying assumptions and implications of each approach.[1] In addition, the Gordon and Dietz essay clearly identifies the testable implications of each theory and then compares them to the empirical literature on the effects of dividend taxation; the authors conclude that the signaling version of the traditional view model is best able to explain the empirical regularities that characterize this literature.

The Gordon and Dietz chapter is an excellent one, and I have only a couple of minor quibbles with the models they have constructed, which are extensions of standard models of these phenomena found in the literature,[2] and their interpretation of the implications of these models. Specifically, in the case of the signaling model, a somewhat unusual feature of the Gordon and Dietz model is that a successful signal in the form of an increased dividend payout raises firm value but does not have the ancillary effect of lowering its cost of capital, as is the case for most of the signaling models that have appeared in the literature. If this were the case, for example, if the costs of capital declined due to a lower interest rate or lower required returns to shareholders, then investment might increase with a cut in the dividend tax rate as would be expected; by comparison, in the Gordon and Dietz model, a dividend tax cut unambiguously leads to a decline in investment simply because it encourages payouts and thus reduces the funds available for investment. This effect could of course also be enhanced if the model were extended to allow a positive savings response to a reduction in dividend tax rates.

In addition, the authors' argument that there is only limited empirical evidence of any response of investment to the cost of capital, much less the dividend tax component of the cost of capital, seems somewhat overstated. The recent literature, as reviewed in a survey by Hassett and Newmark (2006), suggests that models which include the costs of adjusting the capital stock clearly establish an inverse relationship between investment and cost of capital. The effects of the recent dividend tax cuts are presumably sufficiently large that they could in principle affect the level of investment. Accordingly, empirical tests of the implications of the various views of the effects of dividend taxes using the recent tax changes should be a fertile ground for future research; the recent study by Desai and Goolsbee (2004)—discussed further below—is an excellent example of this approach.

The general conclusion of the analysis by Gordon and Dietz is that although there is still considerable uncertainty about the effects of dividend taxation and neither model adequately explains all of the empirical regularities that have been observed, the signaling version of the traditional view is more consistent with the empirical data. Although this is certainly a reasonable conclusion, let me suggest an alternative interpretation of the existing evidence.

When I surveyed the literature on the traditional and new views of dividend taxation fifteen years ago (Zodrow, 1991), I concluded that there were important theoretical problems with both views, but that virtually all of the existing empirical evidence supported the traditional view. This was also the position taken by the U.S. Department of the Treasury (1992), as it argued that the empirical evidence clearly supported the traditional view, which in turn supported the argument that some form of corporate-individual tax integration was highly desirable. This conclusion was based primarily on three pieces of empirical evidence, each of which supported some version of the traditional view but was inconsistent with the new view: numerous studies demonstrated that dividend tax increases reduced payouts, the often-cited fact the dividend payments are highly stable over time, and the increased importance of share repurchases (which are precluded by assumption in many derivations of the new view). These three factors of course correspond to three of the first four pieces of evidence cited by Gordon and Dietz in their Table 6.1 (the fourth—that firms rather anomalously simultaneously issue new shares and pay dividends—cannot be explained by either view). However, in my view, this consensus has become increasingly suspect over the past fifteen years.

In particular, the three empirically observed regularities noted above seem less compelling as arguments against the new view. First, it is clear that reduced dividend payouts in response to increases in dividend tax rates are inconsistent with the basic new view model. Nevertheless, they are consistent if (1) the tax on interest income simultaneously increases, making debt less desirable and thus increasing equity-financed investment and reducing dividend payouts; (2) the dividend tax increase is perceived to be temporary (and Gordon and Dietz argue that all such increases are "inevitably" perceived to be temporary); (3) the dividends are paid by new firms that are using equity finance in the form of new share issues rather than retained earnings; (4) the firm anticipates using new share issues in the future, and thus reduces current dividends to avoid the use of more expensive new share issues in the future (Edwards and Keen, 1984); (5) firms increase investment in the short run and thus reduce dividend payouts because the equilibrium value of Tobin's q declines; and (6) the reduction in shareholder wealth due to the fall in Tobin's q prompts more saving and investment and thus lower payouts. For all these reasons, it is far from clear that the observed negative relationship between dividend tax rates and payouts provides compelling support for the traditional view.

Second, although it is clear that dividends are stable, the sum of dividends and share repurchases is much more volatile. To the extent the dividends and share repurchases are substitutes, the stability of dividends viewed in isolation may be a misleading indicator of firm payout behavior. In particular, it is clear that for the agency cost model, it is the total payout rather than just dividends paid that matters in terms of limiting managerial discretion. Similarly, dividends and share repurchases are substitutes in some signaling models (although in others share repurchases are assumed to provide a weaker signal of profitability because they are perceived to be temporary and may be subject to asymmetric information problems). Some recent evidence presented by Grullon and Michaely (2002) suggests the dividends and share repurchases are becoming increasingly substitutable. After documenting the significant growth in share repurchases from 1980 to 2000, Grullon and Michaely argue that (1) the increase in share repurchases has been financed with funds that previously would have been used for dividends; (2) share repurchases are very popular not only with new firms but also with established firms, who have been keeping dividends roughly constant and using more share repurchases over time; and (3) although firms that reduce dividend payments typically experience a reduction in market value, this does not occur for firms that reduce dividends but simultaneously use share repurchases. All of these results suggest that dividends and share repurchases have become increasingly substitutable, which in turn suggests that the stability of dividends over time is not a particularly good indicator of firm payout behavior.

Third, although it is clear that share repurchases are becoming increasingly important, it is also important to note that more recent models of the new view attempt to incorporate share repurchases. For example, Sinn (1991) assumes that the ratio of share repurchases to dividends is constant, Bernheim (1991) constructs a signaling model with an optimal mix of dividends and share repurchases that clearly has new view characteristics, and Auerbach and Hassett (2003) discuss such hybrid models as well. Thus, the existence of share repurchases does not by itself preclude the validity of the new view.

Perhaps more importantly, a number of recent studies provide empirical support for the new view over the traditional view. Auerbach and Hassett (2003) argue that under the new view dividends should be negatively correlated with investment and positively correlated with cash flow, and that such behavior is characteristic of about half of the firms in their sample—a result that is consistent with the eminently reasonable observation by Sinn (1991) that the most realistic model is one in which the behavior of some firms is characterized by the new view, others are characterized by the traditional view, and still others are best characterized by behavior that is intermediate between the two views. And, as described briefly by Gordon and Dietz, Auerbach and Hassett (2005, 2006) use the event study methodology to examine the response of stock prices to news about the likelihood of dividend tax reductions as captured by the probability of a Bush reelection in 2004. They show that an increased likelihood of the continuation of the Bush dividend tax cuts benefits higher yield firms less than proportionately, a result that is consistent with the new view (as more time to distribute profits while dividend tax rates are low is not particularly beneficial to high yield firms) but inconsistent with the traditional view (under which the prospect of a lower cost of capital for a longer period of time would be more important for high yield firms). Desai and Goolsbee (2004) estimate the investment effects of the Bush dividend tax cut and the partial expensing provisions passed in 2002 and expanded in 2003 and show that the dividend tax cut had little effect on investment, as predicted by the new view. Finally, Harris, Hubbard, and Kemsley (2001) use a firm valuation model to show that retained earnings distributed as dividends are valued less by the market than the return of contributed equity, a result that is consistent with a value of Tobin's q less than one, as predicted by the new view; similarly, recent work of Sialm (2005) also supports dividend tax capitalization.

To sum up, the importance of several often-cited empirical regularities, especially dividend stability and the inverse relationship between dividend tax rates and payouts, for distinguishing between the two views of the effects of dividend taxation is far from clear. In addition, numerous new empirical studies are consistent with the new view rather than the traditional view. Thus, it is no longer as obvious as it was fifteen years ago that empirical evidence strongly supports the traditional view.

In any case, it is clear that the early insights of Bradford on the effects of dividend taxes have been extremely provocative and sparked a long-standing and fascinating debate. The chapter by Gordon and Dietz provides an excellent overview of the work of Bradford and others on the new view, coupled with an elegant yet straightforward model of the competing signaling version of the traditional view, and identifies and evaluates the testable implications of each of these views. Although this chapter is an important contribution to the literature, the resolution of the debate is still far from clear and will require additional theoretical and empirical research—all of which will no doubt build on the pathbreaking work of David Bradford.

NOTES

1. In the version of the chapter presented at the conference, Gordon and Dietz also constructed an innovative but preliminary model of the agency cost version of the traditional view—an extension that is left to future research in this version of the essay. That model specified explicitly the sources of agency costs and the instruments available to a firm's Board of Directors, which was assumed to represent the interests of shareholders by limiting managerial discretion regarding investment policy. An interesting feature of such a model is the nature of the representation of the asymmetry of information between the Board of Directors and its managers, and the extent to which the use of dividends as a disciplining device may vary as the Board learns more about the "empire-building" tendencies of its managers (Jensen, 1986).
2. In particular, an especially appealing feature of the Gordon and Dietz signaling model is that it allows for an optimal ratio of dividends paid to share repurchases, which reflects the balancing of the tax costs of more dividends against the benefit of a smaller payout and thus a higher level of investment—an approach that is quite similar to that modeled in the important contribution to this literature by Bernheim (1991).

REFERENCES

Auerbach, Alan J. 1979. "Wealth Maximization and the Cost of Capital." *Quarterly Journal of Economics* 93: 433–446.

Auerbach, Alan J., and Kevin A. Hassett. 2003. "On the Marginal Source of Investment Funds." *Journal of Public Economics* 87: 205–232.

Auerbach, Alan J., and Kevin A. Hassett. 2005. "The 2003 Dividend Tax Cuts and the Value of the Firm: An Event Study." *National Bureau of Economic Research Working Paper No. 11449.*

Auerbach, Alan J., and Kevin A. Hassett. 2006. "Dividend Taxes and Firm Valuation: New Evidence." *National Bureau of Economic Research Working Paper No. 11959.*

Bernheim, B. Douglas. 1991. "Tax Policy and Dividend Policy." *RAND Journal of Economics* 22: 455–476.

Bradford, David F. 1981. "The Incidence and Allocation Effects of a Tax on Corporate Distributions." *Journal of Public Economics* 15: 1–22.

Desai, Mihir A., and Austan D. Goolsbee. 2004. "Investment, Overhang, and Tax Policy." *Brookings Papers on Economic Activity* 35(2): 285–338.

Edwards, Jeremy, and Michael Keen. 1984. "Wealth Maximization and the Cost of Capital: A Comment." *Quarterly Journal of Economics* 99: 211–214.

Grullon, Gustavo, and Roni Michaely. 2002. "Dividends, Share Repurchases, and the Substitution Hypothesis." *Journal of Finance* 57: 1649–1684.

Harris, Trevor S., R. Glenn Hubbard, and Deen Kemsley. 2001. "The Share Price Effects of Dividend Taxes and Tax Imputation Credits." *Journal of Public Economics* 79: 569–596.

Hassett, Kevin A., and Kathryn Newmark. 2006. "Taxation and Business Behavior: A Review of the Recent Literature." Paper prepared for presentation at a conference on "Is It Time for Fundamental Tax Reform? The Known, the Unknown and the Unknowable," sponsored by the Tax and Expenditure Policy Program of the James A. Baker III Institute for Public Policy, Rice University, Houston Texas.

Jensen, Michael. 1986. "Agency Costs of Free Cash Flow, Corporate Finance, and Takeovers." *American Economic Review* 76: 323–329.

King, Mervyn. 1977. *Public Policy and the Corporation.* London: Chapman and Hall.

Sialm, Clemens. 2005. "Tax Changes and Asset Pricing: Time-Series Evidence." *National Bureau of Economic Research Working Paper No. 11756.*

Sinn, Hans-Werner. 1991. "Taxation and the Cost of Capital: The 'Old' View, the 'New' View, and Another View." In David F. Bradford (ed.), *Tax Policy and the Economy* (vol. 5, pp.-25–54). Cambridge, MA: MIT Press.

U.S. Department of the Treasury. 1992. *Integration of the Individual and Corporate Tax Systems.* Washington, DC: U.S. Treasury.

Zodrow, George R. 1991. "On the 'Traditional' and 'New' Views of Dividend Taxation." *National Tax Journal* 44: 497–509.

CHAPTER 7

On the General Relativity of Fiscal Language

JERRY GREEN

LAURENCE J. KOTLIKOFF

For David

We are deeply honored to contribute to this volume in recognition of David Bradford. David was our very dear friend and mentor. He was also our steadfast enthusiast, filling us full of encouragement and lauding us with overly generous praise. David was a seeker of core truth, and his marvelous research contributions are replete with fundamental insights that separate economic science from popular perception.

David's research interests overlapped with ours on a wide range of topics, none less than the issue considered here; namely, how to discuss and measure fiscal policy in economically meaningful ways. David was particularly supportive of generational accounting, whose goal is to compare the fiscal treatment of current and future generations. Indeed, David was a driving force behind the development of the first set of generational accounts.

David's laugh, spirit, spark, insight, and support continue to sustain us. He has moved from the physical to the metaphysical, but his presence is no less real in our hearts, souls, and minds and will always be treasured.

1. Introduction

In this chapter we provide a general proof that standard fiscal measures, including the deficit, taxes, and transfer payments, are economically ill defined. Instead these measures reflect the arbitrary labeling of underlying fiscal conditions. Analyses based on these and derivative measures, such as disposable income, private assets, and personal saving, constitute the perusal of nomenclature, not the application of economics.

The argument that any underlying fiscal policy can be reported as entailing any time path of deficit, taxes, and transfer payments and that these measures are, economically speaking, content-free was originally advanced by Kotlikoff (1986). Auerbach and Kotlikoff (1987) and Kotlikoff (2002) provide formal treatments of the point, but neither provides a general proof of the proposition. This chapter fills this gap. It posits a competitive, contingent claims economy that can accommodate uncertainty, information asymmetries, distortions, externalities, public goods, time inconsistent policy, imperfect credit markets, and incomplete/segmented markets.

2. The Model

In this section we demonstrate the proposition described above. Specifically, we show that one can report any time path whatsoever of government deficits independent of the general equilibrium of the economy. The reported time path of deficits requires mutually consistent reports of the time paths of taxes and transfer payments. This consistency requirement means that the time paths of reported fiscal variables are determined relative to each other, rather than being determined independently. That is, what deficits one reports has implications for what taxes and transfer payments one reports.

Our method of demonstrating this proposition is to articulate the equilibrium of a fully general neoclassical model. In presenting this model, we make no reference to "deficits," "taxes," or "transfer payments." This, in and of itself, proves that these measures are arbitrary descriptive constructs, which have no more scientific bearing than does the choice of whether to use French or English as the language in which to discuss the model.

Our model differs from the classical private ownership model only in that it includes a government sector. Government policy is unconstrained in real terms. What we show, therefore, is that for any real policy there are an infinite number of ways that it can be reported making the measured path of deficits in all future periods completely arbitrary.

In what follows, there are K agents, N states, M goods, V firms, and H endowments. Goods include leisure. Endowments include time, various types of physical capital, and natural resources. As in Arrow (1964), a state of the world is defined by a particular date, a particular resolution of uncertainty, and a specification of all economically relevant variables. The terms p_s and q_s reference pre-policy producer and endowment price vectors in state s.

2.1. *Profit Maximization*

There are V firms, which may be operated by private agents, the government, or both. Firm j's profit is

$$\pi_j \equiv \max_{y_{js}} \left(\sum_s p_s Y_{js} - \sum_s q_s \phi_{js} + m_j \right), \tag{7.1}$$

where y_{js} is firm j's $1 \times M$ vector of net goods supply in state s, ϕ_{js} is firm j's $1 \times H$ vector of endowment demands, and m_j is a function determining the government's net payment to firm j. Producers are atomistic and take producer prices, endowment prices, and their net payment functions as given.

Firm j's constant returns production function is given by

$$f_j(y_{j1}, \ldots, y_{jN}, \phi_{j1}, \ldots, \phi_{jN}; Y_{-jl}, \ldots, Y_{-jN}, \phi_{-j1}, \phi_{-jN}, X_1, \ldots, X_N, Z_1, \ldots, Z_N, \omega_1, \ldots, \omega_N) = 0 \tag{7.2}$$

where Y_{-js} is a $1 \times M \times (V-1)$ vector of net supplies of firms other than j in state s, ϕ_{-js} is a $1 \times H \times (V-1)$ vector of state $-s$ endowment demands of firms other than j, X_s references the $1 \times M \times K$ vector of goods demanded by agents 1 through K in state s, Z_s references the $1 \times M$ vector of goods demanded by the government in state s, and ω_s references the $1 \times H$ vector of economy-wide endowments in state s. For future reference we denote by Y_s the $1 \times M \times V$ vector of net supplies of firms 1 through V in state s, and by $Y\phi_s$ the $1 \times H \times V$ vector of endowment demands of firms 1 through V.

Including the Y_{-js}'s, ϕ_{-js}'s, X_s's, Z_s's, ϕ_s's, and ω_s's in equation (7.2) entertains the possibility of production externalities, consumption externalities, externalities from the use of economy-wide endowments, as well as externalities arising from the levels of economy-wide endowments.

Firm j's net payment function, m_j, may depend on its own state-specific net supplies of goods and demands for endowments. But it may also depend on the state-specific net supplies and demands of other firms, the constellation of agents' state-specific demands, the constellation of government state-specific demands for goods and endowments, and the economy's overall endowments. In other words, the firm's net payment function may depend on any real variable in the economy. This potential dependency, which may be highly nonlinear, is expressed in

$$m_j = m_j\,(y_{j1}, \ldots, y_{jN}, \phi_{j1}, \ldots, \phi_{jN}; Y_{-j1}, \ldots, Y_{-jN}, \phi_{-j1}, \ldots, \phi_{-jN}, X_1, \ldots, X_N, Z_1, \ldots, Z_N, \omega_1, \ldots, \omega_N) \tag{7.3}$$

2.2. *Preferences*

Let x_{is} reference the $1 \times M$ vector of goods demanded by agent i in state s, X_{-is} reference the $1 \times M \times (K-1)$ vector of goods consumed by agents other than i in state s, and Z_s reference the $1 \times M$ vector of goods consumed by the government in state s. The utility of agent i is given by

$$U_i = U(x_{i1}, \ldots, x_{iN}; X_{-i1}, \ldots, X_{-1N}, Z_1, \ldots, Z_N, Y_1, \ldots, Y_N, \phi_1, \ldots, \phi_N, \omega_1, \ldots, \omega_N) \tag{7.4}$$

The arguments of these preferences accommodate consumer and producer externalities as well as externalities/public goods generated by producers' and government demands. These arguments can also determine commodity characteristics, like average quality, that can be important determinants of demand and welfare in economies characterized by asymmetric information.

2.3. *Private Budgets*

The budget constraint of agent i is given by

$$\sum_s p_s x_{is} = e_i, \tag{7.5}$$

where e_i is the net resource function of agent i. The net resource function references the amount of resources the government arranges for agent i to be able to spend on state-specific claims. As indicated in (7.6), this function may depend not only on the agent's own demand for claims in states of nature, but also on the claims of other agents, the production of each firm, the government's state-specific goods demands, and the economy's state-specific overall endowments. This dependency may also be highly nonlinear.

$$e_i = e_i(x_{i1}, x_{i2}, \ldots, x_{iN}; X_{-i1}, X_{-i2}, \ldots, X_{-iN}, Z_1, Z_2, \ldots, Z_N, Y_1, Y_2, \ldots, Y_N, \omega_1, \omega_2, \ldots, \omega_N), \tag{7.6}$$

In addition to (7.5), agent i's demands are constrained by

$$x_{is} \in \psi(X_1, X_2, \ldots, X_N, Z_1, Z_2, \ldots, Z_N, Y_1, Y_2, \ldots, Y_N, \omega_1, \omega_2, \ldots, \omega_N). \tag{7.7}$$

Equation (7.7) can accommodate a variety of important restrictions on trade, including those arising because of incomplete/segmented markets and borrowing constraints.

2.4. *Market Clearing*

In equilibrium, firms' supplies of goods in each state s must cover agents' and government demands and the economy-wide supplies of endowments must cover firms' endowment demands.

$$\sum_j y_{js} = \sum_i x_{is} + Z_s. \tag{7.8}$$

$$\omega_s = \sum_j \phi_{js}. \tag{7.9}$$

2.5. *The Government's Budget*

Equations (7.1), (7.5), (7.8), and (7.9) imply

$$\sum_s p_s Z_s = \sum_s q_s \omega_s + \sum_j \pi_j - \sum_i e_i \sum_j m_j. \tag{7.10}$$

The economy's overall resources consist of the value of its overall endowments plus the value of pure profits. These overall resources less the amount of net resources that the government provides to agents and firms must finance the government's demand for goods.

2.6. *Government Policy*

Government policy consists of a set of $e_i(^2)$ and $m_j(^2)$ functions as well as state-specific government product demand functions given by

$$Z_s = Z_s(X_1, X_2, \ldots, X_N, Z_1, Z_2, \ldots, Z_N, Y_1, Y_2, \ldots, Y_N, \omega_1, \omega_2, \ldots, \omega_N). \tag{7.11}$$

As equation (7.10) indicates, these four sets of policy functions are not mutually independent.

2.7. *Equilibrium*

In equilibrium, households maximize equation (7.4) subject to (7.5) and (7.7); firms maximize (7.1) subject to (7.2); the government jointly chooses its $m_j(^2)$, $e_i(^2)$, and $Z_s(^2)$ functions consistent with (7.10); and the market clearing conditions (7.8) and (7.9) are satisfied.

2.7.1. Reporting Policy

Agent i's net resources, e_i, can be reported as reflecting the market value of a $1 \times H$ vector of state-specific private endowments, a_{is}, proportionate holdings of firm j of θ_{ij}, less a $1 \times K$ vector of state- and good-specific net tax functions, τ_{is}; that is,

$$e_i = \sum_s q_s a_{is} + \sum_i \theta_{ij}\pi_j - \sum_s p_s \tau_{is} \tag{7.12}$$

Since the elements a_{is} and agent i's reported share of firm profits will be described as constants, the T_{is} functions must contain the same arguments as the e_i function; for examble,

$$\begin{aligned}\tau_{is} = \tau_{is}(&x_{i1}, x_{i2}, \ldots, x_{iN}; X_{-i1}, X_{-i2}, \ldots, X_{-iN}, Z_1, Z_2, \ldots, \\ &Z_N, Y_1, Y_2, \ldots, Y_N, \omega_1, \omega_2, \ldots, \omega_N).\end{aligned} \tag{7.13}$$

Note that in equilibrium, endowment and producer price vectors depend on the same arguments as τ_{is}, namely $X_1, \ldots, X_N$, $Z_1, \ldots, Z_N$, $Y_1, \ldots, Y_N$, $\omega_1, \ldots, \omega_1$, so there is no need to list them in (7.13) as separate arguments.

Let Ω_s reference a $1 \times H$ vector of reported government endowments in state s. Since endowments are held either by agents or the government, reporting, for agent i, endowments of a_{is} in state s also requires, for consistency, announcing a government net endowment vector Ω_s satisfying

$$\Omega_2 = \omega_s - \sum_i a_{is}. \tag{7.14}$$

Combining equations (7.10), (4.12), and (7.14) yields the more conventional expression for the government's budget, namely

$$\sum_s p_s Z_s + \sum_s \sum_j m_{js} = \sum_s q_s \Omega_s + \sum_j \theta_{gi}\pi_j + \sum_s \sum_i p_s \tau_{is}, \tag{7.15}$$

where references the government's reported ownership share of firm j. Equation (7.15) can be described as the government financing its goods and its net subsidies payments to firms from its net worth (the sum of the first two terms on the right-hand side of (7.15)) plus its net taxation of agents.

$$\theta_{gi} = 1 - \sum_i \theta_{ij} \tag{7.16}$$

Given an equilibrium, any party, be it a private agent or government official, is free to report any constellation of private endowments and corresponding government endowments he or she wants. Assume, for example, that there is a single endowment, capital, and that agent k reports private asset values of $\hat{a}_{\text{is}}$ for $i=1,\ldots,$ K and $s=1,\ldots,$ N and private firm ownership shares θ_{ij}. The corresponding announcement of government net tax payments by agent i in state s—denoted by $\hat{\tau}_{is}$, and government assets in state $s, \hat{\Omega}_{is}$, must satisfy equation (7.17) and (7.18).

$$e_i = \sum_s q_s \hat{a}_{is} + \sum_i \hat{\theta}_{ij} \pi_j - \sum_s p_s \hat{\tau}_{is}. \tag{7.17}$$

$$\hat{\Omega}_s = \omega_s - \sum_i \hat{a}_{is}. \tag{7.18}$$

If agent k is a fiscal conservative (liberal) and is reassured by contemplating a large government surplus (debt) and low (high) taxes, agent k can simply declare very low (high) values of private assets, $_{\text{is}}$, which will lead, according equation to (7.17) and (7.18), to high (low) reported values of $\hat{\Omega}_s$ and low (high) reported values of $\sum_s p_s \hat{\tau}_{is}$. Thus the reported levels of these fiscal variables are completely undetermined as individual magnitudes, but they are linked to each other by (7.17) and (7.18). In this sense these variables are mutually determined, but not individually determined. As we discuss below, however, many economic analyses in macroeconomics and public finance have used the levels of taxes or deficits as measurable, identifiable variables, as if these levels had an unambiguous, independent meaning.

Equations (7.17) and (7.18) complete the demonstration of the proposition that is our main objective, as stated at the beginning of this section. One can see from these equations that a change in $\sum_i \hat{a}_{is}$ and a corresponding change in $\hat{\Omega}_s$ and $\sum_s p_s \hat{\tau}_{is}$ leaves the real value of each i's net resources constant while changing the reported government assets to any desired level. Of course, taxes and private assets need to be restated consistently. But there no an intrinsic meaning to the level of the deficit, the level of taxes paid, transfer payments received, or private assets held. Stated differently, there is are an infinite number of mutually consistent sets of fiscal labels that one can attach to any neoclassical model without providing the slightest economic insight concerning the model's true underlying fiscal policy, including the impact of that policy on the welfare of current and future economic agents.

2.8. Deficits

Time is one of many characteristics of our model's states of nature. If we consider two states, s' and s'', that differ with respect to their measure of time, the difference in government net debt (the negative of government assets) between the two states constitutes their intervening deficit. Since one can report any size debt or surplus for states s' and s'', one is free to report any size deficit (reduction in net assets) across those two states and, indeed, across any two states that one wants. Hence, each agent is free to concoct whatever deficit and associated net tax payment times series, past or present, that one wants.

2.9. Tax and Transfer Payments

Net taxes are defined as gross taxes minus transfer payments. Given one's reported level of net taxes, one can report any level of gross taxes minus a corresponding level of transfer payment. Hence, gross taxes and transfer payments are just as ill defined as net taxes. The same holds for any measures that rely on gross taxes and gross transfer payments such as average tax rates, the unfunded liabilities of transfer programs, disposable income, or personal private/saving.

2.10. Intuition

There is an old joke in which a husband claims to be in charge of his household. As he puts it to his friends, "I make the important decisions—I determine our household's foreign policy and let my wife handle everything else." Knowing who is really in charge in a marriage is tough business, and determining who owns what can be even harder. Indeed, if the household resides in a community property state, it is impossible to allocate ownership. The husband and wife may have "separate" bank and other accounts, but neither can withhold the corpus of "their" accounts from the other. Indeed, a variant of the quoted joke is "I own the money and my wife spends it."

The private sector and the government are no different from a couple living under community property law. They jointly own everything and jointly determine how to spend it. Whether the government says (a) "It's all mine, but I'll let you [the private sector] have some"; (b) "It's all yours, but I'll take whatever I'd like"; or (c) "It's partly mine and partly yours, but I'll determine how much of mine to give you and how much of yours to keep" does not make an iota of economic difference.

3. Illustrating the Model

The canonical model of government debt is Diamond's (1965) two period life-cycle formulation. We now show how the above general formulation accommodates this model. Agents are assumed to consume a single good and leisure when young and old. Labor supplied by young and old is homogeneous. Output of the good, call it corn, is produced via constant returns to scale with capital and labor. There is neither population nor productivity growth. We normalize each cohort's population to unity. The endowment of time that can be used for work or leisure is one per generation per period. For simplicity, we assume the government makes no net payments to firms, but does have a demand for consumption of the economy's single good.

Let c_{yt}, l_{yt}, c_{ot+1}, and l_{ot+1} stand, respectively, for consumption and leisure when young and old of the generation born at time t. The lifetime utility of the generation born at time t is given by

$$u_t = u_t(C_{y,t}, l_{yt}, C_{ot+l}, l_{ot+1}). \tag{7.19}$$

Consider the economy as of time $t = 0$. The budget constraint facing the old at time 0 is given by

$$C_{o0} + W_0 l_{o0} = e_{o0}. \tag{7.20}$$

For generations born at time $t \geq 0$, the budget constraint is given by

$$C_{yt} + \frac{c_{ot+1}}{1+r_{t+1}} + W_t l_{yt} + \frac{W_{t+1} l_{ot+1}}{1+r_{t+1}} = e_t. \tag{7.21}$$

In equations (7.20) and (7.21) $e_{o,0}$ stands for the remaining lifetime net resource function of the old at time 0, and e_t is the lifetime net resource function of the generation born at time t. Each generation's net resource function can depend freely and in a highly nonlinear way on its consumption and leisure decisions. And, since each generation will consider how its consumption and leisure decisions affect its net resources both inframarginally and at the margin, this formulation fully accommodates distortionary policy.

The production function is

$$Y_t = F(K_t, L_t). \tag{7.22}$$

The government's demand for corn at time t is g_t. The economy's endowment of capital evolves according to

$$K_{t+1} - K_t = Y_t - C_{yt} - C_{ot} - g_t. \tag{7.23}$$

Labor supply is determined by

$$L_t = 2 - l_{yt} - l_{ot}. \tag{7.24}$$

Using (7.22) and (7.24), rewrite (7.23) as

$$K_{t+1} - K_t = F(K_t, 2 - l_{yt} - l_{ot}) - C_{yt} - C_{ot} - g_t. \tag{7.25}$$

In hiring capital and labor, firms equate marginal factor products to pre-policy factor prices; that is,

$$\begin{aligned} F_K(K_t, 2 - 1_{yt} - l_{ot}) &= r_t \\ F_L(K_t, 2 - l_{yt} - l_{ot}) &= W_t \end{aligned} \tag{7.26}$$

3.1. Policy

In equilibrium, the government announces a time path of net resource functions—the terms e_{oo} and e_t—and a time path of corn demand, g_t, that satisfy (7.25) in each period given utility maximization subject to (7.19) and (7.20), and given the determination via (7.26) of pre-policy factor prices.

3.2. Labeling

Suppose the economy is in dynamic equilibrium given government policy as determined by its net resource and spending functions. Denote by an upper bar this equilibrium's variables. Now consider announcing/reporting any time path of official debt, $\hat{D}_t$ starting at time 0. If one reports $\hat{D}_0$ as the amount of government debt prevailing at time 0, the corresponding report of private assets at time 0, $\hat{a}_0$, is determined by (7.27) for $t=0$. The consistent report of net taxes facing the elderly at time 0, $\hat{\tau}_{o0}$, is determined by (7.28). The reported debt for time $t>0$ determines $\hat{a}_t$ from (7.27). This determines $\hat{\tau}_{yt}$ from (7.29), and, given $\hat{\tau}_{yt}$, the reported value of $\hat{\tau}_{t+1}$ is determined by (7.30).

$$\hat{a}_t = \hat{D}_t + \bar{K}_t. \tag{7.27}$$

$$\bar{e}_{o0} = \hat{a}_0(1+\bar{r}_0) + \bar{w}_0 - \hat{\tau}_{o0}. \tag{7.28}$$

$$\hat{a}_{t+1} = \bar{w}_t(1-l_{yt}) - \bar{C}_{yt} - \hat{\tau}_{yt}. \tag{7.29}$$

$$\bar{e}_t = \bar{w}_t + \frac{\bar{W}_{t+1}}{1+\bar{r}_{t+1}} - \hat{\tau}_{yt} - \frac{\hat{\tau}_{ot+1}}{1+\bar{r}_{t+1}}. \tag{7.30}$$

3.3. Relationship to the General Formulation

In the above example, equation (7.20) and (7.21) are specific cases of (7.5), (7.24) is a specific case of (7.8), and the equation of economy-wide capital and time endowments with firm demands for these endowments in (7.26) is a specific case of (7.9).

Although we have presented this example assuming that all cohort members are identical, the example can readily be modified to include cohort-specific heterogeneity. One need simply apply an individual-specific subscript to each of the cohort-specific variables. Doing so does not rule out anonymous net resource functions. Subscripting net resources by an agent's identity does not imply that the function determining those resources (as opposed to the arguments of the function) is agent-specific. Hence, Mirrlees' (1971) optimal income tax can be relabeled as freely as any other tax, with no alteration in his underlying optimal net resource function.

3.4. A Second Illustration with Adverse Selection, and Credit Constraints

Our second example, informed by Jaffee and Russel (1976) and Hayashi (1987), shows that the relativity of fiscal language is not compromised by incomplete information, adverse selection, or credit constraints.

Agents again live for two periods. But each cohort now features two types of agents—*A* and *B*. An agent's type is private information. Type *B* agents are honest. They always repay what they owe, whether they owe payments to private parties or the government. In contrast, type *A* agents are dishonest.

Define C^*_{Ay} by

$$V_A = u(c^*_{Ay}, 0), \tag{7.31}$$

where for $i = A, B$,

$$V_i \equiv \max_{C_{iy}, C_{io}} (C_{iy}, C_{io}) \text{ such that } C_{iy} + \frac{c_{io}}{1+r} = e_i. \tag{7.32}$$

Note that for standard concave utility functions, $C^*_{Ay} > e_A$.

If type A agents are permitted to consume more than C^*_{Ay} when young, the present value of their consumption will exceed their lifetime net resources.

Denote by the utility maximizing value of c_{iy} and c_{io}. Consider a separating equilibrium in which

$$\hat{C}_{By} > C^*_{Ay} \tag{7.33}$$

and "financial" and "fiscal" institutions permit agents to set their consumption when young as high as C^*_{Ay}, but no higher.[1] Since type A agents are indifferent between X, consuming C^*_{Ay} when young and zero when old and Y, consuming less than C^*_{Ay} when young and a positive amount when old, we assume they choose option i. In contrast, given (7.33 the consumption of type B agents is given by

$$C_{By} = C^*_{Ay} \quad \text{and} \quad C_{Bo} = (e_B - C^*_{Ay})(1+r). \tag{7.34}$$

The consumption of type A agents is given by $\hat{c}_{Ay}$ and $°c_{Ao}$.

Note that we have described this economy with no reference to the terms "borrowing," "taxes," or "transfer payments." The budget constraint in (7.32) is a specific case of (7.5), and the constraint on agent B's consumption when young and old in (7.34) is a specific case of (7.7).

If we want, we can describe type B agents as "facing high taxes when young, but being able to borrow large amounts." or as "facing low taxes, but being able to borrow small amounts." A "policy" of "raising current taxes" and "cutting future taxes" that leaves lifetime net resources unchanged can be described as engendering an increase in "private lending" that leaves type B agents with the same first and second period consumption values.

4. Research and Policy Implications

The fact that one can construct an infinite number of equally meaningless time series of government debt, deficits, taxes, transfer payments, private assets, private saving, and disposable income vitiates a vast number of economic analyses predicated on these measures. Recent examples include Gale and Orszag's (2004) and Engen and Hubbard's (2005) studies of the effects of budget deficits on interest rates; Bell and Bosworth's (2005) study of the decline in personal saving; Banks, Blundell, and Smith's (2001) study of financial wealth inequality; Slemrod's (1994) study of tax progressivity and income inequality; the Organization for Economic Cooperation and Development's (OECD) (1997) analysis of inequality in disposable income; the International Monetary Foundation's (IMF) study of fiscal policy and financial development (Hauner 2006); and the World Bank's study of fiscal sustainability (Burnside, 2005).

The failure to distinguish economics from linguistics also undermines theoretical research. Consider, for example, Barsky, Mankiw, and Zeldes' (1986) paper on Keynesian tax cuts. Their policy entails a short-run across-the-board "tax cut" coupled with a long-run progressive "tax hike," which is present value neutral in terms of the government's net receipts. The policy provides earnings insurance, which leads to more current consumption. The authors suggest that this provides a neoclassical basis for the Keynesian view that tax cuts expand aggregate demand.

In fact, it does no such thing since the policy could equally well be run/described/labeled as entailing a tax hike. No doubt someone will someday write a paper arguing, from the perspective of this model, that a tax hike policy and a tax cut policy are equivalent. This projected essay will add to the long list of papers purporting to identify "equivalent policies"—policies that can be run/implemented differently, but that generate the same economic outcomes. Such papers miss a central point. There are no equivalent policies in neoclassical economics. Policies are unique. What is different is simply the words we use to describe the same underlying policy.

Fischer's (1980) famous paper on the time inconsistency provides yet another example of the confusion of economics and language. In Fischer's two-period model agents fail to save out of fear of *ex post* efficient, but *ex ante* inefficient capital levies. But from the perspective of the second period, Fischer's capital levy is no different, apart from labeling, from a second-period inframarginal labor income tax. Were Fischer's agents to adopt such a nondistortionary labor tax in their second period and also in their first, they'd achieve a first-best equilibrium.

So why does Fischer conclude that his economy ends up in a third-best equilibrium in which no one saves for fear of a capital levy? The answer is his assumption that only proportional labor income taxes may be levied/announced. But this assumption is not based on any economic feature of his model. Instead it boils down to a noneconomic restriction on language since, from the perspective of the second period, a "capital levy" could just as well be called "an inframarginal labor income tax." Fischer's rational agents will surely realize this and also realize that if they can infra-marginally tax labor in the second period, they can do so in the first. Having figured this out, they will end up in the first-best.[2]

A third example of theoretical confusion over real policy and labels is the ubiquitous invocation of transversality conditions requiring that government debt grow, in the long run, no faster than the economy's return on capital,[3] and the presumption that economies that violate such conditions are dynamically inefficient. As indicated here, there is no limit to the growth in reported debt, nor is there any economic association between the growth rate of reported debt and what matters for dynamic efficiency—namely, the deviation between the growth rate of the economy and its return to capital.

To see this in a less abstract framework, consider a dynamically efficient two period life-cycle model with a zero intrinsic growth rate. Assume the economy is sitting in a stationary state with a positive return to capital of r. Also assume the economy's government consumes nothing and takes, on net, nothing from any generation either when it is young or when it is old. Now, starting at time 1, let us label this policy as the government's "borrowing $m^t h$ from each agent born at time t, making inframarginal transfer payments of $m^t h$ to each agent born at time t, repaying principal plus interest of $m^t h(1 + r)$ at time $t+1$ to each agent born at time t, and inframarginally taxing at time $t + 1$ each agent born at time t in the amount $m^t h(1 + r)$." This economy's reported debt at the beginning of time $t + 1$ is $m^t h$. If $m > 1$, the economy's debt and deficit will head to infinity with no affect whatsoever on the economy or any agent in the economy.[4]

Turning to actual policy, one need only consider the Maastricht Treaty limiting members of the European Union to 3 percent deficits, the Stability and Growth Pact that sanctions EU members with deficits above 3 percent, the IMF's enduring use of the deficit to assess fiscal prudence, the Gramm-Rudman-Hollings Act to limit U.S. deficits, or the ongoing movement for a U.S. balanced budget amendment to realize that official reports of deficits are (a) dramatically influencing policy decisions and (b) diverting attention from fundamental and meaningful measures of fiscal policy.

5. Conclusion

A century ago, everyone thought that *time* and *distance* were well-defined physical concepts. But neither proved absolute. Instead, measures/reports of time and distance were found to depend on one's direction and speed of travel making our apparent physical reality, in Einstein's words, "merely an illusion."

Like time and distance, standard fiscal measures, including deficits, taxes, and transfer payments, depend on one's reference point/reporting procedure/language/labels. As such, they too represent numbers in search of concepts that provide the illusion of meaning where none exists. Economists must accept this fact and acknowledge that much of what they have been writing and saying about fiscal policy has been an exercise in linguistics, not economics.

NOTES

We thank Alan Auerbach, Daniel Shaviro, Kent Smetters, and other participants at the New York University Law School's conference, "Key Issues in Public Finance: A Conference in Memory of David Bradford" for very helpful comments.

1. Condition (7.32) could arise because type-B agents have higher net lifetime resources than type-A agents or because type-B agents have relatively strong preferences for consuming when young.
2. Kotlikoff (2002) discusses both Barsky, Mankiw, and Zeldes (1986) and Fischer (1980).
3. See, for example, Blanchard (1985).
4. If $m < -1$, the government's surplus heads to infinity. If $-1 < m < 1$, the governments reports a declining debt or surplus through time.

REFERENCES

Arrow, Kenneth J. 1964. "The Role of Securities in the Optimal Allocation of Risk-Bearing." *Review of Economic Studies* 31; 91–96.

Auerbach, Alan J., and Laurence J. Kotlikoff. 1987. *Dynamic Fiscal Policy.* Cambridge: Cambridge University Press.

Banks, James, Richard Blundell, and James P. Smith. 2001. *Financial Wealth Inequality in the United States and Britain.* Los Angeles: The Rand Institute.

Barsky, Robert B., Gregory Mankiw, and Steven P. Zeldes. 1986. "Richardian Consumers with Keynesian Propensities." *The American Economic Review* 76(4): 676–691.

Bell, Linda, and Barry Bosworth. 2005. "The Decline in Household Saving: What Can We Learn from Survey Data." Mimeo, The Brookings Institution.

Blanchard, Olivier. 1985. "Debts, Deficits, and Finite Horizons." *Journal of Political Economy* 93(2); 223–247.

Burnside, Craig (ed.). 2005. *Fiscal Sustainability in Theory and Practice.* Washington, DC: The World Bank.

Diamond, Peter A. 1965. "National Debt in a Neoclassical Growth Model." *American Economic Review* 55: 1126–1150.

Engen, Eric M., and R. Glenn Hubbard. 2005. "Federal Government Debt and Interest Rates." in Mark Gertler and Ken Rogoff (eds.), *NBER Macroeconomics Annual 2004* Cambridge, MA: MIT Press (pp. 83–138).

Fischer, Stanley. 1980. "Dynamic Inconsistency, Cooperation, and the Benevolent Dissembling Government." *Journal of Economic Dynamics and Control* 2; 93–107.

Gale, William and Peter R. Orszag. 2004. "Budget Deficits, National Saving, and Interest Rates." *Brookings Papers on Economic Activity* 2: 101–210.

Hauner, David. 2006. "Fiscal Policy and Financial Development." IMF Working Paper, WP/06/26, January.

Hayashi, Fumio. 1987. "Tests for Liquidity Constraints: A Critical Survey." In T. Bewley (ed.), *Advances in Econometrics II: Fifth World Congress* (pp. 91–120). Cambridge: Cambridge University Press.

Engen, Eric, and glenn Hubbard. 2005. "Government Debt and Interest Rates." in M. Gertler and K. Rogoff, (eds.) *NBER Macroeconomics Annual 2004.* Cambridge: MIT Press.

Jaffee, D. M., and T. Russel. 1976. "Imperfect Information, Uncertainty, and Credit Rationing." *Quarterly Journal of Economics* 90: 651–666.

Kotlikoff, Laurence J. 1986. "Deficit Delusion." *The Public Interest* 84 (Summer): 53–65.

Kotlikoff, Laurence J. 2002. *Generational Policy.* Cambridge, MA: MIT Press.

Mirrlees, James A. 1971. "An Exploration in the Theory of Optimal Income Taxation." *Review of Economic Studies* 38: 175–208.

OECD. 1997. "Income Distribution and Poverty in Selected OECD Countries." *OECD Economic Outlook.* Paris: OECD.

Slemrod, Joel. (ed.). 1994. *Tax Progressivity and Income Inequality.* Cambridge: Cambridge University Press.

CHAPTER 7

Comment 1

On the Relative Generality of Fiscal Language

DANIEL N. SHAVIRO

1. Introduction

Laurence Kotlikoff has played a vital role in demonstrating that prevailing fiscal language terms, such as "taxes," "spending," and "budget deficits," lack fundamental economic content, causing them to be misleading and manipulable. He has also been at the forefront of developing a better fiscal language, in particular through his work on generational accounting. This work remains mystifyingly underappreciated and underutilized by the economics profession.

This volume's chapter by Jerry Green and Kotlikoff goes a step further than previous work, suggesting that a term I regard as a cornerstone of generational accounting, "net taxes," is no better than any of the rest. The argument is logically sound, but I regard it as not comparably important, and as not requiring similar revision of the vocabulary used to describe fiscal policies. Green and Kotlikoff, in my view, make overly broad claims about the significance of their analysis by not addressing how constraints on fiscal language use can limit the degrees of freedom (and hence manipulability) that it shows exist in theory.

I begin by briefly reviewing why "taxes," "spending," and "budget deficits" are so descriptively inadequate. I then explore the Green and Kotlikoff critique of "net taxes," starting with its logic and then turning to the question of its significance.

2. Fiscal Language Changes That Ought to Be Uncontroversial

2.1. Taxes and Spending

Cash is constantly flowing back and forth between the government, on the one hand, and individuals or legal entities, on the other. With limited exceptions, such as flows of debt principal or payments denominated user fees, these cash flows are labeled as "taxes" when they go to the government, and as "spending" when they come from the government.

One might think that people, or at least sophisticated economists, would recognize that, in this basic sense, taxes are merely negative spending and spending is merely negative taxes. And one might think that such experts would generally recognize that net cash flows between a given individual and the government, rather than gross cash flows in either direction, would be the point of real interest, whether one is thinking about incentives or about distribution. Sadly, one would be mistaken in thinking that they generally recognize this.

If I may indulge one last time in mentioning my favorite whipping boys on this subject (see Shaviro, 2004, 2007), consider Milton Friedman and Gary Becker. Friedman (2003) has said: "I never met a tax cut I didn't like." Presumably, then, there are few "spending increases" that he would like. Becker and colleagues have urged that "taxes" be cut so that "government spending" will decline (Becker, Lazear, and Murphy, 2003). A hypothetical followed by a real-world example should suffice to show how lacking these categories are in the substance that Friedman and Becker evidently ascribe to them.

The hypothetical comes from David Bradford (2003), who imagined the replacement of $60 billion in military appropriations by a $60 billion "weapons supplier tax credit" (WSTC) made tradable to ensure that it could fully be used. The WSTCs would go to exactly the same companies that would otherwise have gotten the appropriations, in exchange for exactly the same weapons. This purely formal change would be treated, under existing practice, as a $60 billion "tax cut" financed by a $60 billion "spending cut." In fact, however, nothing would actually have changed beyond trivial administrative details.

Lest this example seem too fanciful, consider the enormous tax cuts of 2001 and 2003, hailed at the time by small-government conservatives because they reduced gross cash inflows to the government. This fed the expectation that they would "starve the beast," or bring about reductions in the government's gross cash outflows. Yet, as I have shown elsewhere, these changes, given the financing that will eventually be necessary, may actually result in making the government bigger rather than smaller, if one defines government size in terms of the magnitude of its redistributive and distortionary effects (Shaviro, 2007)

For example, a current tax cut that results in future Social Security benefit cuts may increase redistribution—presumably a hallmark of "big government"—from younger to older generations. It also may fail to reduce economic distortion, since it increases the net tax on younger generations imposed by Social Security, and since Social Security benefits are a cash grant that the recipient can decide how to use, rather than being the equivalent of building "bridges to nowhere." Whether or not this particular argument is correct, one must look at substance rather than labels in order to analyze it. And in doing so one must use meaningful concepts, such as allocation and distribution, rather than formal and meaningless ones.

2.2. Budget Deficits and Explicit Public Debt

"Budget deficits," the historical sum of which roughly equals existing national debt, are no better terminologically than "taxes" and "spending." The better-known problem is their limited time frame and hence myopia. This was keenly exemplified when the U.S. Congress in 2006 pretended to use tax cuts to help pay for tax cuts. The methodology it employed was inducing taxpayers to convert traditional individual retirement accounts (IRAs), which are deductible upfront but excludable on the back end, with Roth IRAs, which are nondeductible but fully tax-exempt. Due to the inducements offered, this change increased the fiscal gap by more than $14 billion, yet it was treated by Congress as raising $6.5 billion, due to the convention of using only a ten-year budget window (Burman, 2006, p. 954).

This was not the first time Congress exploited the myopia of the deficit measure to increase the fiscal gap and yet claim credit for raising revenue, and I doubt that it will be the last. Another recent example was the temporary tax holiday that Congress enacted, permitting U.S. companies to repatriate foreign earnings at a 5 percent tax rate in lieu of being fully taxable sometime in the future. This accelerated revenues but probably reduced them in present value, especially given the lesson that there might in the future be similar tax holidays. More generally, "paying" for tax cuts with tax cuts appears to be a growth area in Congressional behavior, and I would expect ever balder examples of it in the next few years unless budget rules are made more long-term in order to prevent it.

The less well-known problem with the budget deficit as a measure, long emphasized by Kotlikoff, is its sensitivity to labeling given that flows of "debt principal" are disregarded. Thus, for example, suppose we recharacterized

Social Security taxes as payments of debt principal, and Social Security benefits as repayments of principal plus interest, plus a subsidy or minus a tax that was levied in one's retirement years (or perhaps at any other time). This recharacterization would not change actual cash flows at all, yet it would drastically change the path of reported annual deficits.

The arbitrariness of the bright-line distinction between debt principal and other cash flows became prominent in 2005 when supporters of President Bush's private accounts plan for Social Security argued that the plan's effect on explicit government debt, which for decades it would greatly have increased, was irrelevant given the offsetting reduction in implicit debt. They would have been entirely correct had the labeling done nothing to change the strength of the government's commitment, which arguably would have been increased by it. Whether correct or not, however, evaluation of their claim required going beyond labels to look at substance.

3. Beyond "Net Taxes": The Next Step?

Green and Kotlikoff argue that the term "net taxes" is just as content-free as the terms "taxes," "spending," and "budget deficit." While they use sophisticated math in their chapter, the basic argument is easy to understand intuitively. Indeed, Green and Kotlikoff explain it nicely in the following passage:

> The private sector and the government . . . jointly own everything and jointly determine how to spend it. Whether the government says (a) "It's all mine, but I'll let you [the private sector] have some," (b) "It's all yours, but I'll take whatever I like," or (c) "It's partly mine and partly yours, but I'll determine how much of mine to give you and how much of yours to keep," does not make an iota of economic difference.

To put the point in terms of a concrete example, suppose that the government gets 30 percent of the income generated through my labor, while I get the remaining 70 percent. If this is all the government does pertaining to me, we would normally say that I face a 30 percent gross and net tax rate. This reflects, however, the assumption that I initially own the income generated by my labor.

Suppose that, without actually changing any policy, we instead described the government as initially owning my labor income. Then the identical policy could be described as my receiving a 70 percent gross and net wage subsidy. Or suppose, since the starting point is arbitrary so long as the endpoint is the same, that we say the government initially owns 21.76988 percent of my labor income. Now the identical policy is described as my paying a gross and net tax, relative to the assumed baseline of 8.23012 percent of the labor income.

Green and Kotlikoff suggest that to call any one of these the true description of the policy is to confuse the "application of economics" with the "perusal of nomenclature." Hence, "net taxes" is no less ill-defined than "taxes," "spending," and "budget deficit," with the apparent consequence that a "vast number of economic analyses," including some by other contributors in this volume, are "vitiate[d]."

This claim raises the question of what Green and Kotlikoff mean by "economics" and "nomenclature." As it happens, they do not define these terms.

4. What Is the Difference between "Economics" and "Nomenclature"?

The on-line Cambridge University Press *Dictionary of American English* defines *economics* as "the scientific study of the system by which a country's wealth is made and used." This definition plainly embraces nomenclature or linguistics (another commonly used term in Green and Kotlikoff) that affect economic behavior.

A familiar example from behavioral economics involves the situation where gasoline costs, for example, $3 per gallon if you pay cash and $4 per gallon if you use a credit card. Consumers evidently distinguish between (a) a $3 "regular price" with a $1 "credit card penalty" and (b) a $4 "regular price" with a $1 "cash discount," regarding the former as a greater deterrent to using a credit card even though the two are financially equivalent. An empirical study of this effect on behavior clearly would be "economics."

In defense of Green and Kotlikoff, while good economists might study the effect of the alternative labeling conventions, they would themselves regard the difference as purely language and framing, and thus would regard neither as a truer description of the price structure. Likewise, in the labor income example, good economists should recognize that all of the differently described policies are the same, apart from the fact that the choice of convention might affect economic or political behavior.

Does this, however, mean that one is deluded and practicing bad economics if one describes the fiscal rule concerning my labor income as involving a 30 percent tax? The answer to this depends on whether one is making the same error as the gas station consumers, or instead is simply applying a consistent convention.

In the gas station example, there would be nothing wrong with our applying a consistent convention, whereby we always treat the cash price (or, alternatively, the credit card price) as the baseline. Either baseline permits us to describe the entire price structure accurately, and possibly more concisely than if we fully describe both prices. (This would be even truer if, as in the labor income but not in the gas station example, the two components inherently had to add up to a specific number, such as 100 percent.) What matters is that we keep on doing it the same way, and recognize that we are applying a convention rather than stating some deeper truth about the correct description. So, for the term "net taxes," the question of interest is whether we are simply applying a consistent convention, or instead are confusing ourselves as in the cases of "taxes," "spending," and "budget deficits."

5. How Problematic Is the Term "Net Taxes"?

For labor income taxes, there is somewhat of a "natural zero," involving the case where the worker is treated as owning all of the labor income until taxes at a 30 percent rate are levied. This does not mean that the zero baseline is more correct than any other. Rather, the point is that it is salient, prominent, widely assumed to apply, and convenient. It also aids us in applying the standard rule of thumb that doubling the tax rate tends to quadruple the distortion.[1]

This raises the question of whether the Green and Kotlikoff analysis of "net taxes" requires anything more than (in effect) a footnote, clarifying that the term as commonly used reflects an arbitrary convention treating the government's prior share as zero. The need for anything more than this depends on fiscal actors' degree of freedom to vary the baseline (whether deliberately or not), and thus to make "net taxes" a slippery term that fails to convey consistent information. I do not at present see how this might be so.

It is true that the net tax measure must be used with care in various respects. For example, if we are using lifetime net tax rates to evaluate how government policy has affected the members of different age cohorts, we must keep in mind that the measure, for reasons of practicality, leaves out the value of public goods and various noncash services that the government provides, and also leaves out regulatory burdens. Thus, for example, the much higher lifetime net tax rate paid by people born in 1950 as compared to 1850 should not too readily be used to draw distributional conclusions about relative treatment of those two cohorts. However, this point about omitted items is orthogonal to the baseline issue that Green and Kotlikoff raise.

If the government started playing games with the baseline—for example, by raising its assumed pretax share by 10 percent so that it could misrepresent constant policy as a 10 percent tax cut—then clearly there would be more than a conceptual footnote at issue here. Likewise, even so bad a term as "budget deficit" may have been quite adequate until instruments for creating long-term commitments, such as Social Security and Medicare, were invented. In the nineteenth century, annual budget deficits plus outstanding public debt may have provided a reasonable framework for evaluating the sustainability of current fiscal policy, so long as one kept in mind the temporary effects of wars and recessions.

6. Conclusion

Notwithstanding Green and Kotlikoff, I will continue using the term "net taxes" until I become aware of problems with it that are not currently evident to me. Their chapter's critique of the term is logically persuasive, but little may turn on it.

Green and Kotlikoff close by quoting Albert Einstein to the effect that Newtonian physics, treating time and distance as well-defined physical concepts, was "merely an illusion." In fact, however, Newtonian physics works just fine under nearly all circumstances that any inhabitant of our planet is likely to experience any time soon, other than those deliberately contrived in a high-tech laboratory. Newtonian physics generates verifiable predictions, and engineers should and do use it in designing actual products. Moreover, Newtonian physics is not false but rather a special case of Einsteinian physics (which may itself be a special case of something broader). Green and Kotlikoff's use of this metaphor does not encourage heeding in practice the critique it offers of "net taxes."

NOTE

1. The gas station example differs practically, even if not logically, from the labor income example if neither the cash price nor the credit card price is dominant in the same manner as the zero pretax government share. If everyone agreed that

"price" generally means cash price, the two examples would be closer. The broader lesson of the gas station example applies to the labor income example if departing from the zero convention in describing tax rates would affect the labor supply response.

REFERENCES

Becker, Gary S., Edward P. Lazear, and Kevin M. Murphy. 2003, October 7. "The Double Benefit of Tax Cuts." *Wall Street Journal*, p. A-20.

Bradford, David F. 2003. "Reforming Budgetary Language." In Ssjibren Cnossen and Hans-Werner Sinn (eds.), *Public Finance and Public Policy in the New Century*. Cambridge, MA: MIT Press.

Burman, Leonard. 2006. "Roth Conversions as Revenue Raisers: Smoke and Mirrors." *Tax Notes* 111: 953–956.

Friedman, Milton. 2003, January 15. "What Every American Wants." *Wall Street Journal*, p. A-10.

Shaviro, Daniel. 2004. "Rethinking Tax Expenditures and Fiscal Language." *Tax Law Review* 57:187.

Shaviro, Daniel. 2007. *Taxes, Spending, and the U.S. Government's March Towards Bankruptcy*. New York: Cambridge University Press.

CHAPTER 7

Comment 2

KENT SMETTERS

Laurence Kotlikoff and his frequent coauthors, Alan Auerbach and Jagadeesh Gokhale, have convinced me over the years that traditional measures of the government's budget are suspect. Their arguments should be taken seriously by academics and, especially, by practitioners.

The chapter by Green and Kotlikoff goes a step further by arguing that many fiscal policies are arbitrary in their description of the underlying economics. Their chapter is provocative and their underlying message strikes me as an important warning for economists and policy makers to be more precise in their terminology. Indeed, the current federal budget, which fails to book the present value of the implicit liabilities in the nation's entitlement programs, makes the past accounting practices at Enron look rather pristine.

Still, the authors could have been clearer. Green and Kotlikoff never propose a meaningful definition of when a label of fiscal policy is "arbitrary." Instead, they simply show that a reasonably specified model of an economy with a government sector is under-identified, permitting a degree of freedom to construct multiple policies with the same economic outcome. So far, so good. But their subsequent rhetorical statements—usually not tied directly back to their model—suggest to me that they are advancing a much more general impossibility theorem of sorts about language itself.

What does it really mean for a fiscal policy label to be arbitrary? Presumably, a *necessary* condition is that there exists at least one other fiscal policy with a different commonly used label that could produce the same allocations of consumption (and leisure) within and across generations *ceteris paribus*. By *ceteris paribus*, I mean that the model's "deep parameters" (preferences, technology, etc.)—that is, all exogenous parameters except the fiscal policies—remain unchanged between the two policies.

However, a range of alternative interpretations is still consistent with that necessary condition. Two policies might produce equivalent consumption allocations, even with *imperfect* markets, if the two policies produce an identical *timing* of *resource* allocations for each household. Indeed, and Auerbach and Kotlikoff (1987) have demonstrated how a pay-as-you-go social security program can be relabeled as a deficit and tax program without changing the magnitude or timing of net transfers to each household. Let us call this type of equivalence the *strong form*.

Two policies, though, might only produce equivalent consumption allocations under *perfect* market conditions if the two policies generate the same *present value* of *resources* for each household. For example, transferring $1 today to a household and taxing the household $1 plus interest a year from now would have no impact on consumption allocations when markets are perfect. Hence, we could say that such a policy is equivalent to existing policy and so the exact label is arbitrary. But this policy could generate a different economy if borrowing constraints are binding. For example, a *fully funded* social security program that would be neutral in a world with complete markets might be non-neutral in a world with incomplete insurance markets. So let us call this type of equivalency the *weak form*. Inasmuch, two proposed fiscal policies that are strongly equivalent are weakly equivalent but not vice-versa.

The distinction between these two forms of equivalency gives some insight into Green and Kotlikoff's criticism of Fischer's important 1980 paper on dynamic consistency. Green and Kotlikoff claim that capital income taxes are unnecessary because the same revenue could always be sequestered with an *infra*marginal tax on labor. However, inframarginal taxes are very hard to implement when the government cannot observe the continuous skill distribution in the presence of imperfect information. To be sure, Fischer's paper did not formally incorporate the incentive compatibility constraints à la Mirrlees (1971) when formulating his argument. Nonetheless, his model focuses on the set of second-best taxes that respect this constraint. In contrast, the criticism by Green and Kotlikoff relies on the availability of a first-best tax that does not respect incentive compatibility constraints. So while they would be correct to note that Fischer's labeling of capital income taxation is weakly equivalent to an inframarginal labor income tax, the two policies are not strongly equivalent.

In fact, technically speaking, we can go even a step further. Two fiscal policies might produce equivalent consumption allocations under *perfect* market conditions only for *specific values* of the model's deep parameters. As a simple illustration, consider a two-period stationary overlapping-generations economy with inelastic labor supply and a homogenous age-wage

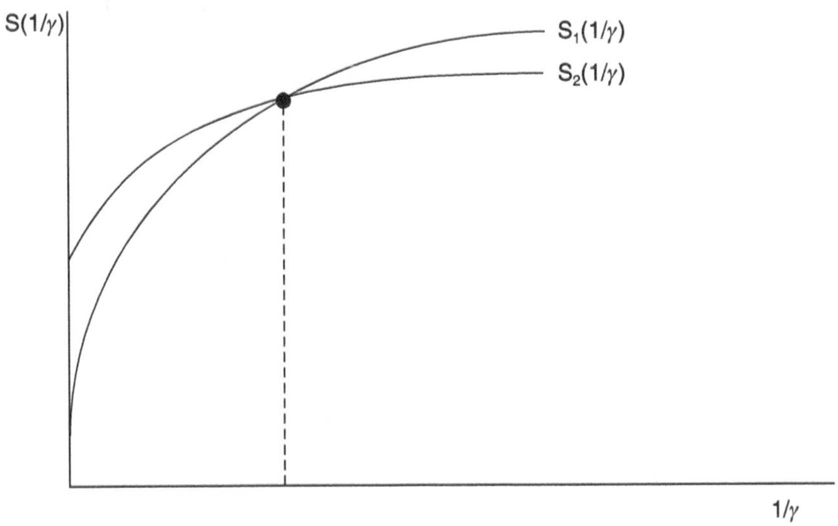

Figure 7.1. Two Savings Policy Functions Corresponding to Two Different Fiscal Policies.

productivity profile. The consumption allocation in this economy can be fully summarized by the economy's savings rate. In Figure 7.1, two savings policy functions (optimal savings rules) corresponding to two different fiscal policies, are shown. The savings rate is shown as a function of the inverse of the rate of time preference, $1/\gamma$.[1] As shown in Figure 7.1, it is possible for two different policies to *not* be weakly equivalent generically yet still produce the same stationary economy (consumption allocations) if the savings policy functions happen to cross. For the sake of argument, I will ignore these *almost nowhere weakly equivalent* policies.

So which form of equivalency are Green and Kotlikoff talking about? Their chapter does not clearly specify. Given their claim that their critique is robust to a wide range of *market settings,* they would seem to be confining themselves to the *strong form* where the exact market setting is unimportant. But given their claim that their critique is also applicable to a wide range of *fiscal policies,* they are hinting at the weak form.

By rhetorically blending the two distinct forms of equivalency, the Green-Kotlikoff critique strikes me as too expansive and bordering on nihilism. I doubt that any sort of labeling could satisfy their critique; notice that they don't even try to propose one. Indeed, even the labels used in the important framework of generational accounting should be in their rhetorical crosshairs. One can always choose to represent the same information provided by generational accounting using different labels.

While the authors analogize their argument to Einstein's General Theory of Relativity, that comparison strikes me as incomplete. To be sure, much of current fiscal language might be relative to the position of politicians and other observers, but Einstein also provided the most straightforward explanation to the Michelson-Morley experiment, thereby producing a new vocabulary in the process. In contrast, the Green and Kotlikoff chapter seems more analogous to Sartre's *Critique of Dialectical Reason;* like these authors, Sartre criticized the existing dialect but failed to provide a new one.

NOTES

I have benefited from conversations with Jerry Green, Laurence Kotlikoff, and the conference participants.

1. I assume that second-period income is sufficiently low such that the "y" intercept is positive; in general, it could be negative.

REFERENCES

Auerbach, Alan J., and Laurance J. Kotlikoff, 1987. *Dynamic Fiscal Policy,* Cambridge: Cambridge University Press. Fischer, Stanley 1980, "Dynamic Inconsistency, Cooperation, and the Benevolent Dissembling Government," *Journal of Economic Dynamics and Control* 2: 93–107.

Mirrlees, James A. 1971. "An Exploration in the Theory of Optimum Income Taxation." *Review of Economic Studies* 38 (114): 175–208.

CONTRIBUTORS

INDEX

Contributors

WILLIAM D. ANDREWS, Harvard University

ALAN J. AUERBACH, University of California at Berkeley

MARTIN DIETZ, University of St. Gallen

ROGER GORDON, University of California at San Diego

JERRY GREEN, Harvard University

JAMES R. HINES, Jr., University of Michigan

R. GLENN HUBBARD, Columbia University

LOUIS KAPLOW, Harvard University

LAURENCE J. KOTLIKOFF, Boston University

KYLE D. LOGUE, University of Michigan

EDWARD J. MCCAFFERY, University of Southern California

CHARLES E. MCLURE, Jr., Hoover Institution

WALLACE E. OATES, University of Maryland

HARVEY S. ROSEN, Princeton University

DANIEL N. SHAVIRO, New York University

JOEL SLEMROD, University of Michigan

KENT SMETTERS, University of Pennsylvania

ALVIN C. WARREN, Jr., Harvard University

DAVID A. WEISBACH, University of Chicago

GEORGE R. ZODROW, Rice University

Index

www.ingramcontent.com/pod-product-compliance
Lightning Source LLC
LaVergne TN
LVHW091517200926
848483LV00005B/443/J

* 9 7 8 0 6 7 4 0 3 0 9 7 8 *